LYN

Teaching E

D0188998

Routledge Education Books

Advisory editor: John Eggleston
*Professor of Education
University of Warwick*

Teaching English as a Foreign Language

Second Edition

Geoffrey Broughton,
Christopher Brumfit,
Roger Flavell,
Peter Hill and Anita Pincas
University of London Institute of Education

London and New York

First published 1978 by Routledge & Kegan Paul Ltd
Second edition published 1980
Reprinted 1981 and 1985
Reprinted with updated bibliographical references 1988
Reprinted 1990, 1993, 1994 and 1996
by Routledge
11 New Fetter Lane, London EC4P 4EE

Simultaneously published in the USA and Canada
by Routledge
29 West 35th Street, New York, NY 10001

Transferred to digital printing 2003

British Library Cataloguing in Publication Data

Teaching English as a foreign language – (Routledge
education books).
1.   English Language – Study and teaching – Foreign students
I.   Broughton, Geoffrey
428' .2' 407   PE1128.A2   78–40161

ISBN 0–415–05882–1

Printed and bound by Antony Rowe Ltd, Eastbourne

428.2407

Contents

Preface

The increased learning and teaching of English throughout the world during recent years in both state and commercial educational institutions has produced a new cadre of professionals: teachers of EFL. Some have moved across from teaching English as a mother tongue, others from teaching modern languages; many have been drawn into service for no other reason than that their own spoken English is good, or perhaps because they are native English speakers. Many have started without specific training, others feel they need to rethink the basis of their teaching.

This book is written for teachers of all backgrounds. Our aim is to discuss a wide range of teaching problems − from classroom techniques to school organisation − in order to help practising teachers in their daily tasks. We have adopted an eclectic approach, recognising that the teaching of English must be principled without being dogmatic, and systematic without being inflexible. We have tried to show how the underlying principles of successful foreign language teaching can provide teachers in a wide range of EFL situations with a basic level of competence which can be a springboard for their subsequent professional development. We gratefully record our debt to colleagues and students past and present at the London University Institute of Education, whose experience and thinking have helped shape our own. Particularly, we would like to thank our colleague John Norrish for compiling the bibliography.

Chapter 1

English in the World Today

English as an international language

Of the 4,000 to 5,000 living languages, English is by far the most widely used. As a mother tongue, it ranks second only to Chinese, which is effectively six mutually unintelligible dialects little used outside China. On the other hand the 300 million native speakers of English are to be found in every continent, and an equally widely distributed body of second language speakers, who use English for their day-to-day needs, totals over 250 million. Finally, if we add those areas where decisions affecting life and welfare are made and announced in English, we cover one-sixth of the world's population.

Barriers of race, colour and creed are no hindrance to the continuing spread of the use of English. Besides being a major vehicle of debate at the United Nations, and the language of command for NATO, it is the official language of international aviation, and unofficially is the first language of international sport and the pop scene. Russian propaganda to the Far East is broadcast in English, as are Chinese radio programmes designed to win friends among listeners in East Africa. Indeed more than 60 per cent of the world's radio programmes are broadcast in English and it is also the language of 70 per cent of the world's mail. From its position 400 years ago as a dialect, little known beyond the southern counties of England, English has grown to its present status as the major world language. The primary growth in the number of native speakers was due to population increases in the nineteenth century in Britain and the USA. The figures for the UK rose from 9 million in 1800 to 30 million in 1900, to some 56 million today. Even more striking was the increase in the USA (largely due to immigration) from 4 million in 1800, to 76 million a century later and an estimated 216,451,900 today. Additionally the development of British colonies took large numbers of English-speaking settlers to Canada, several African territories and Australasia.

It was, however, the introduction of English to the indigenous peoples of British colonies which led to the existence today of numerous independent states where English continues in daily use. The instrument of colonial power, the medium for commerce and education, English became the common means of communication: what is more, it was seen as a vehicle for benevolent Victorian enlightenment. The language policy in British India and other territories was largely the fruit of Lord Macaulay's Education Minute of 1835, wherein he sought to

> form a class who may be interpreters between us and the millions we govern – a class of persons Indian in blood and colour, but English in tastes, in opinions, in morals and in intellect.

Although no one today would defend the teaching of a language to produce a cadre of honorary Englishmen, the use of English throughout the sub-continent with its 845 distinct languages and dialects was clearly necessary for administrative purposes.

The subsequent role of English in India has been significant. In 1950, the Central Government decided that the official language would be Hindi and the transition from English was to be complete by 1965. The ensuing protestations that English was a unifying power in the newly independent nation, a language used by the administration, judiciary, legislators and the press for over a century, were accompanied by bloody riots. Mr Nehru acknowledged in parliament that English was 'the major window for us to the outside world. We dare not close that window, and if we do it will spell peril for the future!' When in 1965 Hindi was proclaimed the sole official language, the Shastri government was severely shaken by the resulting demonstrations. Only after students had burnt themselves to death and a hundred rioters had been shot by police was it agreed that English should continue as an associate official language. The 65 million speakers of Hindi were a strong argument for selecting it as India's national language. But a number of newly independent nations have no one widely spoken language which can be used for building national unity. In West Africa (there are 400 different languages in Nigeria alone) English or French are often the only common languages available once a speaker has left his own area. English is accordingly the official language of both Ghana and Nigeria, used in every walk of daily life. Indeed, English has become a significant factor in national unity in a broad band of nations from Sierra Leone to Malaysia. It is the national language of twenty-nine countries (USA and Australia, of course, but also Lesotho and Liberia) and it is also an official language in fifteen others: South Africa and Canada, predictably, but also Cameroon and Dahomey.

There is, however, a further reason why English enjoys world-wide currency, apart from political and historical considerations. The rapidly developing technology of the English-speaking countries has made British and American television and radio programmes, films, recordings and books readily available in all but the most undeveloped countries. Half the world's scientific literature is written in English. By comparison, languages like Arabic, Yoruba and Malay have been little equipped to handle the concepts and terms of modern sciences and technology. English is therefore often the only available tool for twentieth-century learning.

When Voltaire said 'The first among languages is that which possesses the largest number of excellent works', he could not have been thinking of publications of the MIT Press, cassette recordings of English pop groups or the world-wide successes of BBC television enterprises. But it is partly through agencies as varied and modern as these that the demand for English is made and met, and by which its unique position in the world is sustained.

English as a first language and second language

It is arguable that native speakers of English can no longer make strong proprietary claims to the language which they now share with most of the developed world. The Cairo *Egyptian Gazette* declared 'English is not the property of capitalist Americans, but of all the world', and perhaps the assertion may be made even more convincingly in Singapore, Kampala, and Manila. Bereft of former overtones of political domination, English now exists in its own right in a number of world varieties. Unlike French, which continues to be based upon one metropolitan culture, the English language has taken on a number of regional forms. What Englishman can deny that a form of English, closely related to his own -- equally communicative, equally worthy of respect -- is used in San Francisco, Auckland, Hong Kong and New Delhi? And has the Mid-West lady visitor to London any more right to crow with delight, 'But you speak our language -- you speak English just like we do', than someone from Sydney, Accra, Valletta, or Port-of-Spain, Trinidad?

It may be argued, then, that a number of world varieties of English exist: British, American, Caribbean, West African, East African, Indian, South-east Asian, Australasian among others; having distinctive aspects of pronunciation and usage, by which they are recognised, whilst being mutually intelligible. (It needs hardly be pointed out that within these broad varieties there are dialects: the differences between the local speech of Exeter and Newcastle, of Boston and Dallas, of Nassau and Tobago are on the one hand sufficiently different to be recognised by speakers of other varieties, yet on the other to be acknowledged as dialects of the same variety.)

Of these geographically disparate varieties of English there are two kinds: those of first language situations where English is the mother tongue (MT), as in the USA or Australasia, and second language (SL) situations, where English is the language of commercial, administrative and educational institutions, as in Ghana or Singapore.

Each variety of English marks a speech community, and in motivational terms learners of English may wish to feel themselves members of a particular speech community and identify a target variety accordingly. In several cases, there is little consciousness of choice of target. For example the Greek Cypriot immigrant in London, the new Australian from Italy and the Puerto Rican in New York will have self-selecting targets. In second language situations, the local variety will be the goal. That is, the Fulani learner will learn the educated West African variety of English, not British, American or Indian. This may appear self-evident, yet in some areas the choice of target variety is hotly contested. For example, what kind of English should be taught in Singapore schools to the largely Chinese population? One view is that of the British businessman who argues that his local employees are using English daily, not only with him, but in commercial contacts with other countries and Britain. Therefore they must write their letters and speak on the telephone in a universally understood form of English. This is the argument for teaching British Received Pronunciation (RP), which Daniel Jones defined as that 'most usually heard in the families of Southern English people who have been educated at the public schools', and for teaching the grammar and vocabulary which mark the standard British variety. The opposite view, often taken by Singaporean speakers of English, is that in using English they are not trying to be Englishmen or to identify with RP speakers. They are Chinese speakers of English in a community which has a distinctive form of the language. By speaking a South-east Asian variety of English, they are wearing a South-East linguistic badge, which is far more appropriate than a British one.

The above attitudes reflect the two main kinds of motivation in foreign language learning: instrumental and integrative. When anyone learns a foreign language instrumentally, he needs it for operational purposes – to be able to read books in the new language, to be able to communicate with other speakers of that language. The tourist, the salesman, the science student are clearly motivated to learn English instrumentally. When anyone learns a foreign language for integrative purposes, he is trying to identify much more closely with a speech community which uses that language variety; he wants to feel at home in it, he tries to understand the attitudes and the world view of that community. The immigrant in Britain and the second language speaker of English, though gaining mastery of different varieties of

English, are both learning English for integrative purposes.

In a second language situation, English is the language of the mass media: newspapers, radio and television are largely English media. English is also the language of official institutions – of law courts, local and central government – and of education. It is also the language of large commercial and industrial organisations. Clearly, a good command of English in a second language situation is the passport to social and economic advancement, and the successful user of the appropriate variety of English identifies himself as a successful, integrated member of that language community. It can be seen, then, that the Chinese Singaporean is motivated to learn English for integrative purposes, but it will be English of the South-east Asian variety which achieves his aim, rather than British, American or Australian varieties.

Although, in some second language situations, the official propagation of a local variety of English is often opposed, it is educationally unrealistic to take any variety as a goal other than the local one. It is the model of pronunciation and usage which surrounds the second language learner: its features reflect the influences of his native language, and make it easier to learn than, say, British English. And in the very rare events of a second language learner achieving a perfect command of British English he runs the risk of ridicule and even rejection by his fellows. At the other extreme, the learner who is satisfied with a narrow local dialect runs the risk of losing international communicability.

English as a foreign language

So far we have been considering English as a second language. But in the rest of the world, English is a foreign language. That is, it is taught in schools, often widely, but it does not play an essential role in national or social life. In Spain, Brazil and Japan, for example, Spanish, Portuguese and Japanese are the normal medium of communication and instruction: the average citizen does not need English or any other foreign language to live his daily life or even for social or professional advancement. English, as a world language, is taught among others in schools, but there is no regional variety of English which embodies a Spanish, Brazilian or Japanese cultural identity. In foreign language situations of this kind, therefore, the hundreds of thousands of learners of English tend to have an instrumental motivation for learning the foreign language. The teaching of modern languages in schools has an educational function, and the older learner who deliberately sets out to learn English has a clear instrumental intention: he wants to visit England, to be able to communicate with English-speaking tourists or friends, to be able to read English in books and newspapers.

Learners of English as a foreign language have a choice of language variety to a larger extent than second language learners. The Japanese situation is one in which both British and American varieties are equally acceptable and both are taught. The choice of variety is partly influenced by the availability of teachers, partly by geographical location and political influence. Foreign students of English in Mexico and the Philippines tend to learn American English. Europeans tend to learn British English, whilst in Papua New Guinea, Australasian English is the target variety.

The distinctions between English as a second language (ESL) and English as a Foreign Language (EFL) are, however, not as clear cut as the above may suggest. The decreasing role of English in India and Sri Lanka has, of recent years, made for a shift of emphasis to change a long established second language situation to something nearer to a foreign language situation. Elsewhere, political decisions are changing former foreign language situations. Official policies in, for example, Sweden and Holland are aiming towards a bilingual position where all educated people have a good command of English, which is rapidly becoming an alternate language with Swedish and Dutch − a position much closer to ESL on the EFL/ESL continuum.

It may be seen, then, that the role of English within a nation's daily life is influenced by geographical, historical, cultural and political factors, not all of which are immutable. But the role of English at a given point in time must affect both the way it is taught and the resultant impact on the daily life and growth of the individual.

The place of English in the life of many second and foreign language learners today is much less easy to define than it was some years ago. Michael West was able to state in 1953:

> The foreigner is learning English to express ideas rather than emotion: for his emotional expression he has the mother tongue. . . . It is a useful general rule that intensive words and items are of secondary importance to a foreign learner, however common they may be.

This remains true for learners in extreme foreign language situations: few Japanese learners, for example, need even a passive knowledge of emotive English. But Danish, German and Dutch learners, in considerably greater contact with native speakers, and with English radio, television and the press, are more likely to need at least a passive command of that area of English which expresses emotions. In those second language situations where most educated speakers are bilingual, having command of both English and the mother tongue, the functions of English become even less clearly defined. Many educated Maltese, for example, fluent in both English and Maltese, will often switch from one language to the other in mid-conversation, rather as many Welsh speakers do. Usually, however, they will select Maltese for the most intimate uses of language: saying their prayers, making love, quarrelling or exchanging confidences with a close friend. Such a situation throws up the useful distinction between public and private language. Where a common mother tongue is available, as in Malta, English tends not to be used for the most private purposes, and the speaker's emotional life is expressed and developed largely through the mother tongue. Where, however, no widely used mother tongue is available between speakers, as in West Africa or Papua New Guinea, the second language, English, is likely to be needed for both public and private language functions. It has been argued that if the mother tongue is suppressed during the formative years, and the English taught is only of the public variety, there is a tendency for the speaker to be restricted in his emotional and affective expression and development. This situation is not uncommon among young first generation immigrant children who acquire a public form of English at school and have only a very restricted experience of their native tongue in the home. Such linguistic and cultural deprivation can give rise to 'anomie', a sense of not belonging to either social group. Awareness of this danger lies partly behind a recent Council of Europe scheme to teach immigrant children their mother tongue alongside the language of their host country: in England this takes the form of an experimental scheme in Bedford where Italian and Punjabi immigrant children have regular school lessons in their native languages.

Why do we teach English?

Socio-linguistic research in the past few years has made educators more conscious of language functions and therefore has clarified one level of language teaching goals with greater precision. The recognition that many students of English need the language for specific instrumental purposes has led to the teaching of ESP — English for Special or Specific Purposes. Hence the proliferation of courses and materials designed to teach English for science, medicine, agriculture, engineering, tourism and the like. But the frustration of a French architect who, having learnt the English of architecture before attending a professional international seminar in London, found that he could not invite his American neighbour to have a drink, is significant. Specialised English is best learnt as a second layer built upon a firm general English foundation.

Indeed, the more specialised the learning of English becomes — one organisation recently arranged an English course for seven Thai artificial inseminators — the more it resembles training and the less it is part of the educational process. It may be appropriate, therefore, to conclude this chapter with a consideration of the learning of English as a foreign/second language within the educational dimension.

Why do we teach foreign languages in schools? Why, for that matter, teach maths or physics? Clearly, not simply for the learner to be able to write to a foreign pen friend, to be able to calculate his income tax or understand his domestic fuse-box, though these are all practical by-products of the learning process. The major areas of the school curriculum are the instruments by which the individual grows into a more secure, more contributory, more total member of society.

In geography lessons we move from familiar surroundings to the more exotic, helping the learner to realise that he is not unique, not at the centre of things, that other people exist in other situations in other ways. The German school-boy in Cologne who studies the social geography of Polynesia, the Sahara or Baffinland is made to relate to other people and conditions, and thereby to see the familiar Königstrasse through new eyes. Similarly the teaching of history is all about ourselves in relationship to other people in other times: now in relation to then. This achievement of perspecttive, this breaking of parochial boundaries, the relating to other people, places, things and events is no less applicable to foreign language teaching. One of the German schoolboy's first (unconscious) insights into language is that *der Hund* is not a universal god-given word for a canine quadruped. 'Dog, chien, perro — aren't they funny? Perhaps they think we're funny.' By learning a foreign language we see our own in perspective, we recognise that there are other ways of saying things, other ways of thinking, other patterns of emphasis: the French child finds that the English word *brown* may be the equivalent of *brun*, *marron* or even *jaune*, according to context; the English learner finds that there is no single equivalent to *blue* in Russian, only *goluboj* and *sinij* (two areas of the English 'blue' spectrum). Inextricably bound with a language — and for English, with each world variety — are the cultural patterns of its speech community. English, by its composition, embodies certain ways of thinking about time, space and quantity; embodies attitudes towards animals, sport, the sea, relations between the sexes; embodies a generalised English speakers' world view.

By operating in a foreign language, then, we face the world from a slightly different standpoint and structure it in slightly different conceptual patterns. Some of the educational effects of foreign language learning are achieved — albeit subconsciously — in the first months of study, though obviously a 'feel' for the new language, together with the subtle impacts on the learner's perceptual, aesthetic and affective development, is a function of the growing experience of its written and spoken forms. Clearly the broader aims behind foreign language teaching are rarely something of which the learner is aware and fashionable demands for learner-selected goals are not without danger to the fundamental processes of education.

It may be argued that these educational ends are achievable no less through learning Swahili or Vietnamese than English. And this is true. But at the motivational levels of which most learners are conscious there are compelling reasons for selecting a language which is either that of a neighbouring nation, or one of international stature. It is hardly surprising, then, that more teaching hours are devoted to English in the classrooms of the world than to any other subject of the curriculum.

Suggestions for further reading

P. Christophersen, *Second Language Learning*, Harmondsworth: Penguin, 1973.

P. Strevens, *New Orientations in the Teaching of English*, Oxford University Press, 1977.

P. Trudgill, *Sociolinguistics*, Harmondsworth: Penguin, 1974.

Chapter 2

In the Classroom

The previous chapter has described something of the role of English in the world today. It is against this background and in the kinds of context described that English language teaching goes on and it is clearly part of the professionalism of a teacher of English to foreigners to be aware of the context in which he is working and of how his teaching fits into the scheme of things. However, for most teachers the primary focus of attention is the classroom, what actually happens there, what kinds of personal encounter occur there -- and teaching is very much a matter of personal encounter -- and especially what part teachers themselves play there in facilitating the learning of the language.

It may be helpful, therefore, to sketch briefly one or two outline scenarios which might suggest some of the kinds of things that happen in English language teaching classrooms around the world.

Lesson 1

First then imagine a group of twenty-five girls in a Spanish secondary school, aged between 14 and 17, who have been learning English for two years. Their relationship with their teacher is one of affection and trust which has been built up over the year. They are about halfway through the second term. They are familiar with the vocabulary and structures necessary to describe people, jobs, family relationships and character — in very general terms, also to tell the time, describe locomotion to and from places and to indicate purpose.

Phase 1

The teacher has a large picture on the blackboard. It has been enlarged, using an episcope, from one in *What Do You Think?* by Donn Byrne and Andrew Wright. It shows a queue outside a telephone box. The characters in it are to some extent stereotypes — the fashionable bored girl, the pin-stripe-suited executive with his briefcase, two scruffy loung-ing boys, and a rather drab hen-pecked husband type. The girls and the teacher have been looking at the picture and dis-cussing it. The girls have identified the types fairly well and the teacher is probing with questions like 'What's happening here?' The English habit of queuing is discussed. 'What time of day is it?' The class decides on early evening with the people returning from work or school. 'Who are the people in the picture? What are their jobs? Do we need to know their names? What might they be called? Where have they come from? Where are they going? Who are they telephoning? What is their relationship? Why are they telephoning? What is the attitude of the other person? How does each person feel about having to wait in the queue? Is there any inter-action between them?' and so on.

Phase 2

The girls are all working in small groups of about four or five. The teacher is moving round the class from group to group, supplying bits of language that the pupils need and joining in the discussion. There is some Spanish being spoken, but a lot of English phrases are also being tried out and when the teacher is present the girls struggle hard to communicate with her in English. There is also a good deal of laughter and dis-cussion. One girl in each group is writing down what the others tell her. The class is involved in producing a number of dialogues. Most groups have picked the teenage girl who is actually in the phone box as the person they can identify with most easily, and each dialogue has a similar general pattern: The girl makes a request of some kind, the person she is telephoning refuses, the girl uses persuasion, the other person agrees. However, there is one group here who have decided their dialogue will be between two of the people in the queue. . . .

Phase 3

The girls are acting out their dialogues in front of the class. Two girls from each group take the roles of the people actually speaking, the others, together with any additional pupils needed to make up the numbers, form the queue, and are miming impatience, indifference, and so on.

This is what we hear:

(The talk with the boy friend — first group)

Ring ring . . .

Ann:	Hello, is Charles there?
Mother:	Yes, wait a minute.
Charles:	Hello, who is it?
Ann:	Who is it? It is Ann.
Charles:	Oh, Ann. I am going to telephone to you now.
Ann:	Where did you go yesterday?
Charles:	I stayed at home studying for my test.
Ann:	Yes, . . . for your test . . . my friend Carol saw you in the cinema with another girl yesterday.
Charles:	Oh no, she was my cousin.

(Man taps on glass of phone box. Ann covers mouthpiece. To man:)

	In just a moment I'll finish.
(to Charles:)	No, she wasn't your cousin, because she lives near my house and I know her.
Charles:	Oh no!
Ann:	I don't want to see you any more. Goodbye.
Charles:	No, one moment. . . .
Ann:	Yes.

(Ringing home — second group)

Jane:	Hello, is Mum there?
John:	No, she's at the beauty shop. What do you want to tell her?
Jane:	Well, I'm going to the movies with my boy-friend, but we haven't any money. Can you bring me some money? I promise you I'll give it back to you tomorrow.
John:	You are always lying. I don't believe you any more. You owe me more than £9.
Jane:	I'm going to work as babysitter tomorrow, but I need money now. Please hurry up — I have no money for the phone and there are a lot of people waiting outside.
John:	All right.

(Leaving home — third group)

Monica:	Hello, grandfather. How are you? This is Monica.
Grandfather:	Hello, Monica. What do you want?
Monica:	I need money. Help me.
Grandfather:	Money? Why do you need it?
Monica:	I need, because I want to go out of my home.
Grandfather:	What?
Monica:	Yes, because my parents don't understand me. I can't move.
Grandfather:	Have you thought it?
Monica:	Yes, I thought it very well.
Grandfather:	You can come to my house if you want.
Monica:	Thank you, grandfather. I will go with you. I must go now. A lot of people are outside. Bye Bye.

(The pick-up — fourth group)

Man:	Excuse me, have you got a match?
Girl:	No, I don't smoke.
Man:	Oh. *(pause)* It's a long queue.
Girl:	Yes, it's very boring to wait.

In the Classroom

Man:	Do you like to dance?
Girl:	Sometimes.
Man:	Would you like to come to dance with me tonight?
Girl:	No, I shall be busy.
Man:	We can dance and then go to my apartment and drink champagne.
Girl:	I don't want. Go and leave me. You're an old pig.

Lesson 2

Our second classroom contains eighteen adults of mixed nationality most of whom have been studying English for from five to eight years. Their class meets three hours a week in London and they have virtually no contact with one another outside the classroom. They have had this teacher for about a month now and are familiar with the kinds of technique he uses.

Phase 1

The teacher has distributed copies of a short text (about 400 words) to the students and they are sitting quietly reading through it. Attached to the text are a number of multiple choice questions and the students are attempting to decide individually which of the choices in each question most closely matches the sense of the text.

Phase 2

The students are working in five small groups with four or five of them in each group and discussing with one another why they believe that one interpretation is superior to another. Part of the text reads:

The singing and the eating and drinking began again and seemed set to go on all night. Darkness was around the corner, and the flares and coloured lights would soon be lit. . . .

One of the multiple choice questions suggests:

The singing and the eating and drinking
(a) had begun before nightfall
(b) had begun just before nightfall
(c) began when darkness arrived
(d) had been going on all day

(with acknowledgments to J. Munby, O. G. Thomas, and M. D. Cooper and their *Comprehension for School Certificate* and to J. Munby's *Read and Think* — see Chapter 6 following).

In one group the discussion goes like this:

Mohammed: Well, it can't possibly be (d) because there is nothing in the text to say that it had been going on all day.

Yoko: But what about that 'again' in the first sentence, surely this must mean that the singing and so on had been going on beforehand, something interrupted it and it started again.

François: Yes, but that does not mean it went on 'all day'.

Yoko: Yes, I suppose you are right, so it cannot be (d). What about (c)?

Giovanni: It cannot be (c) which says 'when darkness arrived'. 'When' here means 'at the very moment that', but the text says 'Darkness was around the corner' which must mean 'near but not actually present' and this idea is supported by the phrase 'the lights would *soon* be lit.'

Juan: All right, so it cannot be (c). What about (a)?

Yoko: That could be right because clearly the singing and that had begun some time earlier in the day, but it is a very vague suggestion, (b) must surely be the better answer.

Giovanni: No, this is like (c) and suggests that the singing and so on began at the very moment being described, that is when darkness was still

17

'around the corner'. But Yoko pointed out that 'again' must imply that the singing had started earlier, stopped for some reason and started again, so it originally started well before this time. So (b) will not do.

Juan: Well that brings us back to (a), which is vague but correct, while all the others are wrong. So we must say that (a) is the *best* answer.

While this is going on the teacher is moving from group to group, asking them to justify their rejection or acceptance of suggested interpretations. One group has missed the significance of 'again' as expounded by Yoko above so the teacher asks specifically 'What does "again" mean here? What must we understand about the time sequence of events from its use?' The group is launched into discussion again.

Phase 3

On the blackboard the teacher has drawn up a grid with five vertical columns — one for each group — and ten horizontal rows — one for each multiple choice question. He has been asking each group to indicate which choice they had made for each question. The grid now looks something like Figure 1. All the groups agreed that (a) was the best answer for Q 1 and the teacher got one of the students to justify that choice, and others to justify the rejection of (b) (c) and (d). Over Q 2 there appears to be some disagreement. The text reads:

Jim, of course, had never been to a party at the Great Hall before, but his mother and father had. His great-grandfather claimed he hadn't been to the last one because he was the oldest inhabitant. He was the oldest inhabitant even then, but he had been Father Time in the pageant.

The questions read:

Great-grandfather
(a) had been to the last party and the reason was that he was the oldest inhabitant.
(b) had been to the last party and the reason was that he

	A	B	C	D	E
1	(a)	(a)	(a)	(a)	(a)
2	(b)	(b)	(c)	(b)	(c)
3					
4					
5					
⋮					

Figure 1

had been in the pageant.

(c) hadn't been to the last party and the reason was that even then he was the oldest inhabitant.

(d) hadn't been to the last party and the reason was that he had been in the pageant.

Groups A, B and D argue that the sentence in the text beginning 'His great-grandfather . . .' should be read with a rising tone on 'inhabitant' at the end. Groups C, and E argue that it should be read with a falling tone. Readings like these clearly justify the positive or negative interpretation of the facts about great-grandfather being at the party. However groups A, B, and D come back to point out that the significance of 'but' in the last sentence of the text is such as to make (b) easily the most likely choice since the meaning must be that the reason he was at the party was *not* that he was the oldest inhabitant, though that would have been a good enough reason for him to be invited but that as a member of the cast of the pageant he was automatically invited.

And so the teacher leads and guides the students through the text so that they arrive at sound interpretations which are properly justified.

Lesson 3

Phase 1

In our third classroom the teacher has just announced, 'This morning we are going to learn about the Simple Present Tense in English. The forms for the verb "to be" are these. Copy them down.' He writes on the blackboard:

Simple Present Tense 'to be' Positive Declarative

		Example:
1st Person Singular	I am	I am a teacher.
2nd Person Singular	you are	You are a pupil.
3rd Person Singular	he, she, it is	He, she is a pupil.
		It is an elephant.
1st Person Plural	we are	We are people.
2nd Person Plural	you are	You are pupils.
3rd Person Plural	they are	They are elephants.

He comments as he writes up the forms for the third person singular, 'Note that "he" is used with masculine nouns, "she" with feminine nouns, and "it" with neuter nouns.' He continues writing:

The Negative Declarative is formed by placing 'not' after the verb thus:

		Example:
1st Person Singular	I am not	I am not a teacher.
2nd Person Singular	you are not	(At this point he
3rd Person Singular	he, she, it is not	suggests 'I think you can all complete the
1st Person Plural	we are not	remaining examples
2nd Person Plural	you are not	here.')
3rd Person Plural	they are not	

He waits at the front of the classroom while pupils write. The blackboard is almost full so he points to the first paradigm above and asks, 'Can I rub this out now?' A few heads nod, so he erases it and continues writing:

The Positive Interrogative is formed by inverting the order of the verb and subject thus:

		Example:
1st Person Singular	Am I?	Am I a teacher?
2nd Person Singular	Are you?	etc. etc.

Towards the end of Phase 2

The teacher is still writing on the blackboard, pupils are copying busily:

The Negative Interrogative of verbs other than 'be' and 'have' is formed by using the interrogative form with 'do' and placing 'not' after the subject, thus:

1st Person Singular	Do I not walk?
2nd Person Singular	Do you not walk?
3rd Person Singular	Does he, she, it not walk?
1st Person Plural	Do we not walk?
2nd Person Plural	Do you not walk?
3rd Person Plural	Do they not walk?

By this time pupils have written out in full the paradigms for positive and negative declarative, and the positive and negative interrogative for 'be', 'have', and 'walk' with some additional examples where these were felt to be useful.

Phase 3

The teacher cleans the last paradigm off the board and writes:

(1) Give the 3rd Person Singular Interrogative forms of the simple present tense of each of the following verbs: walk, talk, come, go, run, eat, drink, have, open, shut.

He says, 'Do these exercises, please' and writes again:

(2) Give the 2nd Person plural Negative Interrogative forms of the simple present tense of the following

verbs: write, wash, love, be, push, pull, want, hit, throw, ride.
. . . etc. etc.

Here then are scenarios for three very different kinds of lesson, and in Chapter 12 there is a plan for a lesson of yet another kind.

The key questions

In considering these lessons there are at least five important questions that anyone who aspires to be at all professional about teaching English as a foreign language needs to ask. Each question implies a whole series of other questions and they might be something like these:

1 What is the nature of the social interaction that is taking place?

What is the general social atmosphere of the class? What is the relationship between the pupils and the teacher? between pupil and pupil? Is the interaction teacher-dominated? Is the teacher teaching the whole class together as one, with the pupils' heads up, looking at the teacher? Does he ask all the questions and initiate all the activity? Or are the pupils being taught in groups? How big are the groups? How many of them are there? Are they mixed ability groups or same ability groups? Are all groups doing exactly the same work, or different work? Or, are pupils working in isolation, each on his own, with head down looking at his books?

2 What is the nature of the language activity that is taking place?

This is on the whole a simpler question than the first one since it is essentially a matter of asking, 'Are pupils reading, writing, listening, or talking?' But at a slightly deeper level it is also possible to ask, 'Are they practising the production of correct forms or are they practising the *use* of forms they have already learnt? Are they operating a grammatical rule, a collocational pattern, or an idiomatic form of expression? Are they using words, phrases and sentences in appropriate contexts to convey the message they actually intend to convey? Are they concentrating on accuracy or fluency, on language or communication?

3 What is the mode by which the teacher is teaching?

Is he using a purely oral/aural mode? Talking and listening? Is he simply talking or is he using audio aids as well? a tape recorder? radio? record player? Are there sound effects for the pupils to listen to or is it just words? Or, is the teacher using a visual mode? Is he using written symbols: written words, and sentences and texts, numbers, diagrams, charts or maps? or is he using things that represent reality in some sense: actual physical objects, models, pictures, photographs or drawings? Or is the teacher using a mixture of aural and visual modes? Can they be disentangled?

4 What materials is the teacher using?

There are two important aspects to this question. One asks first about the actual content of the teaching materials in a number of senses. What is the actual linguistic content? What sounds, words, grammar or conventions of reading or writing are in it? A good deal of attention is devoted to answering this particular question in subsequent chapters of this book. Then: What is the language actually about – a typical English family, Malaysian schoolboys of different ethnic backgrounds, a pair of swinging London teenagers, or corgies, crumpets and cricket? A tourist in New York, or the polymerisation of vinyl chloride, or the grief of a king who believes himself betrayed by the daughter he loves most?

The second aspect concerns the type of material it is. Is it specially written with controlled grammar and vocabulary from a predetermined list? Or is it 'authentic' and uncontrolled? What kinds of control have been used in terms of frequency of items, simplicity plus functional utility? Does it have a specific orientation towards a particular group of learners — English for electronic engineers — or is it designed to foster general service English? Is its orientation primarily linguistic or primarily communicative?

5 How is it possible to tell whether one lesson is in some way 'better' than another?

Is it to be done in *purely* pragmatic terms? Do pupils learn from a particular sort of lesson more quickly, with less effort, and greater enjoyment than those who learn by some other type of lesson? Is there any difference between teaching adults and children? Is it possible to measure in any real way different degrees of efficiency in learning? For example, is it true that the method which teaches most words is the best method? Or, on the other hand, are there a number of basic underlying principles, fundamental concepts, which can be brought to bear on what is clearly a rather complex form of human activity to illuminate what is going on and help in making decisions, which are wise enough to avoid being simplistic and naive, yet positive enough to ensure effective action in any given set of circumstances?

It is in the belief that pragmatism and principle must walk hand in hand that the following chapters have been written. First some basic principles will be explored, and then the consequences of applying those to particular areas of language teaching will be looked at in the hope that by the time readers reach the end·of the book they will be in a better position to give informed and reasonably well balanced answers to at least some of the questions posed above, not only about the lessons sketched here but about any lesson in English to foreigners.

Further reading and study

R. L. Politzer and L. Weiss, *The Successful Foreign Language Teacher*, Philadelphia: Center for Curriculum Development and Harrap, 1970.
BBC/British Council, *Teaching Observed*, 13 films, with handbook, 1976.

Chapter 3

Language
and Communication

Kinds of communication

All living creatures have some means of conveying information to others of their own group, communication being ultimately essential for their survival. Some use vocal noises, others physical movement or facial expression. Many employ a variety of methods. Birds use predominantly vocal signals, but also show their intentions by body movements; animals use vocal noises as well as facial expressions like the baring of teeth; insects use body movements, the most famous of which are the various 'dances' of the bees.

Man is able to exploit a range of techniques of communication. Many are in essence the same as those used by other creatures. Man is vocal, he uses his body for gestures of many kinds, he conveys information by facial expression, but he has extended these three basic techniques by adding the dimension of representation. Thus both speech and gesture can be represented in picture form or symbolically and conveyed beyond the immediate context.

It is unfortunate that the word *language* is often used to cover all forms of communication, and that the term *animal language* is common. These expressions obscure a very important distinction between communication which is basically a set of *signals*, and communication which is truly language, *human language*. Man, in common with other creatures, uses signals, but he also uses language with a subtlety and complexity and range far beyond anything known to exist among other forms of life.

Features of language

Language has two fundamental features which mark it as quite different in kind from signals: *productivity* and *structural complexity*.

First, language allows every human being to produce utterances, often quite novel, in an infinite number of contexts, where the language is bent, moulded and developed to fit ever-developing communicative needs. Old expressions are changed, new ones coined. Humans are not genetically programmed to use fixed calls or movements. They have an innate general capacity for language (often called the Language Acquisition Device — LAD), but it is a creative capacity. Given the opportunity to learn from their environment, all humans can communicate in a limitless variety of ways.

Second, language is not a sequence of signals, where each stands for a particular meaning. If words were merely fixed signals of meaning, then each time a word occurred it would signal the same thing, irrespective of the structure of the whole utterances — in fact there would be no 'whole utterances' beyond individual words. So

	John plays football
and	plays football John
and	football plays John

would all mean the same thing, i.e. each would be a string of the same three meanings, merely presented in different order.

Language, clearly, relies as much on its structure as on its semantic properties to convey meaning. Communication can be infinitely varied and infinitely complex just because the language is a highly structured system which allows an infinite range of permutations. The structure is of many types: the organisation of a fixed range of sounds, the ordering of words in phrases and sentences, the use of inflections, the semantic and grammatical relationships between words, the interplay of stress, intonation and rhythm in the actual production of speech, and the dovetailing of paralinguistic features.

The transmission of information

As the major and most complex technique we have of communicating information, spoken language allows us to produce a sequence of vocal sounds in such a way that another person can reconstruct from those sounds a useful approximation to our original meaning. In very simple terms, the sender starts with a thought and puts it into language. The receiver perceives the language and thus understands the thought.

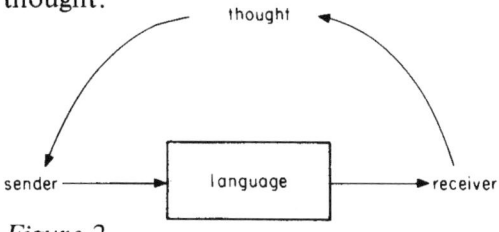

Figure 2

The sender has to *encode* his thought, while the receiver *decodes* the language. Most of the time, these processes are so fast that one could say that both sender and receiver perform them instantaneously and virtually simultaneously. When thoughts are very complex, the process takes longer. Likewise, when an unfamiliar language, or dialect, is being used, the process is slow enough for the distinction between thought and language to be quite clearly observed.

Language and thought

The best way to regard the relationship is to say that 'language is a tool in the way an arm with its hand is a tool, something to work with like any other tool and at the same time *part of* the mechanism that drives tools, part of *us*. Language is not only necessary for the formulation of thought, but is part of the thinking process itself' (Bolinger, 1975, p. 236).

Language is related to reality and thought by the intricate relationships we call *meaning*. For language to be able to convey meaning the reality which it has to represent must be segmented. We abstract things from their environment so

27

that we can name them (the wind, a wave), even though in many cases we would find great difficulty in defining, as objects with definite boundaries, the things which we have abstracted. When we isolate parts of reality through our language, we necessarily leave out considerable detail. Thus, whether we are responding to the sound of a cry, or the appearance of a small hand among the pram covers, we can use the word *baby* and expect our hearer to supply his knowledge of the whole complex of perceptions really involved in the thought of a baby.

Language presents reality in chunks which can be referred to by chunks of language. The continuum of time, for example, can be seen metaphorically as a dimension along which events move in a straight line. Language, however, imposes divisions on that line, in order to be able to refer to parts of it. English can indicate different parts of the continuum, as follows:

I *used to* go swimming, when I was little.
I *had been swimming before* I went there.
I *went* there yesterday.
I *am* here *now*.
I *will have* my lunch at 1 o'clock.
After I *have had* my lunch I will go on working.
By 8 o'clock I *will have been* working for two hours.

There are many such continua which language treats as distinct units for communication purposes. They range through (i) aspects of the world around us, e.g. time, place, quantity; (ii) activities we are involved in, e.g. action, assertion, commitment and (iii) our own moods, emotions and attitudes, e.g. belief, anger, concession. On any of these dimensions there is in fact a gradient, but language imposes divisions in it. Thus, the gradient of anger is divided, in English: irritation . . . annoyance . . . anger . . . exasperation . . . rage . . . fury . . . blind fury. . . .

Translatability

There is nothing necessarily universal about these divisions in reality, though to the native speaker of any one language his own categories are so familiar that he finds them the only logically possible ones and can hardly imagine that other languages segment reality in different ways. But a naive view of languages as all conveying basically the same meanings overlooks fundamental differences and is vitiated by learners' errors; witness 'I am here since 5 o'clock' (from a French speaker whose language has a different cut-off point between near past and present).

Not only do different languages cut up the same continuum in different ways, but, perhaps even more significant, different languages emphasise different kinds of continua. Hopi, a North American Indian language, has a view of time that concentrates on the aspect of duration. Events of short duration which can be nouns in English, e.g. 'flash', 'wave', 'wind', must be verbs in Hopi. Hopi verb forms express different relations in time, also. They do not refer to the position of the events along a time-line as in English, but rather to their relation to the observer.

This is not to say that either language cannot express the meanings of the other, but rather that there is a distinction between the meanings built-in, and the meanings that must be thought about and expressed. In this sense, different languages predispose their speakers to 'think' differently, i.e. to direct their attention to different aspects of the environment. Translation is therefore not simply a matter of seeking other words with similar meaning, but of finding appropriate ways of saying things in another language. Very often, the segments of reality which are structurally built-in to one language may have to be ignored in another language. Thus, dual number, though it can be expressed ('both', 'couple', etc.) has no place in the grammatical structure of English. But there are many languages (e.g. Arabic) in which the form of words (of the nouns, pronouns, or verbs) has to be appropriate to singular, dual or plural number and speakers are unable to avoid observing the distinctions. Therefore, a speaker of English learning a language with dual number built in will have to learn to pay attention to it.

Different languages, then, may categorise reality differently or may express similar categories by different linguistic forms. But the forms are only one aspect of the difference between two language systems. The second major aspect pertains to the ways in which language is used as part of behaviour in the numerous contexts of everyday life. In order to communicate effectively, a speaker must be able to express himself in the right ways on the right occasions. It is not enough to be able to use the linguistic forms correctly. One must also know how to use them appropriately.

Communicative competence

From babyhood onwards, everybody starts (and never ceases) to learn how to communicate effectively and how to respond to other people's communications. Some people are better at communicating than others, but every normal human being learns to communicate through language (as well as with the ancillary signalling systems). It may be a matter of intelligence (as well as motivation and experience) to communicate well, but it is not necessary to have any more than normal intelligence to communicate sufficiently for everyday life.

In the process of communication, every speaker adjusts the way he speaks (or writes) according to the situation he is in, the purpose which motivates him, and the relationship between himself and the person he is addressing. Certain ways of talking are appropriate for communicating with intimates, other ways for communicating with non-intimates; certain ways of putting things will be understood to convey politeness, others to convey impatience or rudeness or anger. In fact, all our vast array of language use can be classified into many different categories related to the situation and purpose of communication. For a foreign learner, it might sometimes be more important to achieve this kind of communicative competence than to achieve a formal linguistic correctness.

Varieties of language

The ways in which we use our language can be divided first of all into two broad aspects: (i) the factors determined by the context, and (ii) the factors determined by the mood and purpose of the speaker. Every time we speak, we operate from a complex of choices, involving selection of vocabulary, structure, and even modes of pronunciation, constantly adjusting our language to suit the moment, fitting in always with the conventions of the group we are part of.

Context

The first factor which operates is on the choice of the language itself, or the appropriate dialect. The choice of language is not as self-evident as it may seem to speakers living in countries where only one language exists, as in the English-speaking countries like England, America or Australia. But in many countries, speakers are bilingual or multilingual, and two or more languages exist side by side, to be used with different purposes to different people on different occasions. Thus, a French speaker in Brussels, might switch between French, Dutch or Flemish, depending on whether he was at home, or in his office, speaking with intimates, friends from his home town, or formal acquaintances. He might even use different languages to the same person, according to whether they were alone or in the presence of others. Similar switching occurs in many countries, including Canada, South Africa, Switzerland, Norway, Nigeria and Paraguay.

Even when there is only one language to use, it may have more than one dialect. Contemporary English has numerous regional dialects which vary in pronunciation, vocabulary and grammar, and although, by convention, a certain prestige usually attaches to one of them — Standard English — many speakers are able to choose between the standard dialect and one of the many regional dialects of Yorkshire, Wales, Ireland, etc. Dialect means primarily the form of a language associated with a geographical region, but geographical boundaries are not the absolute determinants, and one may often find two or more dialects being used within one region, especially in a multi-lingual or multi-dialectal situation where one dialect might be used as a lingua franca (e.g. Swahili).

The second important factor of context is the nature of the participants. The age, sex, social status and educational level of the speaker (or writer) and listener (or reader), all

31

affect the mode of expression used. It is relatively easy for a native speaker to tell, even from a snatch of conversation, who is speaking to whom. Just hearing the sentences, 'Excuse me, please, do you have the time?', 'Find out what time it is, would you?', or 'Try to tell the time for Mummy, dear' is quite sufficient to conjure up a vision of two people who could possibly be involved in each exchange.

The next two factors are closely connected with each other. They are the actual situation in which the language occurs and the kind of contact between the participants. The importance of the situation itself has always been recognised, and is heavily emphasised in 'situational' language courses, as well as in travellers' phrase books, where it becomes clear that the language varies according to whether one is shopping, or asking for directions, or booking a hotel room, etc. Depending on the situation, the contact between the participants could be either in speech or in writing, and at any point on the range of proximity, i.e. face-to-face (close or distant), not face-to-face (two-way contact by telephone or correspondence), or one-way contact (radio, TV, advertisement, notice). Once again, it is relatively simple to suggest appropriate contexts for random items like 'Time?', 'My watch has stopped', 'Have you the time, please?', 'Is there a clock here? I need to know the right time.' Simply by observing the choice of expression, one can postulate circumstances in which one or the other would be likely to be written rather than spoken, used in one place rather than another.

Another parameter that deserves more recognition than it has had in language teaching is the nature of the subject matter or topic or field of discourse. Its influence has been recognised for extreme cases of English for Special Purposes such as technical usage, international aviation English, legal terminology, and the like. But even in very minor and apparently trivial domestic contexts, the topic quite manifestly influences the language. 'He'll come down in 60 seconds' and 'He'll come down in a minute', though they appear to have identical time-reference, are obviously not connected with the same subject matter, any more than are 'The parties agree to abide by the terms hereinafter stated' and 'Let's shake on it.'

All these factors determined by the context are external to

the participant, and are universal only in the sense that they operate in all languages. But just how they operate differs very widely indeed, not only between language, but between different speech communities using the same language. Different languages have different techniques for indicating social status for example. It can be done by special terms like 'Sir', or the use or avoidance of first names, or by special pronouns or verb forms. In English itself, speakers in Southern England may signal the social class they wish to be associated with by using certain accent features in their speech, while in Australia accent is less significant than the vocabulary used.

Mood and purpose

The way people communicate, as well as what they communicate, is, of course, a matter of choice. But it is restricted by the conventions of the speech community and the language itself. The external factors governing usage play their part in decreeing what is appropriate to different circumstances. But

it would be naive to think that the speaker is somehow linguistically at the mercy of the physical situation in which he finds himself. What the individual says is what he has chosen to say. It is a matter of his intentions and purposes. The fact that there are some situations in which certain intentions are regularly expressed, certain linguistic transactions regularly carried out, does not mean that this is typical of our language use. . . . I may have gone to the post office, not to buy stamps, but to complain about the non-arrival of a parcel, to change some money so that I can make a telephone call, or to ask a friend of mine who works behind the counter whether he wants to come to a football match on Saturday afternoon (Wilkins, 1976, p. 17).

And further, I can choose to be vague, definite, rude, pleading, aggressive or irritatingly polite.

Given the freedom to choose the mood he wishes to convey as well as what he wants to say, the speaker is constrained by the available resources of the language to fulfil his aims. It is in this area that foreign language teaching has been of too little help in the past, and attempts are now being made to correct the imbalance in teaching syllabuses. Terms like 'functional syllabus' and 'notional syllabus' reflect concern with aspects of language indicating, on the one hand, certainty, conjecture, disbelief, etc. – all of which relate to the mood or modality of the utterance, and, on the other hand, valuation, approval, tolerance, emotional relationship, etc. – all of which relate to the function of the communication.

Thus, whereas some languages use verb forms to indicate speakers' degree of certainty, English can also use lexical expressions like 'It is beyond doubt that . . .', or special intonation and stress patterns, or grammatical forms of verbs ('If you heated it, it would melt'). The learner must select not only a correct expression but one which is appropriate to his intentions and possibly very different from the equivalent in his native language.

Regarding the *function* of the communication, there are five general functions which can usefully be isolated: *Personal*. The speaker will be open to interpretation as polite, aggressive, in a hurry, angry, pleased, etc., according to how he speaks. *Directive*. The speaker attempts to control or influence the listener in some way. *Establishing relationship*. The speaker establishes and maintains (or cuts off!) contact with the listener, often by speaking in a ritualised way in which what is said is not as important as the fact that it is said at all, e.g. comments on the weather, questions about the health of the family, etc. This is often called phatic communication, and is certainly a vital part of language use. *Referential*. The speaker is conveying information to the listener. *Enjoyment*. The speaker is using language 'for its own sake' in poetry, rhymes, songs, etc. (Corder, 1973, pp. 42–9).

Of course, these functions overlap and intertwine, but they are useful guidelines for distinguishing among utterances like, 'Thank goodness there's a moon tonight', 'The moon is our first objective', 'Lovely night isn't it', 'The moon is in the ascendant', 'The man in the moon came tumbling down.'

Acquiring communicative competence

Learning to use a language thus involves a great deal more than acquiring some grammar and vocabulary and a reasonable pronunciation. It involves the competence to suit the language to the situation, the participant and the basic purpose. Conversely, and equally important, it involves the competence to interpret other speakers to the full. Using our mother tongue, most of us have very little awareness of how we alter our behaviour and language to suit the occasion. We learned what we know either subconsciously while emulating the models around us, or slightly more consciously when feedback indicated that we were successful, or unsuccessful − in which case we might have been taught and corrected by admonitions like 'Say "please"!', or "Don't talk to me like that!'

As far as the foreign learner is concerned, the history of language teaching shows emphasis on a very limited range of competence which has been called 'classroom English' or 'textbook English', and has often proved less than useful for any 'real' communicative purpose. That is to say, as long as the use of English as a foreign language was confined largely to academic purposes, or to restricted areas like commerce or administration, a limited command of the language, chiefly in the written form, was found reasonable and adequate. But in modern times, the world has shrunk and in many cases interpersonal communication is now more vital than academic usage. It is now important for the learner to be equipped with the command of English which allows him to express himself in speech or in writing in a much greater variety of contexts.

Designers of syllabuses and writers of EFL texts are now concentrating on techniques of combining the teaching of traditionally necessary aspects of the language − grammar, vocabulary, and pronunciation − with greater emphasis on the meaningful use of the language. Their aims go well beyond 'situational' teaching because this is merely an attempt to contextualise grammatical structures while still retaining as its objective the acquisition of linguistic forms *per se* in an order dictated by grammatical considerations. Now, the need is recognised for greater emphasis in the selection and ordering of what is to be taught, on the communicative needs of the learners, and it has become the task of everyone concerned to provide teaching materials rich enough to satisfy these needs.

Suggestions for further reading

W. L. Anderson and N. C. Stageberg, *Introductory Readings on Language*, New York: Holt, Rinehart & Winston, 1966.

L. Bloomfield, *Language*, Allen & Unwin, 1935.

J. B. Carroll (ed.), *Language, Thought and Reality: Selected Writings of Benjamin Lee Whorf*, Cambridge, Mass.: MIT Press, 1956.

E. C. Cherry, *On Human Communication*, John Wiley, 1957.

M. Coulthard, *Introduction to Discourse Analysis*, Longman, 1983.

J. P. De Cecco, *The Psychology of Language, Thought and Instruction*, New York: Holt, Rinehart & Winston, 1969.

J. B. Hogins and R. E. Yarber, *Language, an Introductory Reader*, New York: Harper & Row, 1969.

G. Leech and J. Svartvik, *A Communicative Grammar of English*, Longman, 1975.

E. Linden, *Apes, Men and Language*, Harmondsworth: Penguin, 1974.

W. Littlewood, *Communicative Language Teaching*, Cambridge University Press, 1981.

N. Minnis, *Linguistics at Large*, Granada, 1973.

W. Nash, *Our Experience of Language*, Batsford, 1971.

S. Potter, *Language in the Modern World*, Harmondsworth: Penguin, 1960.

E. Sapir, *Language*, New York: Harcourt, Brace & World, 1921.

N. Smith and D. Wilson, *Modern Linguistics*, Harmondsworth: Penguin, 1979.

H. G. Widdowson, *Teaching Language as Communication*, Oxford University Press, 1978.

Chapter 4

Basic Principles

The preceding chapter, in discussing several aspects of language has suggested the complexity of this essentially human activity; whilst the detailed questions posed at the end of Chapter 2 imply a professional dimension no less complicated.

Clearly there are people who teach the English language successfully without professional training or rigorous language study, succeeding by virtue of those sensitive and sympathetic qualities which mark the natural teacher. There are also those whose training for and experience of other kinds of teaching is successfully transferred to language teaching. There are students of linguistics whose studies have provided such insights into English that they are better teachers thereby. Ideally, however, the professional English language teacher should have not only the required personal qualities, but also training in the disciplines and fields of study appropriate to the language teaching process. Training of this kind can be stated in terms of what the teacher should know and what he should do.

Even with the very wide range of educational settings in the world today, from kindergarten groups of twelve in Argentina to strictly audio-visual classes in Senegal, or traditionally taught university seminars in Japan, there are certain basic principles common to all good language teaching, principles derived from the interaction of aspects of those fields of study which contribute to the theory and practice of EFL teaching. The contributory areas of knowledge may be represented in Figure 3.

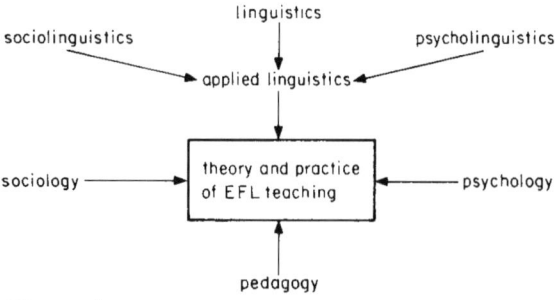

Figure 3

Linguistics, the study of language itself, has drawn on ideas from *sociology* to establish the place and role of language in the sociology of human behaviour, and from *psychology* to investigate among other things how language is learned. The result is two new disciplines, *sociolinguistics* and *psycholinguistics*, which, together with linguistics proper, form the central area of *applied linguistics*. This last field is concerned with many activities involving language – for example, speech pathology, machine translation, mother tongue acquisition, literary analysis. But for the present purpose its chief relevance is to language teaching.

The conjunction of sociology and psychology with the theory and practice box is a reminder that teaching of any kind draws upon knowledge from these fields quite apart from language considerations: group interaction, the status of the teacher and the school in the local culture, the social role of education as a whole – from sociology; and facts about memory span, motivation, cognitive development from psychology. The often forgotten field of *pedagogy* is concerned with class management, questioning techniques, lesson planning and teaching strategies and the numerous daily tricks of the trade that separate the professional teacher from the amateur.

Whether the teacher is well read or not in all the above disciplines, he inevitably makes decisions about the problems involved. Consciously or unconsciously, he reflects in his teaching the beliefs he holds about the needs of the learners, their ways of learning, the best method of motivating them, etc. The more knowledge he can glean from the wealth of writing in the field, the better he will be able to combine this knowledge with practical experience to produce a suitable teaching methodology for his own purposes.

In the light of his knowledge, he can then decide what English to teach, how to give practice in a meaningful way, and how to prepare and execute a progression of enjoyable, well-organised lessons.

Selection and grading

In common with every other subject of the curriculum, English language teaching requires that decisions are made about what is to be taught: the process of selection; and about the breaking down of that body of knowledge or skills into teachable units: the process of grading. Whilst decisions of this kind are usually made for the teacher by textbook writers and syllabus designers, his teaching is inevitably structured and controlled by the underlying theories.

Language teaching presupposes a theory of language, and this is supplied by applied linguistics. The traditional view that the English language consisted of a battery of grammatical rules and a vocabulary book produced a teaching method which selected the major grammar rules with their exceptions and taught them in a certain sequence. This was the grammar-translation method whose rules with examples, its paradigms (like those in the classroom of Chapter 2) and related exercises have for so many years produced generations of non-communicators. The later structural theory of language described the syntax of English as a limited number of patterns into which the lexis or vocabulary could be fitted. Selection and grading them consisted of identifying the major structural patterns and teaching them in a suitable sequence. In its extreme form, the structural approach enabled many learners to use 'language-like behaviour', reflecting a one-dimensional, and essentially non-communicative, view of the nature of language.

Such approaches to language teaching are about as practical as driving lessons in an immobilised car. Language, as a form of human social behaviour, functions within a context of situation. Recognition of this second dimension, and the fact that it is difficult to divorce linguistic forms from their setting, gave rise to situationalised language teaching, or the situational approach. Here, the processes of selection and grading are applied not only to syntax and lexis, but identify a series of appropriate settings: in the classroom, at home, in the shop, at the railway station and so on. Clearly, however, whilst selection from a finite set of rules or structures is possible, it is more difficult to select from an infinite range of situations.

The third dimension of language, which has most recently received the attention of linguists, is that of linguistic functions and notions. The argument is that linguistic forms — sounds, words and structures — are used in situations to express functions and notions.

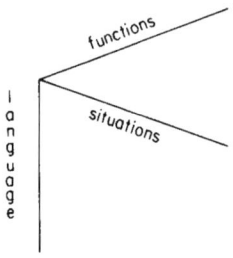

Figure 4

It is possible to identify a wide range of notions: of time, number, length and quantity; of agreement and disagreement, of seeking and giving information, suasion, and concession, to name a few; and thereafter select and grade them into a teaching sequence of communicative goals. The sociolinguistic developments which have in recent years made language teachers more conscious of the functional dimension of language usage have had a number of other effects. At one level, they have given the death-blow to the naive assumption that a particular linguistic form is identifiable with a particular function. As Widdowson (1971) points out:

> One might imagine, for example, that the imperative mood is an unequivocal indicator of the act of commanding. But

consider these instances of the imperative: 'Bake the pie in a slow oven', 'Come for dinner tomorrow', 'Take up his offer', 'Forgive us our trespasses'. An instruction, an invitation, advice and prayer are all different acts, yet the imperative serves them all.

At another level, acknowledgment of the functional dimension has given greater complexity to the basic principle of grading and selection. If these processes are equally applicable to all the three dimensions of Figure 4, which is to have primacy? All must be represented in language courses, but in our present state of knowledge it is the language dimension that is the most completely understood system. The result is that for most non-specialised English teaching in the world today, the principle of grading and selection are applied to the prime dimension of linguistic structure, before those of situation and function.

Contextualisation

Sounds, words and structures, then, are to language what steel, glass, plastic and rubber are to motor cars and the language teacher is no more concerned with teaching philology or transformational grammar than the driving instructor is with teaching car technology. We have seen in Chapter 3 how language is a communicative system representative of reality and thought. Every utterance, to be language, has a meaning, relating to and part of its context. This is why the first two lessons in Chapter 2 were illustrations of English language teaching in a way that the third was not. A sentence like 'My aunt's pen is in the garden' only has meaning when we know who is speaking, and when we can identify the other references and implications. The phrase book for Portuguese learners of English which included the often-quoted and bizarre sentence 'Pardon me, but your postillion has been struck by lightning' demonstrates a total lack of sense of context: who can have said this, to whom, when and in what circumstances?

We know that words and phrases are easier to learn and remember if they are meaningful and in context: it follows

that the foreign language should always be taught and practised in a contextualised form. And when the learning is
being done in a class situation, every member of the learning
group should recognise the context.

Faced with the common need to introduce, exemplify
and practise items of language, teachers often have difficulty
in contextualising them. The immediate classroom environment, with its things and people to identify, count and relate
to each other, is an obvious source of contextualised language
which is common to the experiences of a group of learners.
But its limitations are soon felt after the most elementary
lessons. Supplementation of the classroom's physical resources is possible and many enthusiastic teachers enliven
their lessons by bringing appropriate realities (called *realia*)
into their classrooms. Actual fruit and a knife may be used to
ensure that *apple, orange* and *to cut* are contextualised: but
again there are limits to professional resources and ingenuity.

However, there are no limitations to the introduction of
the physical world at one remove, namely by its pictorial representation. Visual aids are an invaluable contextual resource,
whether completely teacher-produced like blackboard or
over-head projector drawings, or more professional represen-
tations: cut out pictures, maps, wall charts, film strips,
flannelgraphs and film. Of these, it is the former group over
which the teacher has most control in terms of restricting
the context and every language teacher should be able to
produce recognisable blackboard sketches as part of his professional skill.

Visual identification of the physical world, however, is not
the only form of contextualisation available in a given teaching situation. To illustrate one meaning of *to grow*, a teacher
may use the sentence 'Apples grow on trees', verification of
which is not needed from a picture since at least in temperate
climates the fact is part of the common stock of knowledge
of the learners. This contextual source, drawing upon
common experience, is clearly culture-bound, and dependent
upon the learners' ages. But even for a class of students
drawn from the most widely differing backgrounds, there are
many areas of common knowledge. In every culture, the sun
rises in the east and sets in the west, water is wet, people get
hungry and tired, babies cry, metal is stronger than wood and

fire will destroy things: the eternal verities are the basis of any common stock of knowledge. An important second layer is a common cultural background, providing a wealth of events, institutions, people and attitudes, both past and present as a contextual frame of reference.

Clearly, the longer a group of learners continues to work together, the more they build their shared stock of experience. Every happening in that classroom, natural or contrived, is a contextual source of language for as long as the group continues together.

The physical world, however, is of less potential than the world of the imagination. Every shared anecdote or dream, every item of literature becomes part of the class's common experience and therefore the contextual raw material for communicative language work. Given Coleridge's 'willing suspension of disbelief', the world of the imagination is as acceptable as the tangible physical world. Indeed the whole process of foreign language learning is a willing suspension of this kind, where the learners are pretending to be at home in another language. To this end, role play is a useful activity, whereby learners simulate attitudes and roles, which —however briefly and superficially — they adopt as acceptable. The Spanish adolescents in the first lesson described in Chapter 2, by identifying with a manifestly imaginary girl making a telephone call, were role-playing and their resulting dialogues were no less in context than if they had been making an inventory in Spanish of their classroom furniture.

We have argued, then, that the nature of contextualised language for our professional purposes is that the items of language are acceptable or verifiable by all members of the learning group as representing actual or imagined reality. It is clear that a language item which is contextualised in this way is part of a larger body of language (whether realised or not) which the same context may generate. In this way the imaginary dialogues of Lesson 1 and the comprehension discussion of Lesson 2 of Chapter 2 are contextualised in a way that utterances like 'Do we not walk?' in Lesson 3 are not.

Presentation and practice

Just as the processes of language teaching presuppose a theory of the nature of language, they equally need to be based upon a theory of language learning. The one is derived from applied linguistics and sociolinguistics, the other from educational psychology and psycholinguistics.

There is now a considerable body of research on the acquisition of the first language, though much less on the learning of a foreign or second language. The two competing theories about how a language is acquired have had great influence on teaching through methodology books and courses and through textbooks themselves. Whether a teacher has studied the theories, or not, his methods necessarily reflect presuppositions about how language is learned.

The argument is between the behaviourists and the mentalists, in psychological terms, or in linguistics terms, between the structuralists and the generative grammarians. The view on one hand is that language is learned by habit-formation by imitating utterances and then producing new ones by analogy. On the other hand, it is believed that people learn language by utilising certain innate capacities. This view is based on the idea that every human being possesses a sub-conscious language acquisition device (the LAD) which takes in the language encountered, works out the rules that govern it, and then after some trial and error, manages to apply them.

The behaviourist view applied to foreign language learning emphasises the importance of conditioning and reinforcement through the repetition of correct (and only correct) responses to a controlled stimulus. 'Knowing the meaning' is equated with 'giving the correct response'. Learning a foreign language is said to be learning a skill, like riding a bicycle or playing the piano, and these are held to be best learned through automatic and frequent imitation, being positively hindered by conscious awareness on the part of the learner.

The mentalists, or rationalists, reply to this that when a person produces an original sentence of a language he is not repeating something he has learned through imitation — and many of the sentences we produce are original. They may be similar to other sentences in the language, but the actual choice of words and their arrangement is new virtually every time we produce an utterance. (Set phrases, ritual speech as in greetings and farewells, idioms, etc., make a very small list of exceptions.) When the behaviourists answer to this that we make new sentences by *analogy* with those we've learned already, they are, claim the rationalists, contradicting their own stimulus–response theory. For the only way to explain the process of making new sentences by analogy involves the notion of observing the regularities (rules, patterns, structure) underlying them and working out how to operate them to generate new sentences. Language is, thus, rule-governed behaviour. This does not mean that the language-learner indulges in any conscious formulation of rules. The argument is that rules are 'internalised' and their application is quite unconscious. It is not a matter of deliberate problem solving.

But the split between the two schools of thought is not really as fundamental as its proponents may imply. It is extremely difficult to give a water-tight definition of 'habit' or 'rule', and for the practising teacher it seems quite reasonable to say that the oral skill aspects of language (articulation and discrimination of sounds) are acquired as habits which are as hard to change after childhood as other motor habits are hard to change or acquire (learning to play the violin, to skate). But at the same time one can also say that other aspects of language need a knowledge (conscious or unconscious) of rules, but that these are eventually applied habitually, i.e. without conscious attention.

Whether a particular methodology is stricly behaviourist or mentalist, or eclectic, items of language still need to be presented and practised. Presentation consists of introducing each new item of language to the learners in such a way that it can be absorbed efficiently into the corpus of language already mastered.

Whether the new language is lexical or structural, its central meaning must be clear from the context in which it is introduced, but the presentation needs to take place in such a way that the learners' attention is focused upon it. Therefore presentation calls for simple contexts which are at once adequate to demonstrate meaning, but at the same time not so interesting that they distract attention away from the important item of the moment.

45

Another variable in the presentation process is the teaching mode. One cornerstone of behaviourist theory was the insistence on the primacy of the spoken word. Nothing was to be written before it had been said: nothing was to be said before it had been heard. This principle probably continues to hold good for many young learners and for all whose goal is primarily a mastery of the spoken language, but provided that spelling pronunciations are guarded against (and English is not a particularly phonic language) many students find it helpful not only to hear and say new items of language, but also to read and write them during the presentation process. As in any teaching situation, theoretical considerations must give way to considerations of how the learners involved can benefit most.

Basically, during English language lessons the teacher is only involved with three processes: presenting new material, practising familiar material and testing it. And up to 90 per cent of his time is taken up by practice of one kind or another. Ways of practising listening and speaking, reading and writing are dealt with in subsequent chapters, but the way in which this practice is related to presentation and woven into the fabric of each lesson is of the very essence of a teacher's professional expertise. Lessons should be planned and executed so that new language material is soundly integrated with the old. This calls for a sensitive shift from a presentation stage during which the learner's focus of attention is on the new material through early practice where the attention is gradually diverted, into a later practice stage during which the new material is being handled without conscious attention. The shift of attention can be achieved by a gradual increasing of the contextual depth and interest, also by the teacher's sensitive adjustment of the pace of the teaching. Like a stream, a good lesson flows more rapidly over the shallower sections and more slowly over the deeper.

The question of student errors during practice is often hotly debated. A behaviourist would argue that by making mistakes the learner is practising the wrong things and developing undesirable habits: therefore learners should never be put into the position of making errors. A mentalist view assumes that errors are inevitable, that learners at any given point of their growing competence have command of an interim grammar which is by definition imperfect, that we actually learn from our mistakes. There is truth in both arguments. Certainly repeated errors become confirmed and unless the learner is made aware of them he cannot learn from them. On the other hand, that very strict kind of control on a class's language practice which makes error almost impossible is rarely of interest, is rarely motivating. The skilled teacher is able to ensure that during presentation no incorrect language is heard or used and that his gradual relaxation of complete control during the subsequent practice maintains interest and enables him to make the learners conscious of any mistakes as they arise.

Motivation is a basic principle of all kinds of teaching. It is true that there is a certain superficial satisfaction in getting things right. But the student who is satisfied by doing mechanical language exercises correctly has the same superficial motivation as the needlewoman working on samplers, the learner driver operating a simulator or the tyro nurse giving injections to sandbags. The language student is best motivated by practice in which he senses the language is truly communicative, that it is appropriate to its context, that his teacher's skills are moving him forward to a fuller competence in the foreign language.

Ultimately, however, it is the teacher's professional judgment which must count. Every human being is a potential foreign language learner, no less than he is a potential patient: and just as no doctor accepts a patient's own diagnosis and prescription, no professional language teacher can take the view that the customer is always right. Professionalism consists of the operation of a complex of judgment and skills which are soundly based on basic principles of which the layman is usually unaware. It is against the background knowledge of the principles discussed above that the three lessons of Chapter 2 are best evaluated and the procedures and techniques of subsequent chapters are best exercised.

Suggestions for further reading

J. E. Alatis, H. B. Altman, R. M. Alatis, *The Second Language Classroom*, Oxford University Press, 1981.

C. J. Brumfit and J. T. Roberts, *Language and Language Teaching*, Batsford, 1983.

S. P. Corder, *Introducing Applied Linguistics*, Harmondsworth: Penguin, 1973.

J. Haycraft, *An Introduction to English Language Teaching*, Longman, 1978.

E. W. Stevick, *Memory, Meaning and Method*, Newbury House, 1976.

D. A. Wilkins, *Linguistics in Language Teaching*, Arnold, 1972.

Chapter 5

Pronunciation

The skills

Pronunciation teaching deals with two interrelated skills — recognition or understanding the flow of speech, and production or fluency in the spoken language. These skills rely very little on intellectual mastery of any pronunciation rules. Ultimately it is only practice in listening and speaking which will give the learner the skills he requires.

Debates about innate abilities, linguistic creativity, or the pros and cons of habit formation teaching, are hardly relevant to pronunciation. There is no question that using the vocal organs properly for speech is a matter of motor habits, well below the level of consciousness. They can be perfected through constant use, and once established may be difficult to change without serious effort. But they are not as difficult to change as has often been supposed. The drive towards cohesion with a social group is strong enough to change speech habits without any conscious effort or awareness on the part of the speaker in cases, for example, where people move from one area to another and change accent accordingly.

Learning to acquire the pronunciation habits of a foreign language, however, involves a larger number of new skills, especially recognition skills. In order to hear the new language accurately enough to imitate it, the foreign learner must respond to a whole new sound system. Hearing correctly is not always easy, and he is handicapped not only by his lack of control of the new sound structure, but by his lack of knowledge of the new language in general. Understanding the stream of speech involves understanding the vocabulary, grammar and contextual meaning. So that, unlike the native speaker who relies on the heavy redundancy in languages to balance out the normal interference of noise, imperfect transmission of sounds, or muffled articulation, the foreign learner struggles with the whole of the language at the same time, not merely with a few novel sounds.

In order to become proficient in understanding and speaking, therefore, he has to learn skills at many levels at the same time. Every aspect of his knowledge of the language reinforces every other, and pronunciation teaching should always be set in a context of genuine language use. The drilling of isolated sounds has very limited value.

The sound system

The layman who thinks that the stream of speech is merely a sequence of isolatable sounds, which, once learned, merely have to be strung together, is making the same mistake as the person who conceives of language in general as merely strings of words. The truth is that in the area of sounds, as in all other areas of language, structure is all-important. Although separate sounds can be isolated, the characteristics they show in isolation will not be the same as the characteristics they have in the context of neighbouring sounds and the overall structure of the utterance. An oversimplified view of English phonology so frequently leads to a teacher's and his pupil's sense of failure. Having practised all the sounds with considerable effort, the pupils are dismayed to find that they still cannot understand some English speakers, let alone speak like them.

The teacher must understand the way the sounds of English are systematically used within the sound structure of English, not in order to explain this to the students, but rather so that he can clarify his own objectives in pronunciation teaching. *Phonology*, the study of the sound system, is as vital to him as *phonetics*, the study of the physical properties of sounds and their place and manner of articulation in the vocal tract.

The speech process consists of conveying a message through the medium of sound. The message is given shape by the vocabulary and grammar of the language, presented in a train of sounds. These sounds are organised in every language so that it is possible to distinguish one message, i.e. one bit of meaning, from another. Sounds used in a language are therefore distinctive so that words can be distinguished from each other when heard just as they can be distinguished when written. The word *cat* is distinguished from the word *sat* and from the word *cot* and from the word *cad*. In each case the difference of sound which makes the distinction in English is a *phonemic* difference, and the *phonemes* involved can be listed: /k/, /s/, /ae/, /o/, /t/, /d/. In English there are 23 consonant phonemes and 21 vowel phonemes (including diphthongs).

Most descriptions of the sound system of English show how it uses patterns of phonemic contrasts to distinguish words.

The following pairs of messages illustrate, in each case, one phonemic contrast:

'Pull!'	'Bull!'
'It's a pin.'	'It's a bin.'
'There are pears in the garden.'	'There are bears in the garden.'

In every pair, the interpretation of the whole message depends on the distinction between the two phonemes /p/ and /b/ which are similar in being produced by the release of air giving a slight explosion between the two lips, but are different in that the former does not involve the use of voice which characterises the latter. Whole procedures of pronunciation teaching have been based on 'minimal pair' contrasts like these. Useful as they are, however, they often oversimplify matters and ignore further aspects of patterning determined by the context in which the phonemes occur in various utterances.

Although the phonemes /p/, /b/, spoken in isolation differ in respect of voicing and can most readily be distinguished thus, the feature of voicing is not always the most crucial aspect. The features of aspiration and associated vowel length are sometimes of greater weight. For many speakers the /b/

may be hardly if at all voiced, but will not have aspiration — an audible puff of air after it — which the /p/ always has in an initial position. Saying *pear* may suffice to blow out a candle. Not so with *bear*, no matter how loudly or forcefully it is said. Further, at the end of a word like *cap* the /p/ is often not released; the lips simply remain closed. The same is true of /b/ in *cab*. The two words are distinguished, therefore, not by a difference in the articulation of /p/ and /b/, but by a difference in the length of the preceding vowel, which is longer before /b/ than before /p/.

Within any one dialect of English, such facts about the use of the phonemes form a system which is generally referred to as the allophonic sub-system of the general phonemic system of English. Allophonic variations such as those described above, together with facts like the non-aspiration of /p/ after /s/ (*spin* will not blow out a candle), are true for all dialects of English. But allophonic variations like the substitutions of the glottal stop for /p/ varies according to the dialect, and may be found in words like *hopeful* (frequent in RP) or Wapping (in Cockney), which sound as if the /p/ has been left out.

Native speakers are not aware of the way in which they vary the phonemes, and may emphatically deny that they do so. They are to a large extent influenced by the spelling. Teachers in English schools frequently try to exact a pronunciation which is based on the written forms and is quite unrealistic in fact. Such matters as the use of /r/ between *idea* and *of* in *the idea of it*, or the dropping of the /h/ in *I don't like him*, are observed as standard by phoneticians but denied by the layman. The teacher of English to foreign students must be careful to base his pronunciation teaching, especially the recognition practice, on real speech with its allophonic variations. He will be hindered by the spelling system, and this is one strong argument not only against reading aloud for pronunciation practice, but also against the use of a phonic alphabet. The latter does give a more consistent picture of the phonemes of the language, but it ignores allophonic variations just as much as the ordinary spelling system does.

The structure of the sound system involves not only the vowels and consonants, the *segmental* features, but also stress and intonation, the *supra-segmental* features.

Stress – or emphasis, or loudness, or force – functions partly phonemically in words, and partly as a feature of longer phrases or sentences. Depending on the degree of stress, and the prominence thereby given to one syllable rather than another, the following can be different words: *concert, project, desert,* and many others. But the phonemic feature which separates *deserts* (merits) from *deserts* (wildernesses), is not just a simple matter of emphasising the first syllable or the second. An equally important part of the stress system here involves the way the vowel in the unstressed syllable is pronounced. In the first case, the first syllable of *deserts* is unstressed and the vowel is weakened to the short /i/. The neutral vowel (ə) is found in the second syllable of *deserts* in the second case.

Stress is a feature of words not only when the word contrasts phonemically with its minimal pair partner, but also in giving shape to a word as spoken. English does not have as rigid a system of stress patterning as some other languages, where, for example, the stress may fall always on the first syllable (Czech), or on the penultimate syllable (Polish), or on the last syllable (Persian). But there is still a fixed stress pattern for any particular word. Learning this is simply a matter of experience. There are only a few generalisations to be made, for example stress regularly falls on the first syllable of the suffix '-otion', and the suffix 'ity' is always preceded by a stressed syllable. On the whole, learners simply have to get used to the sound shape of a word with its stresses. It is vital that they do so, since they may be virtually unintelligible if they use the wrong stress patterns.

As a feature of phrases and sentences, stress determines the rhythm of English, which is therefore said to be stress-timed. English speakers tend to make the stressed syllables of their utterances come at roughly equal intervals of time, so that all the following sentences would take about the same time to say because they have the same number of stresses (irrespective of the number of syllables):

'I *bought* a *dog.*'
'It's a *dog* I *bought.*'
'But it's a *dog* that I *bought.*'

The unstressed syllables in longer utterances tend to be rushed and slurred so that the total time taken remains the same as long as the number of stressed syllables is the same. In many other languages, Chinese for example, each syllable is given equal time. Such a syllable-timed pronunciation of English gives a machine-gun impression, but is not difficult to understand. The problem for speakers of syllable-timed languages learning English is to understand English speech, in particular to catch the words in unstressed position which are spoken very quickly. For it is not merely a matter of speaking these words fast, but very often of changing their pronunciation as well.

The most frequently observed pronunciation change is that of the weakened vowel, which usually becomes the neutral vowel in most pronouns, articles, conjunction and preposition. Words like *but* and *a* have a strong form and a weak form /bʌt/, bət/, and /ei/, /ə/. Consonants are also affected. For example the consonant of 'is' changes from /z/ to /s/ when the /i/ is dropped in unstressed position after a voiceless consonant, as in 'What's the time?'.

Stress thus functions at two levels. Within a word, one or more syllables have heavier stress than the others. At phrase and sentence level, one or more words are stressed more heavily than the others. The speaker has no choice of which syllable to stress in a word, but at phrase or sentence level he stresses words to suit his meaning. In 'I expect you to bring *John*' the speaker implies that John is to be expected rather than whoever else could be brought. But in '*I* expect you to bring John', he implies that someone else does not expect John. Stress is thus relative. Within the word 'expect', the second syllable is stressed more heavily than the first. But in relation to the whole sentence, the words 'John' or 'I' are stressed more heavily than 'expect' and all the other words.

Stress, at phrase and sentence level, is closely tied with intonation, since the pitch of the voice moves either up or down on the word which is most heavily stressed. Thus, even if a foreign speaker places his stress correctly, he cannot convey his meaning effectively unless he also uses appropriate intonation.

The function of intonation in English is basically very different from its role in tone languages like Chinese or

Luganda, where it is phonemic in distinguishing words from each other just as consonants and vowels do. Thus, two words in these languages may have the same vowels and consonants, but be different words because of a fixed difference in pitch level. In English, tone (or pitch) is not phonemic in this way. On the whole English intonation conveys attitudinal or emotional meaning and is very closely tied to the context of an utterance. Thus 'Please open the window' can sound pleading or peremptory, depending on the intonation used.

(a) Please open the window.   (b) Please open the window.

If the request follows the question 'What shall I open?', however, the heaviest stress, and therefore the main pitch movement, must occur on 'window'. In this case (a), the pleading intonation pattern, would change to

(c) Please open the window.

and (b) would change to

(d) Please open the window.

Since it is often naively supposed that there are universal ways of indicating attitude and emotion, the teaching of English intonation is very often neglected. It is, in fact, so important in spoken communication that many would prefer to give it priority over articulation of segmental sounds in pronunciation teaching.

Pronunciation and grammar

There are a number of important links between English grammar and both segmental and supra-segmental features of pronunciation. The traditionally labelled *s* plural, for example, has a different pronunciation according to which sound it follows, as does the *ed* past tense ending. Thus the final sounds of all the following words are different: *ships, shoes, roses, laughed, loved, hated*. In the sentences 'There he is' and 'There's a man outside', the different stressing and vowel sounds in the first word signal that in the former sentence *there* is an adverb, while in the latter it is an empty slot-filler, the 'existential *there*'.

At the supra-segmental level, stress and intonation show distinctions like that between 'My husband who lives in New York is a banker' and 'My husband, who lives in New York, is a banker' – in this case matched by a punctuation difference. In sentences like 'He didn't go to London because he was ill' only intonation, which cannot be shown by punctuation, distinguishes the two possible meanings (cf. the problem on p. 18).

Variability within the system

There are several ways in which the pronunciation of English can vary. The most obvious one is dialectal variation. Even if RP, or Standard Southern English, is accepted as a convenient general norm for international purposes (as it is in this book), there are many areas in which a local version of English is acceptable and of greater usefulness to students. In this case many features of the sound system will differ from those generally presented in texts and courses covering English phonetics. Whichever dialect is chosen as a model for teaching, students should wherever possible be exposed to other dialects of English so that, at the very least, they will not be too narrowly restricted in their expectations of what English can sound like. There is nowadays such a range of varieties of English in evidence on radio, TV, records and tapes, not to mention films and native speakers living locally, that most learners can gain experience of a range of dialects.

It is inevitable that a language in normal use in a community will in time change in pronunciation, vocabulary and grammar. No amount of formal teaching can prevent the development of local varieties of English, however desirable an international standard might be. As soon as he leaves the classroom, every second language learner will consciously or unconsciously strive to speak in the way that is acceptable to the people he wishes to group himself with. One cannot even say that the retention of RP as the norm at school will ensure that the local dialect does not move too far from international standards. What is more likely to happen is that learners operate two dialects, the school's and the local variety. Since this is very common in Great Britain, as well as many countries, e.g. Nigeria, it is quite a reasonable compromise, though in some cases it may increase the students' learning burden too much.

Within any dialect, there are usually further variations related to social class, educational level and idiosyncratic factors. But these variations are still subject to the rules of the system used by the speech community in general — otherwise communication would break down. That is to say, while speakers have a certain amount of freedom to vary the way they pronounce words, they are by no means totally free. The sound /t/, which can be said clearly and distinctly in isolation, can, in the middle of a word like *matter* sound rather like /d/ or like /ð/ as in *mother*, or like /r/, or even like the sound we make when we cough (a glottal stop — a quick closure and release of the vocal chords). All of these will, in context, suffice for the word *matter*. But if a speaker were to use /f/ he would not be understood. For every sound system, there is a range of possible variations and native speakers do not (except when sleepy, drunk or ill) go beyond the permitted range.

Such variations are a source of difficulty when a foreigner encounters native English speakers after studying English pronunciation in his own country. Since it is impractical for a teacher to teach more than one pronunciation in class, and, in any case, most teachers tend to think of an ideal, careful, way of speech when they are in the classroom, the student gains a limited view of what the actual pronunciation of English really is like. Usually this affects his understanding more than his own speech. It does not matter if he habitually speaks more 'carefully' than native speakers, and, for example, always pronounces the /t/ in *matter* the same way as the /t/ in *term*. He will at least always be understood. He will not mind being recognised as a foreigner, since he will realise that this is usually inevitable and even carries some advantages!

But he can expect his teaching to equip him to follow normal English speech. The teacher therefore has to operate a double standard in his pronunciation teaching. For the students' own speech he can choose a conventional model

57

which is optimally useful for general understanding. But for the students' recognition of speech he must ensure that a good variety of styles is used for practice listening.

Teaching aims

The aim of pronunciation teaching must be that the students can produce English speech which is intelligible in the areas where they will use it. The teacher will have to concentrate on the important phonemic contrasts and select allophonic variations only to ensure intelligibility, not to achieve a total set of native-speaker-like variations. In teaching the different uses of /t/ and /d/ to students who have difficulties with either or both, the distinction of voicing is a useful starting point and examples should be taken of these sounds used between two vowels, as in *rated, raided, sighting, siding, a tin, a din,* etc. In initial position preceding a vowel, the distinction must emphasise presence or absence of aspiration, and in final position lengthening of the vowel preceding /d/.

Other allophonic possibilities such as lateral plosion (as in *little, puddle* or nasal plosion (as in *kitten, goodness*) are not crucial for the students' intelligibility, though they must be able to understand words said in this way.

Teaching techniques

In foreign language teaching, pronunciation is the one area where it is generally agreed that imitation is the essence of the learning process. Some people are better at imitation than others, but one thing is clear: in order to imitate correctly one must have heard correctly what is to be imitated. Unfortunately there is not so much the teacher can do to help his students to hear accurately. He can direct their attention to sound differences, give them plenty of opportunity to listen, but he cannot give them the ability to hear them. On occasion he can make the task easier by separating out the items to be heard. If the students cannot hear a /ts/ combination at the end of words like *cats, mats,* and persistently hear either just /kæt/ or /mæt/ or /kæs/ or /mæs/, the teacher can contrast /t/ with /ts/ and /s/ with /ts/ separately. (Failure to make the plural correctly is often due to a pronunciation problem like this one, as are some other apparently grammatical errors.)

As far as actual pronunciation is concerned, the teacher cannot rely upon explanations of tongue position or even diagrams and the use of mirrors. Apart from a few items such as lip and front of tongue positions, the sensory-motor skills involved are normally well below the level of consciousness and are not easy to deal with consciously. Some kind of intuitive mimicry is necessary. It is sometimes found, incidentally, that when the classroom pronunciation demanded by the teacher does not accord with that which the students hear around them outside the school, they can often mimic the required accent effectively in order to mock it, and their apparent inability to produce it in class is psychological rather than physical. Another source of help may be some noises used by the students when speaking their own language, i.e. onomatapoeic noises for sounds of birds, the wind, trains, etc. In a few cases these might constitute an English phoneme, as the sounds for the buzzing of the bee or for requesting silence do in English.

For successful imitation, students need to listen to themselves. Most people cannot really monitor their own speech, and help from tape recorders can be invaluable. Hearing himself on tape in contrast with the speech model not only convinces the student that he has, or has not, achieved success, but gives him clues for further improvement.

As with all learning, motivation is a highly significant factor in pronunciation. The more it can be made necessary for the student to improve his speech, the more rewarding will the teaching be. Motivation can be real or simulated. Where it is possible, actual contact with speakers outside the class in real communicative contexts (shops, etc.) is of course ideal. Where this is not possible, games in the classroom which are so designed that either hearing correctly or speaking correctly are built in as an essential part of the game provide a context where communication is felt to depend on accurate speech. For example, a class can be divided into teams, standing or sitting in rows. The first person in each row is given an instruction to whisper to the next person, who whispers it to the next, and so on down the line. When the last student has received the instruction he must obey it quickly. If it is worded to highlight a pronunciation point so that an error in speech or recognition at any point along the row might occur, students will in fact be engaged in pronunciation practice in a meaningful context. Thus, if the instruction were 'Draw a ship on the blackboard', and students had difficulty distinguishing /i/ and /I/, the row which produced a drawing of a sheep would not be the winner!

Given the aim of encouraging accurate imitation, the teacher's choice of what to teach and in what order to teach it, depends partly on his decision as to what sound features are essential for intelligibility in the variety of English he has to teach. The degree of difficulty which these sound features present to the students is governed largely by the sound patterns of their native language. By comparing the sets of phonemes and their commonly used allophones in the native language and English, the teacher can assess the areas of pronunciation where difficulty is likely to occur. He will not necessarily be able to predict exactly what errors the student will make, but he will know which sounds or supra-segmental aspects will cause trouble. Although the different languages of the world have all drawn on different sounds and sound features from the infinite range that the human vocal tract could produce, the underlying principle of system of distinctive contrasts with permitted variations is common to all.

Without information about all parts of the system, it is easy to fall into errors of over-simplification. Speakers of German might be thought, for example, to have no trouble with /b/, /d/ or /g/, since these occur in German as well as in English. But inspection of their place in the sound system of German will show that they never occur in final position, so that a German speaker pronounces 'cab' as /kæp/, 'bud' as /bʌt/, and 'dog' as /dok/. The point to remember is that the learners who are not in the habit, in their own language, of hearing certain distinctions will just not hear them in English, and therefore will not pronounce them either. The reason why a German learner might persist in these errors, in spite of being able to say /b/, /d/ and /g/ perfectly well, is that he has simply failed to hear that they occur at the end of words in English. Likewise a French speaker, who uses /i/

and /I/ interchangeably and has never learned to distinguish them, may not even notice the difference between 'live' and 'leave' and may think they are homonyms. Even a speaker of a language like Spanish which has the two sounds but uses them differently (not as different phonemes but as different allophones of one phoneme) will fail to use them correctly in English because he will expect a different degree of significance to attach to them. Attention to the whole system, and adequate recognition practice, are the chief keys to successful pronunciation teaching.

Native language interference applies equally strongly to the supra-segmentals. Foreign judgments of the English as un-friendly, or even as very polite, are often based on faulty interpretation of their intonation, whereas the English judg-ment of certain foreign speakers as rude or aggressive is usually based on a likewise faulty interpretation. The native language habits of intonation and stress and general tone of voice are so all-pervading and deeply ingrained and further out of awareness than vowels and consonants which can often be physically demonstrated, that people find it difficult to accept that there is a systematic variation from one lan-guage to another. Thus, if a foreign speaker makes a segmen-tal pronunciation error, he is excused as a foreigner and his speech is interpreted more or less correctly depending on the context. But if he makes a supra-segmental error, a judgment is made of his personality, not of his language. Thus a German speaker might call someone and use a falling intonation, 'Mr Smith!', as would be appropriate in German. This will make him sound authoritative and possibly impolite in Eng-lish, for gentle polite calling requires a rising intonation. Such intonation differences are a source of misunderstanding even among native speakers of English from different regions.

Classroom procedures

It is very difficult to build up a graded teaching sequence for pronunciation teaching, because, even at beginner level, all the sounds of English tend to occur within the first few months of teaching. Since, as has been seen, the drilling of isolated sounds has little value, it would also be quite unrealistic to attempt to teach the sounds of the language before going on to the language itself.

The teaching sequence must therefore be organised in terms of priorities and degrees of difficulty. The amount of time devoted to specifically pronunciation teaching depends on the larger priorities of the course in general. A useful guide is the precept 'little and often'. The teacher should be prepared to slip a few minutes' pronunciation drill into a lesson at any point where a significant problem is noticed. But random assistance should not take the place of a systematic attempt to integrate pronunciation teaching into the course. It has a natural place in much grammar work, e.g. the teaching of plural endings, third person singular simple present tense, simple past tense and past participles of regular verbs, use of questions of different types, use of adverbial modifiers involving intonation distinctions, and so on.

Pronunciation practice itself might be very short or may occasionally occupy several minutes. In either case a few key principles should be followed:

1 Recognition practice should precede production practice.
2 But since production reinforces recognition, there is no need to wait for perfect recognition before asking for production.
3 The sounds to be heard and spoken should be clearly highlighted in short utterances.
4 But this should not be taken to the extreme of tongue-twisters like Peter Piper.
5 Students should be given the opportunity to hear the same things said by more than one voice as the model.
6 The English sounds can be demonstrated in contrast with other English sounds or else in contrast with sounds from the native language.
7 The target sound contrast should be shown to function meaningfully, i.e. students should realise that it makes an important difference to their intelligibility to use it properly. This can be done by a procedure involving a progression from straightforward drill, where the success or failure is simply measured by the teacher's approval or disapproval, to a simulated communication situation like a picture-word matching exercise, or a game, and then to a

real communication situation like the understanding of a story or joke where the meaning might depend on the sound contrast being taught.

The heart of any drilling or demonstrating of specific sound features is contrast of one kind or another. The most efficient way of showing contrast is by minimal pairs. Any pair of words or phrases or sentences where there is only one feature to distinguish them is a minimal pair. e.g.

part	port
a tack	a tag
He's coming?	He's coming.

Such pairs can be used in the following ways:

(a) The teacher instructs the students to judge whether he is saying two things that sound the same or different. Sometimes he says the contrasting pair, sometimes he says one member of the pair twice.

(b) The teacher says three items, two the same, one different. Students judge which item is the different one.

(c) The teacher says one of the pair and students indicate which one it is, either by referring to numbers (e.g. Sound 1, Sound 2), or by referring to pictures illustrating the words, or by performing an action illustrating the word, or by writing the word on the board or in their books, or by marking a choice in an arranged exercise, etc.

(d) The teacher says one of the pair and students either repeat it after him, or say both members of the pair, or say the other one. This can be done chorally, or by individual students chosen at random, or in turn rapidly round the class.

(e) The teacher says one of the pair and the students have to use the sound feature being highlighted in an utterance of their own, either orally or in writing.

(f) The teacher shows a picture, or performs an action, or gives a clue, or writes a word on the board, or holds up a flashcard, which elicits from the student either a choral or individual production of one or other member of the pair.

But pronunciation teaching does not stop at the drilling

stage. The ultimate step is the recognition and use of the sound feature in normal speech. But the learner should be completely unconscious of his pronunciation, and pronunciation teaching at this stage consists of the teacher's monitoring and making notes of what pronunciation features require further conscious drill.

Where there is a recognition problem, a common teaching error is to falsify the speech to facilitate comprehension. The teacher should always talk at normal speed, rather repeating numerous times till he is understood, or paraphrasing where necessary.The difficulty is not to take the easy way out for the exigencies of the moment, thinking that the problem can be dealt with adequately later. It is, paradoxically, the teacher who is most aware of and sympathetic to his students' problems who is most likely to do this.

Pronunciation then, whilst it can be described and taught in isolation, is not to be regarded as a separate area of language learning, but as a number of contributory strands in the fabric of English, strands to which teachers and pupils give their attention from time to time.

Suggestions for further reading

V. J. Cook, *Active Intonation*, Longman, 1968.

A. C. Gimson, *An Introduction to the Pronunciation of English*, Arnold, 2nd edn, 1970.

B. Haycraft, *The Teaching of Pronunciation – A Classroom Guide*, Longman, 1970.

M. Heliel and T. McArthur, *Learning Rhythm and Stress*, Collins, 1974.

J. D. O'Connor, *Better English Pronunciation*, Cambridge University Press, 1967.

J. D. O'Connor and G. F. Arnold, *Intonation of Colloquial English*, Longman, 2nd edn, 1973.

P. Tench, *Pronunciation Skills*, Macmillan 1981.

Chapter 6

Listening and Speaking

Listening

It is a principle common to this and the previous chapter that listening should precede speaking. Clearly, it is impossible to expect a student to produce a sound which does not exist in his mother tongue or a natural sentence using the stress, rhythms and intonation of a native speaker of the foreign language without first of all providing him with a model of the form he is to produce. It is not possible to produce satisfactorily what one has not heard. The logical first step, therefore, in attempting to achieve oral fluency or accuracy is to consider the learner's ability to listen.

At first sight it appears that listening is a passive skill, and speaking is an active one. This is not really true, since the decoding of a message (i.e. listening) calls for active participation in the communication between the participants. A receptive skill is involved in understanding the message. Indeed, it is essential to the speaker in any interaction that he is assured continually that his words are being understood. This is usually overtly signalled to him in a conversation by the nods, glances, body movements and often by the non-verbal noises (mm, uh-huh, oh, etc.) of his listener. A simple experiment to demonstrate the truth of this is to make absolutely no sound during a telephone conversation (where the verbal cues that the message is being understood are essential, since visual cues by the nature of telephone calls are eliminated) — within a few seconds the person speaking is guaranteed to ask if you are still there.

This visual and verbal signalling confirms to the speaker that listening and understanding has taken place. The receptive capacity for decoding the language and content of the message is a skill which can be trained and developed through teaching, no less than the productive skill of speaking.

Training in listening

There is a clear parallel between the spoken and the written language. On the one hand, listening and reading with understanding are receptive (but not passive) decoding skills; on the other, speaking and writing are productive, encoding skills. But the parallel goes beyond this. The concept of intensive reading (the close study and exploitation of a text for its meaning and the language used) and extensive reading (the more leisurely perusal of a longer text where the learning goes on in a less direct, more unconscious way) is well established and discussed in Chapter 7. There is a similarly valuable and practical distinction to be made between extensive and intensive listening. Indeed, listening is often harder than reading, since it is not often taught and practised, nor is it usually possible to go over again what one hears, whereas it is simple to read and re-read a difficult page in a book.

Both extensive and intensive listening practice should be part of the armoury of a language teacher. Their use will differ in relation to the aim − for example, a French teacher of English may feel that his students are not producing satisfactorily the 'th' sounds in 'this' and 'thin', and confusing them with /z/ and /s/, so he would perhaps, as a first step towards imitation, then production of the sounds, get them to *listen* carefully for the sounds in a given passage (which he has chosen because of the high incidence of these phonemes). There are various books available which provide practice of this type, e.g. Combe Martin's *Exercising Spoken English* (Macmillan, 1970). Trim's *English Pronunciation Illustrated* gives similar practice in quite a different format, as the extract from p. 60 shows (reproduced by permission):

θ,ð/
s,z

a thumb
ə ˈθʌm

a sum
ə ˈsʌm

a mouth
ə ˈmaʊθ

a mouse
ə ˈmaʊs

a path
ə ˈpɑːθ

a pass
ə ˈpɑːs

a race
ə ˈreɪs

a wraith
ə ˈreɪθ

The cook thickens the soup
ðə ˈkʊk ˈθɪkənz ðə ˈsuːp

The soup sickens the cook
ðə ˈsuːp ˈsɪkənz ðə ˈkʊk

This atheist has lost faith
ðɪs ˈeɪθɪɪst əz ˈlɒst ˈfeɪθ

This asiatic has lost face
ðɪs eɪʃɪˈætɪk əz ˈlɒst ˈfeɪs

Figure 5 Intensive listening practice (reproduced from Trim's *English Pronunciation Illustrated* by permission of Cambridge University Press)

On the other hand, the teacher may be aware that his students cannot understand ordinary colloquial English as used by native-speakers. In this case, his aim would be rather to create a more general familiarity not only with the phonological characteristics of conversation (especially the stress, rhythm and intonation patterns), but also with the lexis and grammar typical of this style of discourse. He would then set his class to listen to a passage of natural English speech suitable to their level. e.g. D. Crystal and D. Davy, *Advanced Conversational English*. At intermediate level, V. J. Cook's *English Topics* makes similar use of recorded material. This particular book provides a direct transcript of a spontaneous conversation recorded on tape which should be played to the class. The pupils are asked to listen and answer comprehension questions before they see the written transcript. It is an interesting exercise to ask them then to 'edit' this so that it represents a more normal written representation of a dialogue. The book itself provides an edited version of the same dialogue for the student to check his own efforts against and for the teacher to read from if the tape is not available. An extract from the unedited and edited version of one passage is included below.

Unedited

Richard Parry: Yes, I suppose I suppose that is true. I mean we I suppose it sounds very smug to say it but we do tend to perhaps er see other people rather along our own lines. And perhaps they're not. I don't know I mean. . . .

Vivian Cook: I remember on one of the ...

Richard Parry: . . . . they're fairly discriminating as a as a collection of people.

Vivian Cook: In one of the space shows a few years back that I I happened to turn on and there was this rocket zipping across the sky with sort of smoke belching from all directions. I thought 'Good heavens! How did they get a camera close up like that?' And of course because they'd they'd omitted to show 'simulation' at the bottom um er and it wasn't for five minutes that I sort of realised you know that they hadn't quite achieved such miracles of communication by that stage and um certainly the sort of ersatz um reality is a is a danger.

Edited

Richard Parry: Yes, I suppose that's true. I suppose we do tend to see other people as ourselves. And perhaps they're different.

Vivian Cook: I happened to turn on one of those space programmes a few years ago and saw a rocket zipping across the sky with smoke pouring out of it. I thought 'Good heavens! How did they get a camera close up like that?' But of course they'd forgotten to show the word 'simulation' at the bottom. I didn't realise for five minutes that they hadn't quite achieved such miracles of communication yet. This kind of imitation reality is a danger.

Extensive listening

Extensive listening can be used for two different purposes. A very basic use is the re-presentation of already known material in a new environment. This could be a recently taught structure or, say, a lexical set which was introduced months before and needs revision. The advantage of exposing the student to old material in this way is that he sees it in action in a genuine, natural environment rather than in the classroom context in which it was probably first presented. Psychologically, extensive listening to the 'real' as opposed to purpose-written English is very satisfying since it demonstrates that the student's efforts in the classroom will pay dividends in life in an English-speaking environment. One of the greatest and most common failures of language teaching is that what the student is taught is totally inadequate for dealing with the welter of aural stimuli coming at him from all sides when he first sets foot in England. Extensive listening of this type helps him considerably.

The materials he hears need not of course be only a re-presentation of what is already known.

Extensive listening can serve the further function of letting the student hear vocabulary items and structures which are as yet unfamiliar to him, interposed in the flow of language which is within his capacity to handle. There might be unknown, rather technical words or an unfamiliar verb form, – for instance, the passive for elementary students or the subjunctive for the advanced. In this way there is unconscious familiarisation with forms which will shortly become teaching points in a language lesson. Story-telling, especially appealing to younger age groups, is an example of extensive listening and often includes a considerable proportion of unknown lexis and some untaught structures. Comprehension is not normally seriously impeded since the compelling interest of the story holds the attention and the familiarity of the great body of the language is enough to provide a sufficiently explanatory setting for the unknown material.

The teacher himself is the source of the model in story telling. As one of the aims of extensive listening is to re-present old material in a new way, it is often best that this is done by means of authentic tapes of English people talking together (and so providing the model), where the teacher himself is not involved. Of course it is possible to write a script for recording which illustrates the particular points to be made, but this is a highly-skilled task and the student gets enough specially written material in his textbooks anyway. Much more effective and convincing are extracts of real, live English speech. It is surprisingly easy to build up a library of suitable tapes. An expensive way is to buy commercial tapes put out by the big publishing companies. The tapes that accompany Crystal and Davy's *Advanced Conversational English*, for instance, are invaluable at the most advanced levels. There is also a *Workbook* by K. Morrow to help exploit the material.

Generally, the best resource for extensive listening passages is going to be the recordings which the teacher makes himself. These can be from a wide variety of sources – recordings made whilst in England, recordings of local native English speakers, recordings from local English language TV and radio broadcasts (including advertisements), and, perhaps most accessible of all, recordings from the BBC World Service which can be heard worldwide and has an enormous selection of programmes to choose from.

Once a collection of tapes of this nature has been made, they have to be graded according to language level (elementary, intermediate, advanced) and according to the points they illustrate. They also have to be made available to students to listen to. If the teacher wants the whole class to listen to a passage for revision or to prepare the way for future lessons, this can of course be done in the normal sequence of a lesson. One of the advantages of extensive listening passages is that they need not be under the direct control of the teacher but function as back-up material for the student to listen to in his own time at his own speed. At the most sophisticated level, this can be done in the language laboratory, which should have a library facility providing tapes for extensive listening. The language lab. is particularly useful in providing listening rather than speaking practice.

Many language classrooms today have one or more tape recorders which can be used for individual or small group listening purposes either during class time (with no disturbance to other people working on other things, if good headphones and a junction box are used) or during a fixed period outside regular hours when supervision is provided. The most flexible system, however, is to make available cassette tapes for home loan, since cassette recorders are commonplace in many parts of the world today. The student can then work when and where he likes, as often as he likes. Whichever system, or mixture of systems, is adopted, even greater benefit is possible if a stencilled sheet of instructions and follow-up questions goes with suitable tapes. Occasionally, notes might be provided to introduce and give a setting for the recording. Some types of tapes lend themselves to reinforcement by visuals – a picture guide to London is a good accompaniment to a conversation about the city, and it can be used in class as a visual form of preparation for the tape itself.

Intensive listening

Whereas extensive listening is concerned with the freer, more general listening to natural English, not necessarily under the teacher's direct guidance, intensive listening is concerned, in a much more controlled way, with just one or two specific points. There is one important division to be made – the listening can be primarily for language items as part of the language teaching programme, or it can be principally for general comprehension and understanding. Clearly in this second case the meaning of the language must already be generally familiar.

The vocabulary of conversation is often radically different from the written language with which the student is probably more familiar. Hence listening to conversations is invaluable to him to accustom his ear to what he would hear if he visited England. It is very useful to make available passages with more familiar, colloquial lexical items and concentrate on Anglo-Saxon rather than Romance vocabulary. This is particularly important for speakers whose mother tongue is a Latin Language, as they have a tendency to sound pompous in speech through choosing words like *enter* and *repeat* instead of *come in* and *say it again*. Listening practice for phrasal verbs, fixed expressions such as idioms and generally more colloquial language is one effective means to cure this. It is easiest initially for the student to listen for phrasal verbs, say, in a given passage, then he is asked to put in more formal one-word alternatives. It is usually much harder for students to do this exercise the other way round and listen to a passage (e.g. a formal speech) with a high proportion of Romance vocabulary and then attempt to substitute more colloquial English.

Listening can be for grammatical as well as lexical purposes. Passages with a high incidence of a given grammatical feature provide excellent material. A real football commentary of a match between, say, Liverpool and Manchester United (recorded from 'Saturday Sports Special' on BBC World Service) is a very good introduction to one particular use of the present simple: 'Keegan gets the ball from Toshack, makes a break along the right and tries to beat Gordon Hill outside the penalty box. Hill wins the ball and moves it quickly across the box to Pearson, who skilfully traps it and sends a long, floating pass to the right wing.'

Many other exercises are possible. One area worth mentioning is practice in listening for words or grammatical forms which tell you to expect something else to come shortly, or refer back to something just mentioned. At the simplest level, in the first case, a singular third person subject automatically demands concord with a regular verb in the present tense. As soon as a native speaker hears 'a dog' for instance, he knows the verb, however far away it is, will probably be marked with an 's', e.g. 'a dog . . . barks'. Beyond this elementary level, he must learn that if he hears 'not only', he will certainly get 'but also' or 'but . . . as well' later in the sentence; 'neither the . . .' will automatically precede 'nor . . .'. Pronouns point backwards to the nouns they stand for, so do words like 'former' and 'latter'. Other sentence connections (however, so, but, while, since, etc.) are widely misunderstood and should be the source of intensive listening practice. A very simple way to practise this type of listening is to have the student listen without a written text once or twice to a passage containing several sentence connectors, then give him a written text with blanks where the connectors are. His task is to fill them in without listening to the tape again. In general, listening practice is gravely neglected at the level of discourse. There may be emphasis on the phonology, lexis and grammar of words and even the sentence, but the linguistic links that join sentences into a coherent discourse are usually overlooked, and so the student's aural comprehension is sadly impaired.

As we know, it is perfectly possible to hear, but not listen. Similarly, it is possible to listen but not understand. A technical lecture on nuclear physics is beyond the grasp of most people, regardless of the simplicity or difficulty of language it is couched in. Listening for meaning, therefore, is an important skill to develop, but it goes without saying that the actual content of the message should be within the intellectual and maturational range of the student. There is some gradation possible here, from everyday events of common experience (daily life, current events, etc.) for beginners, to popularisations of more technical material and natural conversations between two native speakers for intermediate students, to a full range of specialist topics and conversations between several English speakers for the advanced. Discussions and debates, which are usually structured somewhat, are useful preliminary listening material before the student is forced to deal with an informal conversation between several participants. As many students at this level of proficiency will be concerned with the study skills necessary for academic English, it is worth giving practice in the format of lectures and their specialist content by first providing practice in listening to the popularising short talks often given on Radio Three or the World Service of the BBC. These can range from talks on composers to political reports in the programme 'From Our Own Correspondent'.

There are other factors to be considered apart from the actual subject matter of the aural text. One is the formality of the language – that is, where it is situated on the following axis:

Slang—familiar—neutral—formal

Most classes have had little practice with anything other than neutral English. Another factor is speed of delivery – is it a rapid conversation or a measured speech? Further, is it prepared and rehearsed, or impromptu? How many speakers are involved? Clearly, the more there are, the more difficult it is. Is the accent of the speaker what the student is accustomed to hear? English regional or class accents are very confusing, on first hearing, for someone brought up on RP. Again, lack of familiarity with these factors can seriously impair the student's understanding of the meaning of the passage.

A final consideration, which applies equally to listening for language or to listening for meaning, is the type of question to be employed. The simplest are yes/no answers to questions and true/false exercises. Blank-filling can direct attention to key-words and phrases. Beyond the purely factual questions such as these, other types depend on inferences being made from the passage. This is a difficult exercise for the student, as it demands that he not only understands what the passage says, but also what it implies. Clearly, it is best with good students at higher levels. Multiple-choice questions are widely used for both factual and inferential exercises. Many of the books mentioned on pp. 75–6 provide this type of practice. Reading comprehension texts, e.g. in J. Eynon's *Multiple Choice Questions in English* at intermediate level, and in L. Peterson, D. Bolton, M. Walker and M. Hagéus' *Work and Leisure*, *Our Environment* and *Other Worlds* at advanced, can be readily adapted for listening comprehension, if necessary.

Many students have a tendency to practise listening comprehension line by line, without attempting to get an overall understanding of the passage. There is room, therefore, for questions on sections of the text, or the whole text, e.g. What are the main points in this argument? What are the reasons for . . . ? What would a suitable title for this text be?

A listening comprehension passage can be a springboard for other work. By asking how the author creates a particular effect, or why he uses a specific word, it is easy to go on to a form of literary appreciation. Although this is restricted to more advanced classes, it is nearly always possible to use an aural comprehension passage as a basis for questions on the student's own experience. A passage on sports naturally leads to personal questions about the student's own participation in, say, tennis, and the ensuing conversation provides good oral practice and reinforces what has just been learnt.

Fortunately for the teacher, intensive listening materials, especially for aural comprehension, are commercially produced and very widely available throughout the world. So far this is not the case for extensive materials. Listed below are a few of the many books and tapes on sale. Several publishers have a range of listening materials available. The *Nelson Skills Programme* has four books by Rosemary Aitken designed to practise listening skills at different levels. Longman and Oxford University Press have their own series of books on similar lines. Other examples of such books and tapes include:

L. Blundell and J. Stokes, *Task Listening*, Cambridge University Press, 1981.

M. Geddes and G. Sturtridge, *Listening Links*, Heinemann, 1979.

R. R. Jordan, *Active Listening*, Collins, 1984.

R. Mackin and L. Dickinson, *Varieties of Spoken English*, Oxford University Press, 1969.

R. McLintock and B. Stern, *Let's Listen*, Heinemann, 1983.

A. Maley and S. Martling, *Learning to Listen*, Cambridge University Press, 1981.

R. O'Neill and R. Scott, *Viewpoints*, Longman, 1974.

D. Scarborough, *Reasons for Listening*, Cambridge University Press, 1984.

M. Underwood and P. Barr, *Listener*, Oxford University Press, various dates.

Speaking

However good a student may be at listening and understanding, it need not follow that he will speak well. A discriminating ear does not always produce a fluent tongue. There has to be training in the productive skill of speech as well. In many cases, listening should lead naturally on to speaking. This is particularly so at the phonological level where it is essential to develop an ability to recognise a sound before success in producing it is possible. The link between these two areas is bridged by techniques such as those discussed in Chapter 5. The rest of this section is primarily concerned with grammatical and lexical problems of oral fluency in communication, but much of what is said is equally applicable to phonological matters.

It has been pointed out earlier that there is much in common between the receptive skills of listening and reading, and the productive skills of speaking and writing. There are controlled, guided and free phases of production in both oral and written work. The speech produced by the student should be tightly controlled at first by the teacher, then as progress is made there should be less rigorous guidance, culminating in situations where the student is free to produce utterances appropriate to the situation. This progression applies to each teaching point at all levels of achievement, though clearly at beginner stages there will be heavy emphasis on controlled and guided practice, and more and more freedom at advanced levels.

In the previous sections of this chapter, considerable stress was laid on listening to as much natural, authentic English as possible. This aims to go some way towards dealing with the problem of understanding and being understood by real, live English people. All too often, past teaching techniques have led to a good passive understanding of the language, but no capacity to use it. More recently through massive pattern practice in audio-lingual and audio-visual courses, there have been many students who could produce perfectly adequate responses in the classroom when given a clear stimulus by their teacher, but who were incapable of dealing at all convincingly with the social situation when they met their first Englishmen talking together. It is particularly important, therefore, that these stages of controlled, guided and free practice should always be seen in relation to the functional use to which the student will have to put his oral fluency. He must be prepared by his teacher for actual communication with others (apart from monologues and talking to oneself, speech is basically a communicative, social art), and the teaching must develop this competence in the learner.

Controlled oral work

One of the most versatile techniques for the presentation and practice of phonological, lexical and grammatical items is the dialogue. It has the further advantages that it can be used for controlled or guided or free work, and a dialogue is by its very nature language interaction between people, which fulfils the communicative criterion. It is possible to use a dialogue at the most elementary level, even in the first lesson. Within minutes of meeting a class of total beginners it is possible to have an exchange like this:

Teacher: My name's Robert Smithson. What's your name?

Student: My name's Janine Riche.

It is very easy to develop this mini-dialogue into pair work. The teacher, after some choral, group and individual repetition to establish the probably very unfamiliar sounds, can proceed round the class, asking a different student each time. Then he can have two of the better and more extrovert students come to the front of the class and say the dialogue, each one taking a part. Then they switch roles. The next step is to indicate by a judicious mixture of example, mime and translation that every member of the class is to do the same as the pair at the front with their immediate neighbour.

The next step might be to use the dialogue in a chain drill:

Teacher: My name's Robin Smithson. What's your name?

Student 1: My name's Janine Riche. *(Turns to Student 2.)* What's your name?

Student 2: My name's Paul Loquefort. *(Turns to Student 3.)* What's your name?

At the guided and free levels, dialogues are endlessly flexible for both presentation and practice. Guided dialogues may have words blanked out, or whole phrases when they are highly predictable from the context. Even complete responses by one of the parties may be omitted, as in the following extract from Millington Ward's *Practice in the Use of English* (Longman, 1966, p. 102, reproduced by permission).

Here is a 'one-sided' telephone conversation. You know what Mr Brown says, but you cannot hear what the other (the hotel reception clerk) replies. You may, however, be able to guess.

Mr Brown: Hello! Hello! I want the Hotel Splendide, please.

The other: . . . .

Mr Brown: What did you say? I can't hear you very well.

The other: . . . .

Mr Brown What did you say? I can't hear you very well.

The other: . . . .

Mr Brown: Oh, you *are* the Hotel Splendide. Something seems to be the matter with this line.

The other: . . . .

Mr Brown: Well, it does sometimes help to do that, but I can't just ring off and try again now because this is a long-distance call. Will you put me through to the Reception, please?

The other: . . . .

Mr Brown: What? Oh you *are* the Reception. Good. I want to book a double room with bath, overlooking the sea. It must be quiet.

The other: . . . .

Mr Brown: Oh, for two weeks beginning August 1st. August 1st to 14th inclusive.

The other: . . . .

Mr Brown: But you must have some!

The other: . . . .

Mr Brown: But surely a hotel of your size could fit in two elderly people at *any* time of the year. Provided it's quiet I don't much mind if it doesn't have a view of the sea.

The other: . . . .

Mr Brown: At the back? Oh. Is it quiet there?

The other: . . . .

Mr Brown: I see. Yes, I suppose there must be a certain amount of noise at the front from the promenade. Is it a good big room — as big as the front ones?

The other: . . . .

Mr Brown: A double bed? Oh no, I meant twin beds in a double room. We are both very light sleepers. We must have single beds.

The other: . . . .

Mr Brown: Right up there? I suppose it's all right provided there's a lift. What about the bath? It has one?

The other: . . . .

Mr Brown: But we *must* have a bath to ourselves. My wife is not accustomed to wandering along corridors with her sponge-bag.

The other: . . . .

Mr Brown: The seventh floor! Oh dear.

The other: . . . .

Mr Brown: A private suite! Oh, I see. Of course, put that way my wife won't mind the seventh floor so much. Er — what does it cost?

The other: . . . .

Mr Brown: Good gracious! That seems a lot.

The other: . . . .

Mr Brown: Yes, of course. And it *is* a private suite. Very well then. Will you please book this private suite on the seventh floor for August 1st to 14th inclusive? Thank you. Goodbye.

The other: . . . .

Mr Brown: Oh yes, of course. How very silly of me.

Brown, R. G. Brown, 125 Duke Street, South Lampton.

The other: ....

Mr Brown: No, no Sou*thamp*ton is very far away from where we live. I said *South Lampton*, and it is in Cheshire.

The other: ....

Mr Brown: Of course. Don't say another word. Many people make the same mistake. Quite often.

The other: ....

Mr Brown: Yes, I agree. They do sound very similar, especially on the telephone.

The other: ....

Mr Brown: Good. Thank you very much. We'll be arriving in the early evening. Goodbye till then.

In controlled oral work there are many types of drills where the student response is so tightly structured that the possibility of error is almost eliminated. To an extent this is valuable as it leads to a certain fluency and confidence in the learner. A typical example of this is the substitution drill:

Teacher: Say this after me: Have you got any coffee?

Class: Have you got any coffee?

Teacher: Instead of 'coffee', say 'tea', like this: Have you got any tea?

Class: Have you got any tea?

Teacher: Milk

Class: Have you got any milk?

Teacher: Sugar. . . .

Substitution drills of this nature are widely used. They are not as effective in this form as they might be, however, since they could with very little extra effort be made into instances of communicative contextualised language use. In this particular case, the teacher could situate the dialogue in a grocer's shop and pretend to be a customer with a large shopping list (which the whole class can see) with coffee, tea, milk, sugar, etc., written on it. A student faces him (playing the role of the shopkeeper) across a desk which has on it a tin of coffee, a packet of tea, etc. The teacher/customer asks, 'Have you got any coffee?' while pointing to coffee on his shopping list. At the simplest, the shopkeeper simply says 'yes' and points at the coffee. The teacher/customer then points again at the coffee on his list and has the whole class repeat 'Have you got any coffee?' After the reply he points at tea on his list and may first say, 'Have you got any tea?' himself or get the class to do it directly. After the shopkeeper has pointed to the tea, he can point to, and say, the next item on the list.

Here essentially the same thing is happening as in the original substitution drill, but this revised version demonstrates much more clearly to the class that this is not simply mechanical drill but language practice with a visually demonstrated communicative function in a real life situation in which the student could easily find himself. This principle of contextualising the oral language practice applies not only to substitution drills but also to any other mechanical, purely manipulative exercise. They become infinitely more valuable when directed to the actual or potential language needs of the students.

Guided oral work

It is probably a mistake to structure so tightly all the utterances demanded of a student that it is difficult for him to make an error. Practically, it is nearly impossible to do, and mistakes in themselves can teach a lot. It seems that making mistakes and learning from their correction is a natural part of the learning process, so too great rigidity in control may well be counter-productive. Guided oral practice aims to give the student a limited freedom to use and practise what he has learnt, yet still be subject to some restraints. In general, it is best to provide the general situation and content of what is to be said, but allow some freedom in the mode of expression. Role-playing, as in the case of the customer and shopkeeper above, is a useful technique at this as at other levels. The class may well have learnt several progressively more polite phrases to ask if anything is needed:

'Can I help you?'
'Can I help you, Mr. . . ./Mrs. . . ./Sir/Madam?'
'Is there anything you want. . . .?'

'Was there anything you wanted?'
'May I help you in any way, Sir/Madam?'

They have also learnt suitable replies:

'No.'
'No, thank you.'
'Not just at the moment, thank you.'
'That's very kind of you, but I don't need anything at the moment, thank you.'

By controlling the situation but allowing variety of expression of this kind, the dialogue has been changed from controlled to guided oral work.

Another way to practise oral proficiency in a guided way is to set up a role-playing situation. Two lines of chairs with a clear space down the middle could be the gangway between rows of passengers on an aircraft. Students are then allocated roles — one is a stewardess, another the head steward, and another the captain on a cabin inspection. Other students play the part of passengers — but passengers with marked characteristics. One is a brusque, rather rude politician, another a terribly polite old lady travelling to see her grandchildren, others ordinary business and holiday travellers. In this way there is some guidance as to appropriate questions and answers, but some flexibility for the students to bring some of their own individuality into the situation.

As in the case of the dialogue, role-playing of this kind is a flexible technique which can be used in a much more structured and predictable way at the controlled stage, or alternatively with less guidance at a later stage in the lesson where continued practice is turning into active production.

Free oral production

It is important that a student should be able to produce naturally the language which has been presented to him and which he has practised in various more or less controlled situations. This is particularly important, not just in the later stages of a given teaching cycle, but at the more advanced levels of attainment, where the pupil feels he now has the basic machinery to say what he wants rather than what he is channelled into saying, and therefore he insists on moving to freer oral production so much more quickly than the elementary or intermediate student. This is not an easy thing to accomplish, and calls for considerable creative thought on the part of the teacher to provide situations and stimuli that will get all the students to make active use in a communicative way of the language they have learnt.

Group work is a generally active tool, but particularly so at the stage of freer production since there must be automatically less teacher control and more pupil-centredness in any work done in groups. Most of the suggested techniques in this and previous sections can be prepared in groups first of all and then brought back to the class as a whole. This is particuarly useful language work, since there is a task in hand – the writing and presentation of a short dialogue, for instance – which has to be discussed and practised in English. The task itself provides the stimulus for a natural use of English: witness the work being done in the first lesson in Chapter 2.

Visual stimuli – maps, photographs, pictures, cartoons, even slides and films – are another useful source of oral language practice. They can all be used simply as discussion starters, or as the material for a short talk (a procedure common in several important examinations), or as the first step to producing role-play situations or dialogues based on them. The teacher can of course guide to a greater or lesser degree according to how explicit he makes his instructions, and how specific the aim he has in mind before he begins. Generally, it is imperative that he knows what he wants from a photograph or map, and then gives just enough instructions to the class to make sure they produce it.

Another type of stimulus is the written word. Magazines, pamphlets, and not-too-serious newspapers lend themselves at the very least to animated discussion or even to set speeches and debates. Aural stimuli are often overlooked as material for freer language production. But selected sound effects, put on a cassette and played one by one to the class, challenge them to build up a story from what they hear. This produces valuable practice in the English used for deduction and possibility, as well as the more general structures necessary in an oral composition.

Dramatisation of scenes which have been written by the class are motivating and useful for fluency. Similarly, the reading of plays by well-known authors is useful in itself, and probably even more so in the discussion it provokes as to how the characters are to be interpreted and how the play, scene or sketch staged. The best choice of play is one by a contemporary author such as Pinter or Wesker with a real feel for the nuances and rhythms of everyday speech.

The conversation class

Conversation classes are very common at intermediate and advanced levels, often with small groups and individuals rather than large classes. They usually take place in private schools or with private teachers rather than in state-run institutions. The general assumption is that simply talking in a free and easy way, preferably to a native speaker, is the best way to improve oral fluency. It is true that listening to and conversing with a native speaker, especially allied to the extra attention that comes to individuals or small groups, is beneficial. However, conversation classes often do not do as much as they might, and of all classes seem to lead most quickly to boredom and a high dropout rate. The reason is usually that not enough thought on the part of the teacher goes into them and the student's own expectations are often wrong. The moderately experienced teacher feels that a conversation class is a soft option and that he will have no trouble filling an hour with chat and talk. The student expects talking to do far more for him than it is capable of doing. The best approach is to give as much attention and preparation time to conversation classes as to any other lesson. It is as imperative to have as clearly defined an aim and as carefully sequenced a plan for oral work as it is for a grammar lesson. Just talking and filling up the time till the end of the hour is no use at all.

The very term 'conversation class' is imprecise as it refers partly to the mode of teaching and may also refer to the content of what is taught. The idea is that, by simply conversing, the teacher shows the student how to hold a conversation himself. But very often the subject matter of a given lesson rightly ranges much wider than this. It may come from the teacher's professional diagnosis of his students' needs: this could be remedial oral work to bring the students up to standard, or straightforward teaching to prepare them for a forthcoming oral examination. Very often a conversation class is informal in character and allows much more scope for the students to put forward topics of particular interest to them. Indeed, the more personal relationship possible from teacher to student is often a distinguishing feature of a conversation class. As time goes on, progressively more and more suggestions tend to come from the students to which the teacher may well wish to respond. It is remarkable how he takes on an explanatory role in answer to questions, and is often in practice a mediator of his own culture and background. It is wise to anticipate this and plan quite deliberately into any teaching scheme a good number of themes connected with English life and culture.

There are many sources of help here. The big 'global' courses put out by the major publishers are often situated in England with quintessentially English characters in them. They give a very good impression of what is characteristic of certain types of English life, and can be used for that purpose. The amount of explaining that needs to be done will of course depend on the closeness of the students' own society to England's – in Western Europe it will be much quicker and easier than in the Third World or the Middle East. There are also quite a lot of books available about Britain. One of the most readable and detailed is A. Sampson's *The Changing Anatomy of Britain* (Coronet, 1983). The yearly publication of her Majesty's Stationery Office, *Britain*, is full of facts and figures and best used for reference. Other official bodies such as the Centre for Information and the British Travel Association put out books, leaflets, fact sheets and so on which are widely available world wide from their own offices, from the British Council and from British Embassies. There is another category of books written with at least one eye on the optional 'Life and Institutions' paper of the Cambridge Proficiency Examination. Some useful titles are:

H. E. Brooks and C. E. Fraenkel, *Life in Britain*, Heinemann, 1982.

G. Broughton, *Know the British*, Hutchinson, 1977.

E. Laird, *Welcome to Great Britain and the USA*, Longman, 1983.

R. Musman, *Britain Today*, Longman, 1982 (3rd edn).
B. E. Pryse, *Getting to Know Britain, Blackwell*, 1983.
J. Randle, *Understanding Britain*, Blackwell, 1981.

Other very important sources of information are the media – BBC World Service has a regular programme 'News about Britain' and 'English by Radio' often deals with cultural topics; the English press is always available in reading rooms and libraries of embassies, consulates or the British Council, and in most parts of the world can be bought commercially from newspaper kiosks and in international hotels.

Materials of this nature, and to a lesser extent the books mentioned earlier in this chapter, are a very direct and lively introduction not only to English culture but also to the contemporary use of the English language. They can be exploited in every conceivable way in the classroom. Many magazines are visually very attractive and an excellent stimulus to discussion. At the simplest level, students can be asked just to describe what they see. Carefully chosen pictures will give scope for them to make deductions about what has happened and what might soon happen. This in turn will probably suggest wider themes which can be expanded and developed. Practice of this nature is very valuable for students taking certain examinations – Cambridge First Certificate and Proficiency Examinations and the ARELS Certificate in Spoken English and Comprehension for non-native speakers of English involve this type of exercise.

Materials from the media are excellent for developing the skill of reporting. In the first place news items are by their nature models to imitate. The ability to narrate events is a ˈeful skill to acquire. Each member of the class might be given a news story, and given the task of putting it across orally to the others from notes. Not only is he asked to tell a coherent story, but also he needs to be able to summarise, make notes and speak in public in an understandable way. As time goes on, the exercise set can become harder – he might be given a non-factual interpretive piece by a political commentator, for example. As in the case of visuals, this can easily be seen as very relevant work by the many advanced examination candidates who are asked to give a short talk, with only a few minutes' preparation, to the examiner.

It would be wrong, however, to think of conversation

classes solely in terms of a final examination or testing. Certainly the exploitation of the teaching materials should never be restricted only to provide practice in examination questions. Variety has got to be present. It is all too easy to sink into an initially successful, comfortable format which never varies from lesson to lesson. For instance, instead of taking a newspaper article and always having the students summarise and report it orally to the class, they may attempt to reconstruct in pairs the original interview and make a list of the reporter's questions, a verbatim statement of the interviewee's replies, and a copy of the reporter's notes jotted down at the time. The article can be rewritten for a very different newspaper in a suitable style for homework.

Variety must be allied to pace. A slow, boring lesson teaches very little, so it is important to keep everyone moving and challenged with something which is just a little beyond his capacity. No topic or device should be overworked, however good an idea it is or however much preparation it has entailed. It is always better to stop whilst everyone is enjoying it and wants more, rather than pursue it to the bitter end. Then a repetition on another day provokes eager anticipation rather than groans.

The class atmosphere is very important, and is greatly helped by a less serious side to class activities. As well as more serious materials and teaching, there should always be room for games, songs and puzzles. There are specially written books on the market that can help (for instance M. Carrier, *Take 5*; C. Granger, *Play Games with English*; J. Hadfield, *Communications Games* and A. Wright *et al.*, *Games for Language Learning*) and records produced for the overseas learner, mentioned earlier in this chapter. But it is best to build up one's own collection of games and puzzles from as many places as possible. The type of book sold on railway stations to keep travellers occupied on their journeys are a rich source, as are the competition pages of weekly and monthly magazines. Some records from the present Top Ten, universally known contemporary classics such as the Beatles' records, and English folk songs are also very exploitable. Of the periodicals listed at the end of this book, *English Teaching Forum* and *Modern English Teacher* are useful for this type of material.

Variety, pace and humour go hand in hand with a necessary lightness of touch on the part of the teacher. They all contribute to the essentially informal nature of the conversation class, which is one of its great strengths. With careful management, the pitfalls of boredom through conversation for conversation's sake can be avoided and a friendly atmosphere established in which the advanced student feels free to develop oral confidence and the ability to project himself and his personality in a foreign language.

Suggestions for further reading

M. Argyle, *The Psychology of Interpersonal Behaviour*, Penguin, 4th edn, 1983.

G. Brown, *Listening to Spoken English*, Longman, 1977.

G. Brown and G. Yule, *Teaching the Spoken Language*, Cambridge University Press, 1983.

D. Byrne, *Teaching Oral English*, Longman, 2nd edn, 1981.

W. Rivers, *Teaching Foreign Language Skills*, University of Chicago Press, 2nd edn, 1981.

W. M. Rivers and M. S. Temperley, *A Practical Guide to the Teaching of English*, Oxford University Press, 1978.

Chapter 7

Reading

What reading is

It is a commonplace of teacher education that teachers tend to teach by the methods which were used by the teachers who taught them. In no area of language teaching is this more true than in that of reading. It is probably for this reason that the procedure of reading round the class has been perpetuated, though anyone who considers it seriously, even briefly, in terms of what it contributes to new learning, or of pupil participation, or of communicative function, realises very quickly that it is a singularly profitless exercise.

It may be well, therefore, to begin by looking carefully at just what 'reading' entails in the context of teaching English as a foreign language – see Appendix 1 for a summary.

First it must be recognised that reading is a complex skill, that is to say that it involves a whole series of lesser skills. First of these is the ability to recognise stylised shapes which are figures on a ground, curves and lines and dots in patterned relationships. Moreover it is not only a matter of recognising the shapes as such but recognising them as same or different, and recognising that shapes which are quite different may for the purposes of reading be regarded as the same, as is the case with upper and lower case letters like 'A' and 'a'. Good modern infant teaching recognises the need for training in this kind of recognition and a good deal of time is devoted to the matching of shapes and patterns and in general cultivating the perceptual apparatus necessary for it.

This is, however, in the nature of a low level skill, which becomes increasingly mechanical; where learners are already literate in a language which uses the Roman alphabet, acquiring this skill presents few problems. It is only where learners are illiterate or literate in a language which uses a non-Roman script that difficulties may be encountered.

The second of the skills involved in the complex is the ability to correlate the black marks on the paper – the patterned shapes – with language. It is impossible to learn to read without at least the capacity to acquire language. The correlation appears to be made between elements of the patterns on the paper and formal elements of language. According to the nature of these formal linguistic elements the nature of the skill involved alters. The elements may be complex groups of sounds which might be called 'words' or 'phrases' or 'sentences' or even 'paragraphs', 'chapters', or 'books'; or they might be the most basic elements, the single 'sounds' called phonemes. Readers who learn to correlate larger groups of sounds with the patterns on the paper might perhaps be learning by 'look and say', those learning to correlate the patterns on the paper with phonemes by a 'phonic' method; both kinds of skill are needed to develop efficient reading. Reading speed, for example, probably depends to a considerable extent on the development of the first; reading aloud would seem to depend at least to some extent on the second.

A third skill which is involved in the total skill of reading is essentially an intellectual skill; this is the ability to correlate the black marks on the paper by way of the formal elements of language, let us say the words as sound, with the meanings which those words symbolise.

We have therefore three components in the reading skill; A, the recognition of the black marks; B, the correlation of these with formal linguistic elements; and C, the further correlation of the result with meaning. The essence of reading then, is just this – the understanding of the black marks on paper A–C. A great many complexities have been grossly simplified in this account, in particular it is important to understand that the process is not a straight linear sequence as might be inferred by the symbolisation that has been used. The scope of the recognitions may be large scale or small, and the correlations involve a to-and-fro scanning between the text both as a physical object and as a linguistic object and the meanings which it conveys. The reader clearly brings his knowledge of the language and his knowledge of the world to bear, he builds up expectations, he makes predictions about what is to come and the extent to which his predictions are accurate is one of the factors in fluent reading. Thus most English native speakers faced with a sentence that began, 'The mathematician soon solved the . . .' would, using their knowledge of the world, of how mathematicians behave and what their work is, and their knowledge of the language, be likely to predict that the sentence might continue with a word like 'problem' or 'equation' and accurate reading would be a matter of confirming the prediction.

The word *reading* of course has a number of common interpretations. It may mean reading aloud, a very complex skill, which involves understanding the black marks first and then the production of the right noises. Most people, if they are asked to read something aloud, like to have an opportunity to 'glance over' what it is they are being asked to read. In the actual process of reading aloud too they usually find that their eyes are several words if not lines ahead of their tongues. The process is something like A–C–B.

If reading involves only the first two of the components discussed above, A–B, the result is 'barking at print'. It is perfectly easy to learn to read an exotic language in this sense. One can learn to make the right noises to correspond with the squiggles on the page without having the slightest understanding of what the sense of it is.

It must be recognised that reading aloud is primarily an oral matter. For those who teach foreign languages it is closer to 'pronunciation' than it is to 'comprehension'. While it is perfectly proper to try to develop the skill of reading aloud it clearly cannot be done using an unfamiliar text the content and language of which stretches the linguistic capabilities of the learners to the utmost. It requires a familiar text whose content and language are clearly understood, detailed explication and practice of the special pronunciation problems in it, and small group techniques. It must also be admitted that the usefulness of the skill of reading aloud is limited. Few people are required to read aloud as a matter of daily routine, radio newscasters, clergymen, perhaps actors and that is all. To the huge majority its importance is minimal.

Reading may also mean 'silent reading' and this is the interpretation which is most likely for the term. This is perhaps the nearest approach to the essence of reading, the A–C of it. It is obvious that by far the greatest amount of reading that is done in the world is silent. A reading room is a silent room. But the nature of the silent reading skill is far from uniform. It varies according to the use to which it is being put. Some of the uses are (i) to survey material which is to be studied, to look through indexes, chapter headings and outlines, (ii) to skim – particularly when one item of information is being sought in a mass of other printed information, (iii) to gain superficial comprehension, as when reading for pleasure or preparing to read aloud, (iv) to study the content of what is read in some detail, (v) to study the language in which the material is written – this may involve textual study in the literary sense or it may involve the kind of language study that a foreigner may need to do. The depth and detail of understanding, of comprehension, increases as we go through these ways of using reading, in sequence. The skilled reader has developed all of these ways of using reading. It is common for the third, fourth and sometimes the fifth of these to be encouraged in schools, though the first and second are almost completely neglected.

Of these five kinds of reading activity the first three, survey reading, skimming, and superficial reading are sometimes grouped together and called *extensive reading*. The object of such reading is to cover the greatest possible amount of text in the shortest possible time. A relatively low degree of understanding is perfectly adequate for this, either because that is all that is being sought in any case, or because the material itself is highly redundant – as is the case for example with newspaper reports. The label indicates that those who use it are not concerned with the actual skills involved but with the effects which the employment of those skills produce, that is to say a familiarity, albeit not a very thorough familiarity, with a large body of reading material. It is by pursuing the activity of extensive reading that the volume of practice necessary to achieve rapid and efficient reading can be achieved. It is also one of the means by which a foreigner may be exposed to a substantial sample of the language he may wish to learn without actually going to live in the country to which that language is native.

The remaining two kinds of reading activity, content study reading and linguistic study reading are also often grouped together and called *intensive reading*. Once again the term indicates that it is not the nature of the skills involved that is of most interest but the results, in this case a deep and thorough understanding of the black marks on the paper. The concern is for detailed comprehension of very short texts. Intensive reading is typically concerned with texts of not more than 500 words in length. The objective is to achieve full understanding of the logical argument, the rhetorical arrangement or pattern of the text, of its symbolic, emotional and social overtones, of the attitudes and purposes of the author, and of the linguistic means that he employs to achieve his ends.

Closely related to degree of understanding is reading speed. Obviously the rate at which material may be covered becomes slower as depth and detail of understanding increase, but there are a number of other factors which enter in here. One of these may be the clarity of the text itself. Another factor is the extent to which the content of a text is already familiar to the reader. Nevertheless it is possible to develop reading speed, and efficient reading involves high reading speeds with high levels of comprehension.

Many people seem to believe that *study* and slow reading are the same, or at least that in order to study well one must read slowly. It is very important that this belief be undermined. Study involves several other sorts of skill besides reading, and may well involve several different sorts of reading skill. The good student will probably want to make a preliminary survey of what he is going to study, this will lead him to formulate a series of questions about the subject he is studying, he will then read, perhaps partly skimming, partly reading intensively to find the answer to those questions, and when he has recorded the answers he will at some future time revise the material. This sequence of operations describes the well-known SQ3R study technique, and it is clear that there is much more to it than just slow reading. (A fuller description of this technique and much practical

advice on the matter of reading quickly will be found in
E. Fry, *Teaching Faster Reading.*)

It should be the concern of every teacher to foster
increased general reading speed in pupils. Fluent silent
reading is specially necessary for anyone who proposes to
venture on to any kind of higher education, and when, as
Fry and many others have clearly shown, it is fairly easy
to double and treble that speed, it is obvious that the effort
to do this ought to be made.

Some relationships, within material to be read

In discussing the complex nature of the reading skill it was
pointed out that reading involves correlating elements of language with meaning. The most familiar of all elements of
language are 'words' and it must be quite clear that part of
what is involved in understanding a text is understanding
the meanings of individual words in that text. Thus if a
reader does not understand the meaning of a word like *fleet*
he may miss the whole point of a passage which concerns
some kind of naval engagement. This particular kind of block
to comprehension is so common that it is frequently taken
to be the whole story, but it is not quite so simple as that.
The failure to recognise a particular lexical item may not be
the result of simple blank ignorance of the kind suggested
above, it may be much more subtle than this. It may be the
product of false association, as in the case of the reader who
understands 'concerted action' as something to do with
music; or it may be due to lack of knowledge of the limits
of derivational morphology as in the case of the reader who
understands 'commando' as the men under a particular
officer's command; it may be due to a kind of folk etymo-
logy as in the case of the reader who understood a 'limpet'
to be a dwarf with one leg shorter than the other; or for
foreigners especially it may arise from the existence of
'false friend' cognates so that a Spaniard or a Frenchman may
understand that a 'library' is a place where books are sold.

Understanding the meanings of individual words is not
the end either. The efficient reader needs to be able to
understand the patterns of relationships between words –

the semantic patterns of lexical items. Thus he must learn to observe for example how a series of synonyms can carry a particular concept through a passage (weapons . . . arms . . . equipment . . .), or how a general term is made more precise (The men were issued with their *weapons*. Each man received a *pistol*, *two clips of ammunition*, and a *dagger*), or how a technical meaning may be assigned to a term so that it may be used as a counter in the development of an exposition (Let us call this first infiltration of the enemy's defences the first *wave*. Once the first *wave* is in position . . . the second *wave*. . . .).

There is still much more to come. The efficient reader must have a clear understanding of *the grammatical relationships* which hold between the lexical items, and he needs to grasp the semantics of a particular grammatical item in a particular context. For instance a sentence like 'We'll change the programme in Bremen', may be spoken in such a way that it is quite unambiguous, but in its written form it may be interpreted either to mean 'We'll change the programme which has been arranged for Bremen', or 'We'll change the programme when we get to Bremen'. This is a question of whether *in Bremen* is related to the whole sentence 'We'll change the programme', as a sentence adverb, or whether *in Bremen* is a prepositional phrase acting as a post-modifier of *programme*.

The good reader also needs to be familiar with the precise meaning of the particular grammatical devices used, structure words, word order, word forms and broad patterns of sentences. (The text says 'The airforce had agreed to create a diversion by bombing the other side of the submarine basin but they were late.' How does this differ from saying '*and* they were late'? 'The aircraft were due at 3.40 precisely. At 3.46 the first anti-aircraft gun opened fire.' Why not 'The first anti-aircraft gun opened fire at 3.46'? The consequences of subordinating one clause to another, or choosing one tense rather than another, or relating sentences by nominalisation ('The men disappeared into the night. Their disappearing so silently was quite eerie') and all the multifarious patterns of the grammar in their almost incredible richness are all the proper subject of the good reader's attention.

So also are the patterns of logical relationships within

texts. The skilled reader makes use of the information, the signals, passed to him by the lexical and grammatical patterns to discover the architecture of a passage, the framework upon which it is built. He can perceive that this sentence is a generalisation, that this paragraph which follows is one bit of the evidence upon which the generalisation is based. Here, and here, and here are time adverbs showing the temporal sequence of the events in the story, and so on. It is from this general overview that he is most likely to gain an understanding of what the text is really about.

There are three other kinds of relationship which concern written texts. The first of these is the relationship which exists between the author and his text. The skilled reader is aware of the author's attitude and purpose whether he intends the passage to be taken seriously or whether he is writing ironically, or with his tongue in his cheek, or whether he is writing light-heartedly or with humorous intent. The author may be writing something purely descriptive, attempting to encapsulate a bit of experience in words, or he may be attempting to present a narrative, expound a theory or develop an argument. An anecdote may be recounted to support a contention, emotion may be deliberately invoked to cover inadequate reasoning, but at every point the author is using what he writes for some end in human communication and it is essential that the reader should be aware of what this is. Reading a joke as though it were serious exposition is a very radical kind of misunderstanding.

The second sort of relationship concerning written texts is that which exists between the reader and the text. Obviously the author's purpose will be related to the reader's reaction to the text, but there is one kind of reader response which involves a kind of extension of the text and which can therefore be very important for a full understanding of it. It may be, for example, that the text is so constructed that it leads the reader very powerfully towards adopting a particular point of view, or accepting a particular generalisation, or value judgment, yet the conclusion may never be explicitly stated in the text. So the logical implications of a text may need to be explored as well as the syllogisms expounded explicitly in it. To fully comprehend the point of a short story, for example, it may be necessary to imagine what the next incident in the narrative might be and the good reader has the ability to make this kind of projection.

The third kind of relationship which is relevant to the understanding of a written text is that which exists between the text and the culture, in the anthropological sense, of the community in whose language the text is written. The understanding reader is aware of the precise cultural value of verbal expressions. It is not sufficient to know that an expression like *Spiffing*! means *Excellent*! or some such thing, it is also necessary to be aware that such an expression places the user, socially, educationally and temporally. The whole realm of literary allusion and quotation, comes in here. It may be necessary to know who wrote the text, when he wrote it and for whom, in order to understand it fully. Such information is often not derivable directly from the text and has to be acquired from some outside supplementary source. There is, however, something of a tendency among teachers to provide too much of this supplementary information at the expense of paying attention to the text itself and what it says and the priority must always be to ensure that the text itself yields up as much as possible of what is really relevant to its understanding. Knowing who wrote it and when may not be relevant at all.

It is not only the cultural value of words and expressions that is important; the ability to identify the kinds of situation, the topics, the social classes, the geographical regions, and the points in time to which they belong; but the value which the text as a whole may have in a particular society. In order to understand a play like *Look Back in Anger* by John Osborne, or a novel like *Saturday Night and Sunday Morning* by Alan Sillitoe and to appreciate why they are regarded as important in post-war British literature it is necessary to have at least some idea of the nature of the social changes that took place in the 1950s and 1960s in England and the kinds of conflict that these changes generated. All of this is part of comprehending a text. It is clearly some way from understanding the plain sense and is beginning to approach literary appreciation, but it remains true that even quite ordinary pieces of writing like advertisements offering French lessons at your home may be misunderstood if the cultural context in which they appear is not known.

Finally every reader must make some kind of evaluation of the texts he reads. Until he does this he cannot be said to have fully comprehended them. He has to relate what the text conveys through its vocabulary and grammar and its rhetorical and logical structure and the attitudes and cultural meanings which it has to his own experience, his own conception of reality. He needs to judge if this is really the way men and women behave under the influence of fear, love, or hate. The whole question of the truth of fiction needs to be examined (is the story of the Prodigal Son a 'true' story?) and so too must the validity of logical and rhetorical structures. (Are the conclusions which the author draws from the evidence he presents justified? Are the conclusions the author leads us to draw valid? Is the language used in this apparently objective description in fact 'loaded' so that we find ourselves approaching this following section of the text with prejudice? and so on.) It is only when all of these dimensions of understanding have been seriously contemplated that full comprehension may be achieved.

This then is a brief exploration of the nature of reading, of the kind of thing it is, and the factors that enter into it. How then is reading to be *taught* and what part does it play in teaching English to foreigners?

Teaching reading

First of all there is the question of teaching the mechanics of reading. As was pointed out earlier, where pupils are already literate in a language that uses the Roman alphabet the mechanics as such present few problems. Where the Roman alphabet is not known then the full panoply of techniques used for teaching initial literacy must be brought into play. A useful account of current methodology is to be found in C. Moon and B. Raban, *A Question of Reading.*

The conventions of reading from left to right, and from top to bottom may have to be taught by such devices as simply getting pupils to follow the tip of a pointer which moves appropriately, picture story series arranged in the appropriate pattern, video or cine projections with moving points or areas of brightness which follow the left to right pattern all help. The shapes of letters may have to be taught by using all kinds of mnemonics which will help to link them with their sound values – *S* is a Snake, *b* is a big fat man with a big belly, and so on. The visual perception may have to be supported by the kinaesthetic, learning to write the letters as they are recognised, sandpaper cut-outs, plastic or wooden letters which can actually be handled, the range of devices available is almost overwhelming. Once the basic conventions are understood, then the combining of phonic analytic/ synthetic approaches and global pattern recognition approaches can proceed. It is at this point that learners should be made aware of the most usual regular English spelling patterns, and encouraged to recognise words by their block shapes thus aeroplane has quite a different block shape from bus. Flashcards, or better, flashboards are of great use here. A flashboard is a piece of black painted plywood or white thin melamine surfaced sheet, like Formica, about 30 cm long and 10 cm wide. The black painted surface can be written on with chalk and easily erased for re-use, similarly the white Formica surface can be written on with water-based felt tip pens. A set of nine or ten flashboards is sufficient for most purposes and avoids the consumption of great quantities of card. Longer boards can be used to encourage quick recognition of whole sentences in their written form and most teachers of complete beginners will find a set of five of these about one metre long extremely useful. Some teachers may have access to such sophisticated pieces of equipment as tachistoscopes or Wordmaster talking cards where the words or sentences being read are recorded onto a magnetic tape strip attached to the card on which the words are printed or written. When the card is run through the Wordmaster machine the printed words are reproduced in the spoken medium. The greater the variety of approaches that can be adopted the greater the likelihood of success.

One relatively mechanical aspect of reading is that related to reading speed. The book by Edward Fry mentioned earlier gives sound guidance here. The simplest technique for improving reading speed is basically to use a series of timed texts, understanding of which is then tested in some way, most often by multiple-choice questions, but mechanical pacers which move a blind or a pointer down a page have also been shown to be useful, as have various types of film projection device. Obviously at very early stages it is possible to encourage rapid recognition by using flashboards as suggested earlier. Most teachers need to learn flashboard technique. The key things to remember are to stand where all pupils can see the board without the teacher having to move the board around, and to keep the board still when showing it. If the teacher holds the board horizontally across his chest so that the writing is upside down and facing him, calls for pupil attention, and then twists the board along its own horizontal axis, a good clear 'flash' can be achieved with the writing revealed right way up for just as long as the teacher may require.

Given that the mechanical aspects of the teaching of reading are satisfactorily dealt with how are the intellectual reading skills to be developed? The classic approach has been by questioning, and a great deal can be done by this means. There are however a number of points that the teacher needs to bear in mind when using questions to help pupils to develop understanding of texts. The first is that there is a great difference between questions intended for teaching and questions aimed at testing. Teaching questions tend to be very numerous, oral rather than written, constructed in ordered sequences which lead the pupil to pay particular attention to various aspects of the text, and are likely to be provocative in the sense that they constitute the opening move in an exchange which might grow into a discussion. Sometimes teaching questions don't have a 'right' answer because they ask for personal reactions, and any one of a dozen idiosyncratic responses may be equally acceptable. Teaching questions should seek to cultivate as many as possible of the different kinds of reading skill. It is therefore inappropriate to tell pupils to shut their books when asking questions which are intended to teach understanding of the text. Questions asked with the books shut test memory, either pure visual memory or memory of what was understood. To learn to comprehend, the pupil must learn to look at the actual black marks on the page and to make sense of them, and this can only be done with the book open.

One useful technique for encouraging the pupils to develop

the skill of skimming is that which is initiated by the instruction, 'Find the sentence that has the word *aircraft* in it.' The pupils then all hunt busily for the word in their texts and put their hands up when they have found it. One pupil is then chosen to identify the place where the word is by some agreed convention 'On line x on page y', and may then be asked to read aloud the sentence in which the word occurs. More complex variations of this technique involve instructions like, 'Find the sentence that tells us that the commandos had to wait for the arrival of the aeroplanes' or 'Find the sentence from which we know that the plans made for the carrying out of the raid did not go through without a hitch.' Notice that while still demanding a skimming reading skill we are also demanding a deeper level of understanding involving making deductions from what has been read.

For cultivating close and repeated reading of a text at the plain sense level, or even at deeper levels, P. Gurrey in his book *Teaching English as a Foreign Language* suggests a technique which may be illustrated by the following series of questions about the sentence above concerning the men who were issued with weapons. Thus, 'Who were issued with weapons? What were the men issued with? Do we know who gave the men the weapons? Can we guess? Do we know whether the men actually received their weapons? How many different things did each man receive? Is a clip of ammunition a weapon? What kind of pistol did each man receive? Was it a revolver? Why do you think so? etc., etc.' These questions would be very numerous and fired off with the utmost speed. They will be so easy that the great majority of pupils will always be ready to answer and even the slowest pupils will have some opportunity to participate. All such questioning is for teaching. It is in fact very close to language manipulation and pattern practice.

Questions for testing, on the other hand, usually are not very numerous, the most common number seems to be about ten or twelve. Very often they are written and it is clear that a written reply is expected. They are not concerned with fostering specific reading skills. They tend to have a high proportion of questions directed at specific vocabulary items, and demand definitions or explanations rather than asking for inferences about meaning to be drawn from the context.

The questions are often directed at apparently arbitrarily chosen points in the text and do not concern themselves with overall pattern or tone. The proportion of questions dealing with logical inferences is high, and the number of questions relating to the plain informational content is low. Often the 'questions' are not questions at all but are instructions for a written exercise involving summary or rewriting the text from a different point of view. Tests of this kind may be perfectly proper, they may indeed help to gauge the attainment of pupils. They may even, education systems being what they are, contribute to the pupil's success in public examinations by virtue of the practice they give in examination technique, but the teacher must be quite clear that they do not 'teach' reading comprehension.

The second point which the teacher needs to bear in mind is that the choice of an appropriate text is very important in building up pupils' reading competence. A text which is too difficult, where every other word has to be explained, or which uses extremely complex grammatical constructions, or which is about some obscure technical subject of small interest to the pupil, is only likely to produce frustration. Similarly a text which is too easy does not extend the pupil and it is fundamental that learning requires effort. So texts must be properly graded and sequenced and varied so that their linguistic content and cultural difficulty matches the abilities and sophistication of the pupils, and ensures a reasonable coverage of the various kinds of reading skill they need to develop. Thus texts should include description, exposition, and argument as well as narrative. Some texts should be short and dense, others should be longer and more slight. Humorous pieces, advertising copy, official regulations, as well as essays, feature articles and news reports should all be included. A collection of pieces like Annabell Leslie's *Written English Today* gives some idea of what is possible.

The third point is that it is important that all the aspects of reading, all the various kinds of relationship, between words in the text, between grammatical constructions, between logical and rhetorical elements, between the author and the reader and the text should be covered by the questioning. Clearly for some texts one aspect may be more important than another but there is something to be said for maintaining a kind of check list to ensure that at some point every aspect receives due attention. On Page 104 you will find a summary list which may be used in this way.

The fourth point the teacher needs to bear in mind when using questions to help pupils to understand what they read is that the form in which the question is put may have a bearing on how easy or difficult it is for the pupil. For example there are those structural patterns of question which lead to the answer 'Yes' or 'No'. The first of these are the ordinary 'general questions' (Did the man beat the dog? Did the aircraft arrive on time?). Then there are those which have the word order of a statement but have a rising intonation which gives them question value (The aircraft arrived on time?), and there are also a range of different kinds of 'tag question' (The aircraft arrived on time, didn't it? The aircraft didn't arrive on time, did it?) The structure of such questions is closely related to, often paralleled by the structure of the sentences of the text, and the one-word answers 'Yes', 'No' are about as simple structurally as it is possible to get in English so that from a purely structural point of view such questions are very easy.

The second formal pattern is that which requires as minimal response a short phrase or word group, not just 'Yes' or 'No'. A great many *Wh*–questions belong to this category. (When did the aircraft arrive? – at 3.46. Who were issued with weapons? – The men.) Similarly alternative questions with *or* are often of this kind. (Were the men soldiers or civilians? – Soldiers.) However alternative questions may also require full sentence or clausal answers – see page 104. Questions which require short phrase answers are slightly more demanding in structural terms, but even these have a structure which is related in a clear and regular way with the structure of the sentences of the text. The structure of the replies can usually be taken ready made from the text.

The third formal pattern is that which requires as minimal response a clause or full sentence. Questions beginning with 'Why?' or 'How?' are frequently of this kind, and one of the most insidious is 'What does . . . mean?' (Why were the men issued with weapons? Because they were going on a raid. How does an ammunition clip work? The clip consists of . . . Perhaps almost a whole paragraph of explanation may be

---

THE DIMENSIONS OF QUESTIONS USED TO HELP PUPILS
TO UNDERSTAND WRITTEN TEXTS BETTER

I DEPTH OF UNDERSTANDING

1 of plain sense within the text
2 grammatical relationships within the text
3 lexical relationships within the text
4 logical relationships within the text
5 rhetorical relationships within the text
6 relationships between the author and the text — attitude, purpose, etc.
7 relationships between the reader and the text — reactions, prejudices, projections, etc.
8 evaluation and acceptance

II STRUCTURAL COMPLEXITY

Type of question	*Type of minimal response*
(a) General	Yes/No
(b) Wh—?	One word/short phrase
(c) Alternative, 'or'	One word/short phrase/ clause/sentence
(d) Why?/What does . . . mean?/How does . . . work?	Clause/sentence/paragraph
(e) Declarative statement	True/False
(f) Multiple-choice questions	Non-linguistic (tick, cross, underlining, etc.)

The cross-multiplication of these two dimensions gives some 48 different types of questions which can be used to help pupils to read with greater understanding.

---

required. What does *wave* mean? In this passage *wave* means the body of men who move into position against the enemy. And an alternative question with *or* might be Did the men get into position first or did the aircraft arrive first? The men got into position first.) Here the relationship between the structure of the question and the structure of the passage — except in the case of alternative questions — is rarely clear cut or explicit, and the structure of the reply may bear very little relation to either. Clearly questions of this kind may make very heavy demands on the ability to produce complex structural patterns, and so must present certain sorts of inherent difficulty which must be taken into account.

There are two other kinds of question which are frequently used to try to help pupils understand texts better. One of these is the True/False variety. Here the structural complexity of the reply is of the same order as for Yes/No questions, but whereas certain sorts of Yes/No questions predispose us to one answer or the other by virtue of their intonation, and hence can be answered in a virtually mechanical, automatic way, True/False questions demand judgments at the level of content so may be just that little bit more difficult. (The weapons the men were given were suitable for attacking tanks. True or False?)

The second kind of question here is the multiple-choice question — frequently abbreviated to MCQ. In a sense this is simply an elaboration of the True/False type since such questions involve making decisions about the relative truth of a number of statements related to the text. In terms of the structural dimension considered above it should be understood that the structural patterns of the questions can be made to match exactly the structural patterns of the text. This means that MCQs have great advantages where the linguistic levels at which pupils are working are at least partly defined in structural terms. The mode of the answer is virtually non-linguistic, it may be a tick in a box or a circle round a letter, or at most a letter or number written down, so the demands made on the pupil in terms of the production of complex structure patterns is nil. This means that all his attention may be devoted to the business of understanding the black marks on the paper. It is very important to remember the distinction between questions for teaching and questions for testing with the multiple choice format. The most important characteristic of teaching-MCQs is that the rubric for them no longer reads 'Choose the *correct* answer' but 'Choose the *best* answer'. Testing-MCQs have one element which is clearly and unambiguously 'correct'. With teaching-MCQs several of the elements may be equally acceptable at one level, and it may require considerable discussion and close examination of both the text and the question to decide which one is the 'best'. It must be very clearly understood that the purpose of framing these questions is not to find out how much of the particular text in question the reader has understood but to help him to develop strategies by means of which he may better be able to understand other texts. Detailed discussion and exemplification of what is involved is to be found in *Read and Think* by John Munby.

It will be noticed that while open-ended questions for teaching are very often oral, leading and guiding the pupil along the road to fuller and fuller understanding, MCQs for teaching are most likely to be written in form. The pattern of classroom interaction for open-ended questions is likely to be teacher centred: the teacher asks the questions, the pupils answer. With MCQs the most profitable pattern of classroom interaction is between pupils in small groups where the discussion of alternatives can go ahead and the close reading of text and question, comparison and interpretation develop freely. The very great success of this technique, illustrated by the second lesson in Chapter 2, is one of the things that recommends it so strongly.

The discussion of using questions to help pupils understand texts better so far, assumes that the questions are formulated by the teacher or the textbook writer, but questions formulated by the pupils themselves can contribute substantially to furthering their understanding of texts. This technique has the advantage that the questions that the pupils ask will in the first instance be real questions, directed at gaining information which is not accessible to them on first reading the text. If the teacher begins by asking each pupil to formulate three questions about the text, questions to which he genuinely does not know the answer, and small group discussion is initiated, some of these questions can be answered by other pupils in the group. If the discussion is then widened to a whole class discussion even more of the questions are likely to be answered and the few remaining ones can be dealt with by the teacher in the ordinary way. With very little guidance pupils soon develop strategies for getting the meat out of a text, and soon acquire the ability to peel layers of meaning off. This seems to be a particularly useful technique for dealing with literary texts like poems, where the layers of meaning may be very numerous. It may of course be necessary for the teacher, keeping the checklist of types of understanding in mind (see p. 104), to use straight questioning techniques to lead his pupils towards full understanding, but pupil-initiated questions have the advantage that they lead the pupil to develop those strategies for understanding which will ultimately take him beyond the tutelage of the teacher, and this must surely be a fundamental educational objective. See Appendix 2 for a summary of questioning techniques.

A recurring problem in helping pupils to understand what they read is that no matter how carefully the teacher chooses his texts, there will always be some pupils for whom they are too easy and some for whom the texts are too difficult. One way round this problem is to attempt to individualise instruction. This involves having available a large number of carefully graded texts with appropriate exercises on them which pupils can work through largely on their own. Creating materials of this kind is a long-term project which would require great dedication on the part of the teacher to carry through successfully. However there do exist published materials of this kind. They are known as the *SRA Reading Laboratories* (Science Research Associates, 1958/60). These materials need to be used with caution since their cultural orientation is largely American and biased towards the native English speaker, but they nevertheless are a valuable source of immediately usable material.

Visual and audio aids to reading

A further series of devices which may help to foster better understanding are those which involve the use of pictures, diagrams, charts and models. For example a map of the submarine base where the commando raid took place — used as an example earlier in this chapter — might make the whole description easier to follow. Similarly a picture of a dagger, or the real thing, or a cut-away drawing of an automatic pistol showing how the ammunition clip fitted into it might help to clarify the conceptualisation of an unfamiliar bit of military technology. A time line, or diagram, showing the relationship between the time of narration and the sequence of events recounted in the story can also help to make comprehension easier — especially in longer pieces of writing like novels where the technique of telling a story in 'flash-back' is often used. L. P. Hartley's *The Go-between* is a good example, and Joseph Conrad often uses the technique. Similarly various kinds of tabulation or graph presentation can make the architecture of a piece of writing clear. It can show how various themes are developed paragraph by paragraph or chapter by chapter, how several themes or sets of characters are treated, with an interweaving of threads of narrative, the giving of prominence to one event here, another there, or it can help in keeping track of what different characters were doing at different times in different places — as for example in a detective story — so that the solution of a mystery is clarified. Such visual displays can often be prepared by the pupils themselves and the exercise of doing it is a training in perceiving the meaningful relation-ships within the text.

The value of aural presentation ought not to be neglected either. At the very simplest level this may involve no more than the teacher reading a text aloud. A reading like this may resolve structural ambiguities like the one in the example about *the programme in Bremen*, but it can also emphasise the organisational signals — *first, second, third* or *as a con-sequence, thereafter* and so on. With a taperecorder or record player the roles and characters of participants in dialogue and even the context of the dialogue can be made much more vivid, since background noises and sound effects may be introduced. In particular, understanding a play can be made much easier and more enjoyable by listening to it well read — though clearly plays should really be seen in performance to arrive at the best understanding of them. A great many courses for the teaching of English to foreigners published today have taped materials to accompany them and it is nearly always valuable to have these available to support the written text, if for no other reason — especially for the teacher who is a non-native speaker of English. A very useful list of recorded spoken materials is published by the English Teaching Information Centre (*Information Guide No. 3. Recorded Material for Teaching English*, 1974) and this is well worth consulting. Many of the records and tapes listed there may be borrowed from British Council Offices in various parts of the world.

Study and reference skills

So far the techniques discussed have related principally to developing the intensive reading skills. It sometimes happens however that pupils learning English as a foreign language need to develop study and reference skills in English. These are skills which they ought of course to have developed in their mother tongue first of all, but for most non-Western Europeans the conventions may be quite different and deliberate teaching of the English conventions may have to be undertaken. Even such fundamental skills as those of using an alphabetical sequence may have to be taught, for example to pupils who are literate in Chinese. Exercises involving thorough familiarisation with the sequence of letters in the English alphabet, and with the arrangement of words in sequences which depend on alphabetic order are basic to quick and easy use of dictionaries, encyclopaedias and other reference works.

Pupils may also, of course, have to develop study skills of the kind required for the SQ3R technique mentioned above. This is where attention given to skimming, reading for specific points of information and practice in formulating pertinent questions pays off. But it will be necessary to set specific assignments for this kind of work. The skills don't just spring into existence of themselves, they have to be worked for. Where the EFL teacher has a clear idea of the kinds of content that his pupils will have to study — sometimes the English teaching marches alongside technical or vocational instruction of some kind — then it is clearly of the greatest importance that the English teacher and the teacher of the subject matter that is being studied through English should get together to devise assignments which will be valuable both in terms of the content and of the language skills the pupil may acquire from them. This kind of co-operation is all too rare, but in the best interests of the pupils departmental and subject boundaries must be crossed.

Teaching extensive reading

Turning now to techniques for encouraging extensive reading it will be found that this territory has already been partly covered, in that setting assignments for skimming, or finding one fact in a substantial body of text, involve one kind of extensive reading at least.

The practice of extensive reading needs little justification. It is clearly the easiest way of bringing the foreign learner into sustained contact with a substantial body of English. If he reads, and what he reads is of some interest to him, then the language of what he has read rings in his head, the patterns of collocation and idiom are established almost painlessly with a range and intensity which is impossible in terms of oral classroom treatment of the language, where the constraints of lock-step teaching and multiple repetitions, however necessary they may be, impose severe restrictions on the sheer volume of the amount of language with which pupils come into contact.

Given properly graded readers whose language and subject matter suit the capabilities of the pupils using them, there is no reason why extensive reading should not form a part of regular EFL teaching from the most elementary stages. Every well-devised reading scheme for native speaker uses this principle. Graded readers do exist, the grading is almost entirely in terms of vocabulary control, and every major publisher in the field has them listed in the catalogue, but the grading and classification is very far from uniform. Even those readers written within a vocabulary of 1,000 words may be written within a different 1,000 words for each publisher. Most publishing houses seem to have private lists specifying the vocabulary and the house style for their graded readers. It is therefore wise to treat publishers' claims with caution. There is a substantial literature on this topic; the main points are well discussed in *Teaching English as a Second Language* by J. A. Bright and G. P. McGregor. Ultimately the only way that a particular simplified reader can be shown to be suitable for a particular pupil or group of pupils is by trying it out. In some countries information on which books have proved successful with pupils has been collected but it appears to be available only in mimeographed form from local teachers' associations or educational authorities, and it often requires persistence to get hold of it — though clearly it is well worth doing so.

There appear to be basically three ways that extensive reading may be encouraged, first by having class sets of titles, second by operating a class library system, and third by using the school library.

Having class sets has the advantage that the teacher can control the rate of progress of all pupils, it is convenient where the class is taught together; particular linguistic or content difficulties can be tackled with the whole class at once; themes, textual structure, character development and so on can be explored in class discussion; technical or historical background information can be supplied to the whole class as necessary. This is perhaps the best treatment for a book which is likely to present difficulty for the class so that it would not be easy and straightforward for them to read the book entirely on their own. It is probably best to set the reading to be done out of class in terms of specific assignments of certain nominated chapters or sections. Such assignments do not need to be directly sequential through the book, they may be discontinuous. For example in reading the *Arabian Nights* if the pupils were to pick out only the story of Scheherazade it might be proper to assign only those sections of the book which dealt with her and omit the sections in which the stories she tells are to be found. In this way the basic framework of the book could be made clear. It is valuable too to set specific questions to which answers must be found; four or five are enough. (What story did Scheherazade begin on the second night? Had she really finished the first one?) It is possible by these means to reduce the amount of class time that needs to be given to checking whether the reading has actually been done and in discussing difficulties that may arise, since these usually are quite closely defined by virtue of the work pupils have done, but it is also of course possible to spend a great deal of time on the discussion. In general this should be discouraged and attention focused on the reading and on deriving meaning over the long term.

A class library system has the advantage that with limited funds available for the purchase of books it is possible to have four copies of ten different titles — and hence the

possibility of exposing the pupils to a greater range of language — instead of forty copies of one title. The books are
distributed among the pupils, who read them more or less
at their own rate. The teacher can exercise as much or little
control over this reading, as he wishes. He can set deadlines
or not, he can devise assignments on the same sort of lines
as those for class sets suggested above — but unless these are
made with MCQs to check on the reading they become
burdensome and complicated to keep track of. More usually
pupils may be required to keep a record of the books they
have read by making an annotated bibliographical entry —
ideally on a 10 X 15 cm index card — showing in the usual
way the author, title, number of pages, publisher and date of
publication, then might follow the date of beginning to read
the book and the date of completing it; a star grading, one to
five stars showing how much the pupil enjoyed and valued
the book (a symbol for books which pupils find totally repel-
lent is also useful, say Ø) and the pupil's own summary of
what he thought the book was about. Index cards like this
as they accumulate give the pupils a real sense of achievement
and provide a ready means of refreshing the memory. Cards
also have the advantage that they are easy to sort and keep in
alphabetical order. The same information can equally well be
recorded in an ordinary exercise book of course but this
somehow seems to lack the effectiveness of index cards.
Many teachers find that keeping a class reading chart for the
extensive reading done is useful. This shows pupils' names on
the vertical axis of a grid and the titles of the books available
in the class library on the horizontal axis. As each pupil takes
out a book the date is entered on the intersection of his name
and the title, when he returns it that date is entered too.
Thus it is easy to see at a glance who is reading many titles
quickly, and who is reading few slowly and appropriate encouragement can be offered in each quarter. The demands on
class time of this class library system may be a little higher
than when using class sets but the sheer volume of reading
done is likely to be much higher. The pupils' index cards
provide a cross check on this record and allow some of the
recording to be done out of class time.

Books chosen for use in class libraries like this should on
the whole be easy for the pupils to read, preferably with high

intrinsic interest and the least possible linguistic difficulty – one rough guide is that fewer than one word in every one hundred should be unfamiliar enough to require glossing or the use of a dictionary; that level is the extreme upper limit, ideally the pupil should not need to look up any words at all in the dictionary and provided context and in-text definition is used this is quite feasible. Obviously for both class sets and class libraries of this kind graded or simplified readers are likely to be required. It must be understood that the kind of extensive reading work being discussed here really has very little to do with the study of 'literature'. It appears to be a very common misapprehension that reading a simplified version of *Robinson Crusoe* or *Oliver Twist* has something to do with the study of Defoe or Dickens as literary artists – the fundamental changes in language and even in the organisation of material which simplification may involve clearly mean that this is just not so. The fact that 'Robinson Crusoe' and 'Oliver Twist' are famous names may contribute to the motivation of the reader, but literary study of 'great writers' is clearly something which requires substantially greater experience of all that is written in English than can be expected of most pupils, who need the kind of extended exposure to the written medium in English that graded readers are intended to provide.

Class libraries of the kind suggested here do require some small amount of storage space. Where this cannot be provided in a classroom it is not difficult to fit all the books needed into a small suitcase which may be no more inconvenient to carry about than the average briefcase.

Using a school library for extensive reading has the advantage that no storage space is required for books in the classroom and the range of books available to the pupils can be considerably widened, but it does depend on the school library being well organised, with a good stock of books in English – including graded and simplified readers such as those mentioned above – it needs to be available and open when the class teacher wants to use it, and it needs to have a librarian who is prepared to co-operate with the teacher in promoting the extensive reading programme. In using the school library – even the best organised – the control and checking of what is read always seems to become more difficult. If borrowing from the library is done in out-of-class time then class time needs to be used to get the reading record up to date – unless the librarian is very co-operative indeed. If borrowing from the library is done in class time then the amount of time taken up always seems to be much more than is ever anticipated and it always seems easy for those who most need encouragement and direction to evade it. The school library is probably most useful for that type of extensive reading which relates to study skills, and where skimming and fact finding assignments are set the resources of even a modest library are likely to be far greater than can be conveniently carried into a classroom.

Literature

There is one final matter related to the teaching of English as a foreign language and reading and that is the place of literature in the scheme of things. Traditionally one of the major reasons given for learning English at all has been that the learner might read Shakespeare in the original. There are those who might deny the importance of this reason for learning the language today but it still carries considerable weight. Clearly learning a language and studying the literature written in that language are different activities, but this is not to say that they are unrelated. Much of what has been written above about reading with understanding, and appreciating stylistic and tonal differences has clear relevance to literary study, and is indeed a basic prerequisite to it. Similarly the 'best writing' is clearly a proper object of study for anyone who wishes to know a language well; the memorable quality of much good literature must surely be one of the contributing factors in the foreigner's building up of a native speaker – like intuition. Literature does not have to wait for advanced knowledge of the language, though clearly some literature is not accessible to the beginning learner. Even the most elementary learner can derive pleasure from traditional rhymes and riddles which are fundamental to a great deal of literary reference, or from linguistically simple but aesthetically complex poems like Christina Rossetti's 'Who has seen the wind?' or some of Blake's 'Songs of Innocence and Experience'. What appears to be much more important than a solid and extensive knowledge of the language itself is that students of English literature should share the cultural assumptions which determine what kind of a thing it is and what it is for. The conception that literature is one of the roads to wisdom, that it enriches the spirit and provides deeper and more significant insights into the human condition is one that really must be appreciated before the colourful patchwork of *Pickwick Papers* or the dark agonies of *King Lear* make sense. Conceptions like these arise out of maturity and that literary sophistication which grows from knowledge of literature in the mother tongue as well as in English. Once such conceptions are gained the linguistic difficulties of reading the literature become manageable, without them the undertaking involves Herculean efforts. Once again there is a considerable amount which has been written on the question of teaching English literature to foreigners, the English Teaching Information Centre has a specialist bibliography on it, but probably the most useful introduction is *The Teaching of Literature* by H. L. B. Moody.

Suggestions for further reading

All books mentioned in the text above, and

J. P. B. Allen and S. Pit Corder (eds), *The Edinburgh Course in Applied Linguistics, Vol. 3, Techniques in Applied Linguistics*, Oxford University Press, 1974.

C. J. Brumfit, 'The Teaching of Advanced Reading Skills in Foreign languages with Particular Reference to English as a Foreign Language', survey article in *Language Teaching and Linguistics: Abstracts*, vol. 10, Cambridge University Press, 1977b.

F. Grellet, *Developing Reading Skills*, Cambridge University Press, 1981.

R. Isaacs, *Learning Through Language*, Tanzania Publishing House, Macmillan, 1968.

W. F. Mackey, *Language Teaching Analysis*, Longman, 1965.

M. Macmillan, *Efficiency in Reading*, British Council, ETIC Occasional Paper no. 6, 1965.

C. Nuttall, *Teaching Reading Skills in a Foreign Language*, Heinemann, 1982.

F. Smith, *Understanding Reading*, New York: Holt, Rinehart — Winston, 1970.

H. G. Widdowson, *Stylistics and the Teaching of Literature*, Longman, 1976.

Chapter 8

Writing

The nature of the writing skill

When we write, unlike when we talk, we are engaged in an activity which is usually at the same time both private and public. It is private because the act of composition is by its nature solitary, but it is public in that most writing is intended for an audience, often one which is extremely difficult to define. The act of writing differs from that of talking in that it is less spontaneous and more permanent, and the resources which are available for communication are fewer because we cannot — as we do in conversation — interact with the listeners and adapt as we go along. For this reason the conventions of writing tend to be less flexible than those of conversation, and the language which is used tends to be standardised. If the goal of the English teacher is to enable students to produce fluent, accurate and appropriate written English, there are a number of aspects which need to be considered. These are:

1 Mechanical problems with the script of English;
2 Problems of accuracy of English grammar and lexis;
3 Problems of relating the style of writing to the demands of a particular situation;
4 Problems of developing ease and comfort in expressing what needs to be said.

In this chapter the last three areas will be discussed. The first area is only of importance when students are moving from a language which uses another form of script, and teaching English script is a specialised skill. The book list at the end of the chapter includes a book which gives advice on this aspect of teaching writing.

Although the teaching of the script can be easily separated from the other aspects of writing, there are a number of fundamentally similar aspects which all teachers of English need to take into account. Students need to be able to copy confidently and accurately, and to observe a number of conventions on (for example) paragraphing and punctuation. However, it is easy to include work on these areas in the course of developing work related to the other areas mentioned.

A great deal of the writing that occurs in the foreign language classroom is not primarily concerned so much with developing writing skills as with reinforcing the teaching of particular structures. This very often consists of copying down sentences in order to establish patterns which have just been orally presented. While such an activity may have a general teaching purpose, it is distinct in intention from work which is aimed at teaching students to write effectively in English, and it is with this last activity that we shall be concerned in this chapter.

A writing programme

Ideally, there should be a programme to develop writing skills which works all the way through the educational system. Such a programme would list the main types of writing which it felt students should be able to master by the end of their education, and would offer guidelines to teachers on ways of achieving success with each of these. It is fairly easy to draft the main points which would need to be included in such a programme, but too little is known about exactly how human beings learn to write effectively to be able to relate these points to a satisfactory learning theory. None the less, it is possible to structure the development of writing skills in the foreign language situation, and there are a number of strong reasons for this being desirable.

The strongest reason is that writing is – to the practised

user – an extremely fluent and easy activity for at least part of the time, but very often foreign learners can only be fluent at the expense of accuracy. At the same time, as the conventions of writing are more restricting than those of speech – we are less tolerant of deviation – the need for the writer to be accurate is very great. In fact, any teacher who has had to try and assess the 'free' writing of inexperienced foreign learners of English will appreciate the need for some kind of controlled or guided writing, at least at the early stages.

It seems convenient, then, to structure a writing course through three main stages. These will be: (i) controlled writing, (ii) guided writing, and (iii) free writing. These terms have been fairly loosely used in the past, and the first two are often used as if they are interchangeable. However, it seems sensible to distinguish between writing exercises in which the final product is linguistically determined by the teacher or materials writer, and exercises in which the final content is determined. Thus a paragraph with blanks to be filled may be a legitimate early part of a writing programme, and can be considered a *controlled* composition, as is one in which, for example, picture prompts, or memory of a model presented by the teacher, leads to the students reproducing more or less exactly the same final product as each other. On the other hand a composition in which the teacher provides the situation and helps the class to prepare the written work, either through written or oral assistance, is a *guided* composition, because each piece of work is different in the language used, even if the content and organisation are basically the same throughout the class. A *free* composition usually means a composition in which only the title is provided, and everything else is done by the student.

After these distinctions have been made though, two points need to be stressed. The first is that they represent three points on a cline, a sliding scale. As a class becomes more confident in working with controlled composition exercises, more and more alternative possibilities become available in the choice of language, and the exercises tend to become more and more guided. At the other end of the scale, no composition in school is likely to be truly free, for the very act of a teacher in proposing the writing, let alone suggesting one or more topics, 'guides' the pupils, while any kind of preliminary discussion by the teacher establishes the 'guiding' principle very clearly. The other point to be made is that the movement from controlled to free is not necessarily a movement from easy to difficult. Indeed, some situational compositions in which writing has to be adapted to a particular style, using specific information provided, may be more difficult than most free topics. At the same time, a great deal of real life writing is of the guided type. Whenever a journalist reports a speech, or a student writes an essay in an academic subject at university, or a secretary writes minutes of a committee meeting, a guided composition is being produced, for a conventional version of a restricted range of material is being manufactured.

None the less, it is useful in discussing the development of writing skills to think in terms of these three levels. Generally, the controlled stage concerns itself with the production of accurate language in context, the guided stage with the organisation of material which is given, and the free stage with the production by the student of both content and language.

Goals of the writing programme

In most language teaching courses, the language is taught sentence pattern by sentence pattern, with vocabulary being fitted in according to the situations used to illustrate the sentence patterns being presented. Even in courses designed on different lines, there is a tendency for language to be presented as a number of separate items, related to situation or communicative act. And when writing is used to reinforce work which has been initially presented, it often reinforces either at the direct sentence level, or in relation to dialogues or situations which are not those usually expressed through writing. It is the responsibility of the writing programme particularly to train students to produce sequences of sentences which express their meaning most effectively. Since, both when we speak and when we write, we work not through isolated sentences but through blocks of sentences, this should be a more natural activity than using exercises which consist of lists of sentences without any context whatsoever. None the less, the ability to put sentences together effectively needs systematic encouragement, and sometimes explicit teaching, and part of the work in a writing course involves teaching students to be sensitive to the rules of discourse in English.

Connected with the problem of discourse is that of functional style, or 'register'. When we use written language, we obey certain conventions which are appropriate to the particular purpose we have in mind. Sometimes this is a matter of layout, as in writing a business letter, or of organisation, as in minutes of a meeting, but sometimes it is a much more subtle process of recognising the level of formality of certain combinations of utterance, or of appreciating what would sound bizarre or inappropriate – for any reason whatsoever – to a native speaker. Clearly it is not possible to teach explicitly everything a writer needs to know about English, but fortunately for teachers the learning of language takes place to a great extent unconsciously. A successful writing course must select the conventions and styles which are most likely to be useful to the students, but a great deal of the sensitivity which the students need in the use of language will develop unconsciously from spin-off from their reading and talking in the rest of the English course, so writing cannot be seen as something completely separated from the other activities.

If we define the main aims of the writing course as developing appropriate ranges of style coherently and easily used, teachers may well feel that the traditional concerns of spelling and basic grammatical errors are being neglected. In fact, while these are of some significance, and should be corrected by students as they learn to write good English, correction of these alone will not ensure that satisfactory English writing results. We would expect a good writing course to help students to correct their mistakes, but natural writing does not result primarily from exercises in avoiding mistakes, so we need to fit help with correction into a framework of more positive development of writing skills.

A basic methodology for written work

In writing, as in other aspects of language teaching, the questions for the teacher to ask himself are: Is the task appropriate for the needs of the students? Is the task within the reach of the students? Is it only *just* within their reach, so that they will be really challenged as they try to complete it? And will they find it enjoyable? In this section ways of dealing with the answers to the second and third questions will be explored. If the teacher is sympathetic and enthusiastic, and the first three questions can be answered with 'Yes', the last should follow.

In dealing with written work, there are a number of ways in which the teacher can bring the task to the level of his class. Basically, this means making the exact solutions to the writing problem more and more explicit the lower down the educational system we go. The teacher can grade the task in the following ways:

1 He can limit the length of the written material to be produced.
2 He can increase the amount of class preparation for the task.
3 He can provide guidance on the final form of the written work, for example with picture prompts, or word prompts, or memory prompts as a result of the oral preparation.
4 He can encourage students to collaborate in the actual process of writing.
5 He can allow cross-checking between the draft stage and the writing of the final product.
6 He can limit the complexity of the writing task itself.
7 He can demand that the task be completed either slowly or quickly.

Any combination of these methods can be used to bring the task to the level of the class.

These strategies provide the teacher with ways of organising his work in the class, but what should be the basis for the development? It is in fact possible to construct a very detailed specification of stages in composition work, which advances from what is really only a copying exercise to become gradually freer and freer until advanced writing of a situationalised or free kind has been developed. To illustrate this principle, consider the gradual advance in the following three stages:

Stage 5

(shown to the class)

(read to the class)

Father has just come home from work. He has bought a copy of the *Evening News*. Mother has just begun sewing John's shirt. John has just returned from a game of football. Mary has started her homework. Father has recently bought a new radio. They have not turned it on because Mary is studying. When Mother has finished sewing John's shirt she will cook supper. Mary will help her to prepare the supper. She will clean up when they have finished eating.

(given to the class)

1 Where has Father just come from?
2 What has he bought?
3 What has Mother just begun?
4 Where has John just returned from?
5 What has Mary started?
6 What has Father recently bought?
7 Why have they not turned it on?
8 What will Mother do when she has finished sewing?
9 Who will help her to prepare the supper?
10 What will Mary do when they have finished eating?

Stage 6. Rajabu's journey

(given to the class and then taken away)

Read the following.

After the train had stopped, Rajabu woke up. He was lying on the seat in an empty compartment. He had fallen asleep twenty minutes before, and now he was feeling very stiff. He stretched himself and then he realised that he had been asleep. His heart began beating very fast, for he suddenly felt frightened. While he was asleep, he had forgotten why he had come in this train.

After a second he remembered everything. He remembered that the train was going to Mwanza, and that a man in red trousers had been in his compartment. The thought of the man in red trousers made Rajabu look round quickly, for there was no one else in the compartment now and Rajabu was all alone.

Then Rajabu remembered his box of clothes which had been under the seat. He poked under the seat quickly, but the box had gone. Rajabu now felt terrified, for he had just bought those clothes and they were all new. He went to the window and then looked out. In the distance he saw the man with red trousers running along the road from the station. He was carrying Rajabu's box. The man had taken the box and got out of the train while Rajabu was asleep. Rajabu opened the door, but he couldn't get out because the train was already moving. The man in red trousers had got away with all Rajabu's new clothes!

(given to the class)

Answer the following questions. By answering the questions, you will find that you are re-telling the story you have just read. Do not start each answer on a new line, but write continuously, like an ordinary composition. If two questions are together on the same line, try to join your two (or more) answers into one sentence.

Paragraph 1:
When did Rajabu wake up?
What was he lying on? In an empty what?
What had happened twenty minutes before? How was he feeling now?
What did he do? Then what did he realise?
What did his heart begin doing? Why?
While he was asleep, what had he forgotten?

Paragraph 2:
After a second what happened?
What did he remember (a) about the train, and (b) about a man in red trousers?
What made Rajabu look round quickly? Was there anyone else in the compartment now? Who was all alone?

Paragraph 3:
Then what did Rajabu remember? Where had it been?
What did he do quickly? What had happened?
What did Rajabu feel now? Why?
Where did he go? Then where did he look?
Whom did he see in the distance? What was he doing? Where? What was he carrying?
What had the man done (*two things*) while Rajabu was asleep?
What did Rajabu do? Why couldn't he get out? Who had got away with all Rajabu's new clothes?

Stage 7

(read to the class)

(*to the teacher only*. Read the following passage to your class, slowly, several times. The pupils do not see this passage. Then give out the questions below, in written form. The groups do the composition orally. Finally, pupils write.)

About thirty years ago a scientist noticed the following facts about yellow-fever. In the jungles of South America, blue mosquitoes live in the tree-tops. Monkeys also live in the same place. These monkeys suffer from yellow-fever. The scientists therefore discovered that blue mosquitoes cause yellow-fever. In the jungles the disease passes from the monkey to the mosquito. Then it passes from the mosquito back to the monkey.

Man also catches the disease if he goes into the jungle. This often happens when men cut down the trees. They disturb the mosquitoes and the mosquitoes begin to bite the men. Then the men return to the city. Now men pass yellow-fever into the city mosquito. The city mosquito passes it to other men. In this way yellow-fever passes from the monkeys into the population of the city.

(given to the class)

(*to the pupil*: Answer the following questions to make a composition similar to the one you have just heard read to you. Divide your composition into paragraphs. Each question should be answered with one sentence.)

When did a scientist notice the following facts about yellow-fever?
In the jungles of South America, where do blue mosquitoes live?
What animals also live in the same place?
From what disease do they suffer?
What did the scientists therefore discover?
In the jungles the disease passes from which animal to which insect?
Then what happens?
What happens if man goes into the jungle?
This often happens when men do what?

What do they disturb, and what begins to bite the men?
Then where do the men go?
Now what do men pass into the city mosquito?
To whom does the city mosquito pass it?
In this way what passes from the monkeys into the popula-
tion of the city?

In the first of these there are three sources of control used;
first the picture, then the student's memory of the passage,
and finally the questions which are given to the pupils to
read, the answers to which enable the original passage to be
reconstructed. In this exercise a paragraph is provided which
is in part a description of the situation in the picture, and
which is at approximately the appropriate level syntactically
for the class. Students therefore are being asked to respond
to a picture and describe it, to remember a piece of consecu-
tive prose, and to answer questions orally in their preparation.

In the second exercise, pupils are asked to read the passage
silently (this may be done more than once or once only,
depending on the teacher's assessment of the class's level),
and the passage is then taken away. The students then have
to answer given questions from memory, but this time the
answers to the questions are grouped in paragraphs and the
answers may be combined together so that answers to several
questions may form one sentence. Students are again remem-
bering, but this time on the basis of their own reading, and
they again have question prompts in front of them.

In the third exercise, a passage is again read to the class,
and again question prompts are given, but this time there is
no picture, as there was in the first example. The questions,
and the techniques for answering them, are more complex
than in the earlier examples. Once again a combination of
memory and question prompts is used, but the demands
made on the student are greater.

These exercises represent stages 5, 6, and 7 of a 35-stage
course in writing, and the principles that they illustrate are
applicable to any writing situation. To use this sort of exercise most fruitfully, the teacher should aim to help pupils so
thoroughly that no one makes any significant mistakes in
the writing. How can this be achieved?

At first the teacher may ask individual pupils to do all or part of the composition orally to show the method, and will help them until the right answer is produced. Then the whole passage may be produced orally in groups or pairs, with the pupils correcting each other until they are sure of what they have to write. Later, with similar exercises, pupils may be confident enough to write without such intensive preparation, but this should only be when the teacher knows that they will be able to produce a confident and accurate response. This means that the exercise may be written in one of four ways:

1 By the whole class, with the teacher or a pupil drafting on the blackboard.
2 In groups — each member of the group writing the agreed version, sentence by sentence.
3 In pairs, using the same method as in groups.
4 Individually, without any consultation.

But it is worth repeating that hardly any mistakes should be made in the final version, and the preparation should be thorough enough to ensure this.

When the composition has been written, the process is by no means finished. No serious writer lets his manuscript go forward without revision, and usually he asks someone else to comment on it. Commenting on his own and others' writing should be an essential part of a student's training — at the lowest level it will equip him for the examination situation when he has to re-read his material for errors, and it should have greater educational benefit in encouraging co-operation and openness in practical activities. Thus, if the exercises are well enough prepared to allow only a limited number of syntactic mistakes (apart from the obvious copying and spelling ones), the students can work in groups, pairs or individually to improve their work. In groups, a final version (or versions as the exercises become freer) has to be agreed upon. Pupils may start by changing books in pairs within the group, and finish by reading accepted answers around the group — while the others pounce on mistakes. In pairs, the two will examine one book at a time, and the writer will defend his answers, or adapt them if he is convinced of his mistakes. Finally, pupils may like to check each others' books, without teacher help, separately, before the teacher looks at them. All of these activities demand that the teacher goes round the groups helping and encouraging, and of course the teacher will still have to take in written work from time to time to check through it. However, it should be very clear to pupils that the purpose of this activity, and of all the discussion, is to *help* them to write accurately and effectively, and not to *test* what they can do. If tests of written work are essential, they need to be administered quite separately from this teaching procedure.

These techniques should be varied with each exercise tried, to avoid monotony. As the class becomes confident within each stage, new exercises within the same stage may be worked on without oral preparation, or at great speed. Writing may start with groups, pairs or individuals, and at the early stages, about half an hour each might be allowed for preparation, writing and revision/correction. Certainly the exercise should be short enough to allow ample time for the revision after it is written and the preparation before.

As the exercises become less and less controlled, the nature of the revision will change, so that discussion of layout, organisation, and criteria for what is or is not appropriate subject matter becomes more important. An example of an advanced, and fairly difficult, guided composition is as follows:

Stage 34

(given to the class)

A large new secondary school is to be built in this area. Some government officials have been considering the possibility of making this a co-educational school where both boys and girls will be educated together. Other government officers have opposed the plan.

Last week, a public debate on this subject was held in the Town Hall. Speakers for both sides presented their points of view. Below, listed in random order, are some notes on the arguments offered by both the proposers and the opposers.

Write the speech which might have been given by *either*

the proposer *or* the opposer; you will need to select relevant material only. You may add examples of your own to make the points clearer.

Hobbies, e.g. drama, better with both sexes.
Education given to boys and girls should be different; different needs; girls' subjects e.g. Health Science and Cookery not necessary for boys.
Concentration in class difficult with mixed sexes.
Competition in class between boys and girls: higher academic standards.
Living and working in same school a good preparation for marriage and future life in society.
Girls just as able as boys.
Boys hate being beaten in class by girls.
Experience in other countries: students in mixed schools — not such good results as students from single-sex schools.
School no training for life if sexes separated.
Girls: good influence on boys.
Girls as technical engineers?
Co-educational schools: boys more careful about conduct and speech.
Most girls not good at science.
Great problems of discipline.
Outside interests of boys very different from those of girls.
Recreation, sports.
Boys dress more smartly in mixed schools. Behave better.
Administration problems; bathing, dormitories, washing clothes.
Mixed schools: much time wasted by pupils.
More interesting and varied social life of co-educational school.
Girls not interested in same hobbies as boys.
Sexes develop at different speeds.

Here, the same procedure as that outlined for the earlier examples will be appropriate, but the discussion, both before and after writing, will be far more concerned with content and organisation than with basic errors — though of course by now students should have been trained to pick out most of those where they occur.

It will have been noticed that the sample compositions

given in this chapter show a variety of different kinds of writing: factual as well as story-telling or narrative. If a course such as this is developed, using material from some of the textbooks which are available (and these procedures can be adapted to any teaching materials), it should cover all the main types of writing that the student may need to produce later in his career. What happens through this methodological procedure, of course, is that the student is exposed at the early stages to a variety of short passages which are coherent and which exemplify a number of types of writing. He is asked to reconstruct these passages with the help of a number of aids, and this process, both in language and in the ideas used, is made explicit through the constant discussion and checking which is carried on in the group and pair work. (That also gives a good opportunity for fluency practice in oral English, incidentally.) As he progresses through the course, the student becomes more and more able to correct himself and to evaluate what he is doing. Since the course can incorporate exercises on note-taking and reference work (as in the example above, which requires the pupil to understand note form) if these are appropriate activities, it can be turned into an effective 'study-skills' course for those who need such skills.

Writing and 'creating'

One possible objection to a course such as that outlined above is that it is severely functional. While it is true that most people learn foreign languages for functional reasons, it may well be asked what role there is in EFL for a creative approach to writing.

It should be said at once that the kind of scheme outlined can be exciting, particularly when students genuinely feel that they are progressing successfully, and also that it can include imaginative story writing, both guided and free. At the same time, in the early stages, there is a tendency to emphasise accuracy at the expense of the fluency which can add genuine pleasure to the process of composition, particularly for the able student, in a foreign language. In practice, it may be sensible at the early stages to divide the aims, and to tell students that the purpose of the main writing course is to develop accuracy in the first instance, but that the teacher will be delighted to look at − for example − a diary or anything else written solely for pleasure in English. However, it is inadvisable to express willingness to 'correct' mistakes, otherwise the situation is back to that of approaching a random mass of errors which cannot be systematically treated, and the whole purpose of the early controlled composition work was to avoid that. At the same time the teacher should be willing to discuss the content of freely written work with the students and to encourage them in every way, but they need to be made aware that they must have an ability to do 'normal' writing in English before they can justify being experimental. The emphasis in this chapter has been on controlling, defining and organising the writing course. It is clearly advantageous to the teacher to know exactly what he is doing, but even more the organisation enables the student to see his own progress in terms of a scheme. This builds up his confidence, and with language teaching confidence can be enormously important.

Suggestions for further reading

Books with useful discussion of writing skills include:

L. G. Alexander, *Guided Composition in English Teaching*, Longman, 1971.

J. A. Bright and G. P. McGregor, *Teaching English as a Second Language*, Longman, 1970, chapter 4.

D. Byrne, *Teaching Writing Skills*, Longman, 1979.

Josie Levine, *Developing Writing Skills*, Association for the Education of Pupils from Overseas, 1972.

Hazel McCree, *From Controlled to Creative Writing*, Lagos: African Universities Press, 1969.

A. Pincas, *Teaching English Writing*, Macmillan, 1982.

R. White, *Teaching English Writing*, Heinemann, 1980.

Textbooks on composition include:

Gerald Dykstra, Richard Port, Antoinette Port, *Ananse Tales*, Columbia: Teachers' College, 1968.

T. C. Jupp and John Milne, *Guided Course in English Composition*, Heinemann, 1968.

T. C. Jupp and John Milne, *Guided Paragraph Writing*, Heinemann, 1972.

Writing

Mary S. Lawrence, *Writing as a Thinking Process*, Ann Arbor: University of Michigan Press, 1972.

D. H. Spencer, *Guided Composition Exercises*, Longman, 1967.

Further discussion on correction in groups will be found in:

C. J. Brumfit, *'Correction of Written Work'*, Modern English Teacher, September 1977a.

On teaching script:

J. A. Bright and R. Piggott, *Handwriting, A Workbook*, Cambridge University Press, 1976 (+ Teacher's Book).

Note: The 35-stage course in writing referred to on p. 126 and the ideas for exercises are based on a scheme originally developed in Tanzania by Ann Brumfit, and the exercises given are based on unpublished exercises written by Tanzanian teachers of English. The basic scheme was published in *A Handbook for English Teachers*, Institute of Education, University of Dar es Salaam, 1969.

Chapter 9

Errors, Correction and Remedial Work

The last four chapters have been concerned with good teaching and effective learning. But however good the teaching and however effective the learning, there will always be a place for remedial work of one kind or another because it is beyond the capacity of a human being to absorb perfectly and retain indefinitely everything he is presented with. Hence, from one point of view, every learner needs remedial teaching after the first lesson. It is unfortunately not uncommon to find a student who is quite incapable of using the present simple tense accurately at the end of the first year of English, even though it has been one of the main teaching points. Before considering what can be done about this sort of situation, it is worth looking first at some of the possible reasons for error.

Poor teaching is of course one culprit. But very often there are circumstances quite beyond the teacher's control which produce a remedial situation. The syllabus, for example, is usually not within the control of most ordinary teachers. Some older courses follow a 'linear' progression from one teaching point to the next. First, for instance, the present simple tense is taught quite exhaustively. That is 'done', and the class moves on, without a backward glance, to the past simple, and so on. In this way, over the years, the syllabus covers in some depth all the major structural points. The difficulty is that the students get indigestion from doing too much of one thing all together, and that once a topic is finished, it is only incidentally referred to and practised later.

Of course, many courses take care to build in the regular repetition of lexical and structural material, thereby reinforcing the original learning and increasing the students' exposure to it in new contexts. Regular revision of this kind is a very important means of preventing a serious remedial situation. Several course books provide periodic revision tests to make sure that the material thus far presented has been assimilated. The 'spiral syllabus' is another means of ensuring that good teaching and effective learning achieve the right results. The idea here is that only one or two aspects of the present simple are introduced and practised before moving on to another topic. But the teaching plan comes back round to the present simple fairly shortly and the original structures are reinforced, then extended. Similarly with the second topic. After a while the present simple is reintroduced for the third time, reinforced and extended. And so on for all the structures, notions and lexis in the syllabus.

Another important factor which can produce poor learning and a potential remedial situation is the many choices of materials to teach from. They must not only be constructed on sound educational and linguistic principles but also be suitable for the age groups of the students and suitable for the part of the world they are to be used in. There is little point in using a course designed for teens and twenties who are learning in Europe (with all the presuppositions this entails of a modern sophisticated life style in big cities), with an older age group in a developing country. Many courses are not well suited to the less developed part of the world for the very reason that they are culturally bound to Western Europe.

Apart from the syllabus, the materials and the teacher, another potential source of trouble is the learner himself. Even with optimal conditions, there will still be room for remedial work as there is no such thing as perfect learning. Clearly it is inevitable that learners do make errors. But is this a good or bad thing? At first sight it appears self-evident that errors are a very bad thing and signal a breakdown in the teaching and learning situation. Certainly this was the accepted view for many years. Behaviourist psychologists in particular emphasised the importance of massive manipulative practice of the language, often in a rather mechanical fashion, to ensure correctness. The drills were structured in such a way that it was difficult for the student to make many mistakes. Hence he heard only good models and was encouraged by producing acceptable English sentences all the time.

More recently, the mentalists have put forward a different view of errors, which has gained wide acceptance. The argument in its strong form runs that a learner must make errors as an unavoidable and necessary part of the learning process, so errors are not the bad thing once thought but visible proof that learning is taking place. As the student learns a new language, very often he does not know how to express what he wants to say. So he makes a guess on the basis of his knowledge of his mother tongue and of what he knows of the foreign language. The process is one of hypothesis formulation and refinement, as the student develops a growing competence in the language he is learning. He moves from ignorance to mastery of the language through transitional stages, and the errors he makes are to be seen as a sign that learning is taking place.

Errors will always be made, and have direct implications for remedial work because they are by their nature systematic infringements of the normal rules of the language. The teacher needs to plan his remedial treatment of them into the syllabus for the coming weeks and months. Quite different are the minor errors of speech or writing which everybody makes — native speakers as much as non-natives. Spoken language, for instance, is punctuated by pauses, unfinished sentences, slips of the tongue and so on. The unedited transcript on p. 68 is a good example of this. These lapses would quickly be put right if pointed out. They call for on-the-spot correction rather than remedial work.

The insight that errors are a natural and important part of the learning process itself, and do not all come from mother tongue interference, is very important. It has long been known that learners from very diverse linguistic backgrounds almost universally have difficulty with certain things, whether they existed or not in their mother tongue. For instance, nearly all second language learners — like children learning their mother tongue — produce forms like 'he musted do it yesterday', 'he throwed the ball', 'five womans', etc., at some stage. The problem here is that they generalise a rule they know (the past tense is formed by adding -ed; plural forms have an -s at the end) to apply to all cases. The restrictions on the application of the rule have not been learnt.

Recent experimental evidence suggests that even in adult learners where the mother tongue system is deeply entrenched and transfer errors are at their peak, still only a minority of errors are attributable to mother tongue interference. In the case of children, errors attributable solely to interference represent a tiny percentage of all errors committed.

It was a widespread belief until recently that contrastive analysis (comparing the learner's mother tongue with the target language) would predict the difficulties a learner would encounter and so enable the teacher to concentrate on them and avoid them. Recent findings, plus observation in the classroom, that all predicted errors did not in fact prove to be difficulties have led to the conclusion that contrasting the learner's mother tongue with English is primarily useful as an *explanatory* rather than *predictive* procedure. It is one of the possible causes for error which the teacher must consider, not a basis on which stands all his teaching.

In short, it is clear from this brief discussion that the learner brings with him one source of error: his mother tongue. Even more importantly, the learning process itself is the source of other errors. The most sensible course of action, with present knowledge, for the teacher is to reject the extreme positions – on one hand that errors are wrong and must be avoided at all costs by very carefully controlled drilling; on the other that incorrect forms are necessary, even vital, and so should be actively planned into the teaching process – and attempt to blend the best features from both approaches into his error correction. The rest of this chapter suggests some practical procedures for dealing with errors.

The first stage is to establish what the error is. The basic question to ask is whether what the learner intended to state is the same as the normal understanding of what he actually said or wrote. He may have wanted to communicate the idea that John entered the room, but his actual words were 'John came to the room'. This is a superficially well-formed sentence. It would, however, give the listener a slightly different impression than the speaker intended, since to come to somewhere need not necessarily imply that the person actually entered. He may, but he may not. The speaker's intention was to convey the meaning that the person actually entered the room. The imprecise use of prepositions, although giving a plausible interpretation, caused the speaker to misrepresent his actual meaning. Very often the teacher in a case like this senses something is wrong. It is of course much easier where there is a clearly erroneous sentence such as 'John entered into the room'. In either circumstance, the teacher can ask questions directly in an attempt to discover the learner's original intention. Also there are elicitation techniques available (translation, or multiple-choice tests, for example) to enable the teacher to isolate more exactly the specific error.

The second stage is to establish the possible sources of the error, to explain why it happened. It is important to do this as a full knowledge of the causes of an error enables the teacher to work out a more effective teaching strategy to deal with it. The main reasons for error were given earlier in this chapter: poor materials, bad teaching, errors from the learning process, and mother tongue interference. The last two factors are of most immediate practical use, since it is extremely difficult to identify errors which are solely attributable to the teaching and materials. If a French adult, for instance, said 'John entered into the room', it would be sensible to consider first the possibility of interference from 'Jean est entré dans la salle'.

It is not enough simply to have located the error and analysed its cause. The third step is to decide how serious the mistake is. The more serious the mistake, generally speaking, the higher priority it should have in remedial work. An obvious approach is to look at the error in linguistic terms and see what rules are broken. As a general principle, errors in the overall structure of sentences are more important than errors affecting parts of sentences, though there is no general agreement about a scale of error gravity. As a rough guide it has recently been suggested that the error-types considered most serious are: transformations, tense, concord, case, negation, articles, order, lexical errors.

There is the further possibility of looking at a mistake in

terms of its tolerability in the eyes of native speakers rather than its linguistic correctness. It is very probable that native speakers will tolerate lexical errors far more than grammatical ones. But even within the area of the grammatical, there is some uncertainty about what is acceptable and what is not. It is very common to hear native speakers come out with:

'It's me.'
'He does it better than me.'
'He didn't do nothing wrong.'
'We was going to the City when. . . .'

The educated native speaker would probably show more and more unease as he heard a student produce these forms, since he would not accept a non-native speaker using what he would probably consider in the last two cases at least to be sub-standard English. For similar reasons, it is necessary to teach something close to RP pronunciation, not a strong Geordie, London or West Country accent. The last three would certainly be inappropriate for the learner in all but the most exceptional circumstances, even though they are widely used in England. So it is important to consider the social tolerability of errors as well as the degree to which they transgress the linguistic rules.

As a prior step to deciding on a remedial teaching strategy, it is best to relate the error to the system of English and to its use, allocating it to a level of the linguistic system (spelling, morphology, syntax or lexis) or deciding if the problem is the inappropriacy of a correct linguistic form in a communicative situation, e.g. register. A systematic knowledge of English grammar is vital here. For example, there is a misuse of a preposition in the following extract from a written composition: 'The family were playing happily together on the beach with a ball. Father threw it very gently at his young son, who in turn threw it at his mother.'

The error lies in the preposition *at* instead of *to*. This is a semantic rather than grammatical mistake, since the preposition *at* with verbs of action carries an idea of aggressiveness which is totally foreign to the context. An explicit awareness of the meaning of prepositions will allow the teacher to isolate the main feature of the error and plan his teaching in such a way as to make these differences clear to the learner.

Cases of inappropriacy of correct linguistic forms call for a sensitivity to language in use. An instance of this is found in the following extract from a dialogue. The task for an advanced group was to write a dialogue between a Company Director and his manager who had not come to work.

Company Director: Hello. This is Dr Robinson. I would like to speak to Mr Garrard, please, on a matter of great urgency. Is he available?
Mrs Garrard: OK, hang on. I'll get him.

Clearly the student had heard the expression 'hang on' but had not realised it is informal in style. The problem posed for the teacher is that of teaching the appropriate use of forms in their social context.

The last step after establishing the area of error is its correction. It hardly needs stating that the teacher must tread very cautiously — everyone knows the feeling when a piece of written work comes back covered with red ink, and many students complain bitterly of their teacher correcting their speech so often that they no longer dare open their mouth. For even the best intentioned teacher, there is no easy way to know how much to correct or how often. It is perhaps best to consider this in relation to two factors: the sensitivity of the student and the nature of the task. Some people are always going to support correction (often construed as 'criticism') less well than others. What a student will accept is very variable, and clearly the teacher must exercise his personal judgment.

Secondly, some exercises call for very different techniques in correction, and these must not be used in the wrong place. When listening for accurate pronunciation of sounds and supra-segmentals, it is legitimate to pick up even quite small deviations from the norm, and do this fairly regularly. It will be clear to the student that this intensive listening, production and correction procedure can only be maximally helpful when there is precise and regular review of his efforts. But this technique would be quite inappropriate where the aim of the exercise was oral fluency, for instance. To stop a student giving a two minute impromptu talk because of a wrong pronunciation of a phoneme, even repeated mispronunciation of it, would be quite at variance with the goal of practising

139

fluent and confident delivery. In this case it would be much better to make a note of all errors (phonetic, grammatical and lexical) and deal with them at the end. Too many mistakes might suggest that it was the wrong task in the first place, for no exercise should be so difficult that it produces more incorrect than correct utterances.

But apart from this, the teacher must decide first the gravity of the errors committed in relation to the particular aim in view, as mentioned earlier, then whether to deal with the most important immediately or later. Immediate feedback is extremely valuable to a student. This often follows the pattern of the teacher pointing out the mistake, explaining what is wrong, and attempting on the spot to give some extra practice. There is nothing wrong with explanations of mistakes, particularly with adults, but it is much more effective when followed by extra practice. As this is not always easy to provide on the spur of the moment, another strategy is to postpone some items to another date and, after adequate preparation, make a teaching point of them in another lesson.

Immediate feedback is possible with regard to written as well as oral work, for this is exactly what the teacher provides as he moves round the class supervising his pupils' work in the written stages of the lesson. A more integrated approach comes when the class's books or papers are collected in by the teacher. As mentioned before, it is always best to avoid seas of red ink over the page, perhaps by means of a technique found successful by many teachers over the years. Instead of simply writing in the correct version and telling the student to think about it, an alternative is to put single code letters in the margin (a simple and self-evident code is essential: T — tense mistake; P — preposition mistake; V — vocabulary (word) mistake; etc.). This procedure has the advantage of much reducing the red ink, and forcing the student to think out the error himself and provide his own corrected version. The teacher can incorporate the main, general mistakes in his next teaching lesson, and work towards a 'fair copy' version with the whole class for comparison with their own efforts.

It is by no means necessary or advisable, however, that all the correction should come from the teacher. In written or oral work, students should be responsible in the first instance for their own mistakes. Written work must always be read through and carefully checked before handing in. In the case mentioned above, immediately after a two minute impromptu talk the student himself can say what he feels he has said wrong. This is very good for developing an awareness of one's own errors, and the faculty for self-criticism is a useful one to have in later years when one no longer attends English classes.

Correction might also come from another source apart from the student himself and the teacher. The other members of the group can correct both written and oral work. It is possible, for instance, for the better students to work with the weaker ones in pairs, and for them to suggest improvements and corrections. Group work provides another alternative — many groups will willingly discuss the members' written work and suggest better phrasing and different structures where appropriate. The teacher can go round checking, or be called in where there is doubt in the group. In oral work, a class can be trained to listen closely for mistakes in a talk, and should be given the chance to discuss them with the speaker and teacher afterwards. This produces a discriminating ear, and has the added advantage of making everyone listen closely if they may soon be called on to analyse the errors! Using other members of the group obviously has to be handled sensitively by the teacher, as an aggressive and critical spirit in any member of the class can be very damaging.

It has been assumed so far that the teacher himself will deal with an individual's errors with the whole group listening in. As a general principle it is best to avoid this where the error is not common to a sizeable proportion of those present. It quickly leads to boredom in the rest when the teacher goes on at length about the mistakes which just one person has committed, with the whole group sitting idly by. Individual correction is therefore necessary, but this is obviously very difficult in most teaching situations where a class may number thirty or forty students. It may be necessary on occasions, however, when the pupil himself needs personal attention and explanation, or when one person has not grasped a point and the rest of the class has moved on. In these circumstances, this can be done whilst the rest of the class is busy with some other work. Alternatively, there is scope for individualised work. Work cards can be made on different grammatical topics and lexical sets. Exercises can be set from standard textbooks, or from a series such as *English Language Units* (Longman), which deals with major points of grammar. These units have an accompanying tape which can be used on the classroom taperecorder with earphones, or in the language laboratory. An extensive tape library is very valuable for individual remedial work.

When dealing with the errors of the whole class, it is generally best to present the remedial point to a class as a part of the normal teaching plan, almost as though it were a new item and not something that has been taught unsuccessfully once. It would be integrated into the syllabus, and hardly remarked upon if the class were used to the 'spiral' approach mentioned earlier. In this case, however, it is vital to be different and varied in the re-presentation of the material. Classes quickly get bored. Variety is equally important in the practice and production stages.

Freshness of approach and variety are especially important when dealing with the 'Remedial Class' in the narrow sense. Remedial classes are formed when the standard of a minority of students in the regular classes is so far removed from that of the majority that it seems better to create a class especially for their particular needs. Failed students in an examination — the Cambridge First Certificate, for example — are often put in a group apart from the normal courses to prepare them for the re-sit. Motivation is the key to remedial groups like these, and this is largely dependent on the sensitive handling of the teacher. One very useful technique is to change totally the whole approach. Rather than go back over the same book in the same way and hope that a double dose of the same medicine will cure the problem, it is advisable at the very least to use a different textbook.

Better still is to choose a course written on entirely different principles. When a remedial class has failed at a structural course in which grammatical criteria are paramount in ordering the material for presentation, they will accept a reworking of familiar material if it is organised in a non-structural way. A notional syllabus looks first at the uses to which language is put in communication, and attempts to isolate different semantic notions – how to persuade people to do things, how to express intentions, how to complain and so forth. These notions may be expressed in simple language or complex grammatical patterns, but linguistic factors of this type are of secondary importance. A quite different type of course like this is useful for remedial classes because of its novelty and because its functional goals are readily identified and achieved. In a notional course, particularly when used for remedial classes, there is no long slow build-up to establish a necessary grammatical base before any meaningful communication is possible, and notional teaching makes for strong motivation with its emphasis on communication in practical situations. Such visible signs of success are very valuable to motivate the remedial student. Members of remedial classes are very sensitive to failure, for obvious reasons. An understanding of this is an essential quality in their teacher, since a dismissive, condemnatory attitude will only have very negative results. Patience is another virtue greatly needed, since one's best efforts often seem to produce nothing but the same errors yet once more. Progress is often slow. There are cases where it is almost non-existent, since some people are endowed with a great desire and willingness to learn English, but apparently limited ability to do so. It is also possible that people may have a natural language-learning ceiling beyond which they cannot go. It is best for the teacher gently but firmly to discourage them from continuing – yet another delicate task for the remedial teacher to perform! The demands are great on teachers concerned with error correction, but there are compensatory rewards in seeing one's charges grasp a point at last which seemed totally beyond them or in receiving their evident gratitude for one's efforts. It is all part of the job's satisfaction.

Suggestions for further reading

From a theoretical point of view:

S. P. Corder, *Introducing Applied Linguistics*, Harmondsworth: Penguin, 1973, chapter II.

S. P. Corder, 'Learner language and teacher talk', *AVLJ* 16, 1, 1978, pp. 5–13.

J. A. Norrish, *Language Learners and their Errors*, Macmillan, 1983.

J. C. Richards (ed.), *Error Analysis*, Longman, 1974.

At practical level, there is much good advice in:

J. A. Bright and G. P. McGregor, *Teaching English as a Second Language*, Longman, 1970.

M. K. Burt and C. Kiparsny, *The Gooficon, A Repair Manual for English*, Newbury House, 1972.

P. Hubbard *et al.*, *A Training Course for TEFL*, Oxford University Press, chapter 4.

Chapter 10

Assessment and Examinations

Basic terms

A great deal of the language teacher's time and attention is devoted to assessing the progress pupils make or preparing them for public examinations. One of the problems in discussing this area of English language teaching is that the words used to describe these activities are used in a number of different ways. First of all, the term *examination* usually refers to a formal set-piece kind of assessment. Typically one or more three-hour papers have to be worked. Pupils are isolated from one another and usually have no access to textbooks, notes or dictionaries. An examination of this kind may be set by the teachers or head of department in a school, or by some central examining body like the Ministry of Education in various countries or the Cambridge Local Examinations Syndicate − to mention only the best known of the British examining bodies. This usage of the word *examination* is fairly consistent in the literature on the subject and presents few difficulties.

The word *test* is much more complicated. It has at least three quite distinct meanings. One of them refers to a carefully prepared measuring instrument, which has been tried out on a sample of people like those who will be assessed by it, which has been corrected and made as efficient and accurate as possible using the whole panoply of statistical techniques appropriate to educational measurement. The preparation of such tests is time-consuming, expensive and

145

requires expertise in statistical techniques as well as in devising suitable tasks for the linguistic assessment to be based on.

The second meaning of *test* refers to what is usually a short, quick teacher-devised activity carried out in the classroom, and used by the teacher as the basis of an on-going assessment. It may be more or less formal, more or less carefully prepared, ranging from a carefully devised multiple-choice test of reading comprehension which has been used several times with pupils at about the same stage and of the same ability, so that it has been possible to revise the test, eliminate poor distractors and build up norms which might almost be accepted as statistically valid, to a quick check of whether pupils have grasped the basic concept behind a new linguistic item, by using a scatter of oral questions round the class. It is because of the wide range of interpretation that is put on this second meaning of *test* that confusions and controversy often arise. The important question to ask is always 'What kind of test do you mean?' and it is for this reason that there is perhaps some advantage in talking about *assessment* rather than *testing*.

The third meaning which is sometimes given to *test* is that of an item within a larger test, part of a test battery, or even sometimes what is often called a *question* in an examination. Sometimes when one paper in an examination series is devised to be marked objectively it is called a test, and once again it is important to be careful in interpreting just what is meant.

Subjective and objective testing

There is another pair of terms used in connection with assessment — one of them was used in the last sentence — which also need to be clarified. These are the terms *subjective* and *objective*. There is often talk of *objective tests*. It is important to note that these words refer only to the mode by which the test is marked, there is nothing intrinsically objective about any test or test item. The understanding is that objective tests are those which can be marked almost entirely mechanically, by an intelligent automaton or even a machine.

The answers are usually recorded non-linguistically, by a tick or a cross in a box, a circle round a number or letter, or the writing of a letter or number. Occasionally an actual word or punctuation mark may be used. Typically such tests take the multiple-choice format or a blank-filling format but no real linguistic judgment is required of the marker. Subjective tests on the other hand can only be marked by human beings with the necessary linguistic knowledge, skill and judgment. Usually the minimum requirement for an answer is a complete sentence, though sometimes single words may be sufficient. It must be recognised, however, that the creation and setting of both kinds is ultimately subjective, since the choice of items, their relative prominence in the test and so on are matters of the knowledge, skill and judgment of the setter. Furthermore, evaluating a piece of language like a free composition is virtually an entirely subjective matter, a question of individual judgment, and quasi-analytic procedures like allocating so many marks for spelling, so many for grammar, so many for 'expression' and so on do almost nothing to reduce that fundamental subjectivity. A checklist of points to watch may help to make the marking more consistent but it is well to recognise that the marking is none the less subjective.

It is frequently claimed that the results obtained from objective tests are 'better' than those obtained from subjectively marked tests or examinations, and books like the classic *The Marking of English Essays* by P. Hartog *et al.* with their frightening picture of the unreliability and inconsistency of marking in public examinations give good grounds for this claim. However, there are two devices which may be used to improve the consistency and reliability of subjective marking. One is to use the Nine Pile Technique and the other is to use multiple marking.

The Nine Pile Technique is based on the assumption that in any population the likelihood is that the distribution of abilities will follow a normal curve, and that subjective judgments are more reliable over scales with few points on them than over scales with a large number of points on them. In other words a five-point scale will give reasonable results, a fifty-point scale will not. Suppose a teacher has ninety-nine essays to mark. He will begin by reading these through quickly and sorting them into three piles on the basis of a straight global subjective evaluation: Good, Middling, Poor. In order to get an approximately normal distribution he would expect about seventeen of the ninety-nine to be Good, sixty-five to be Middling, and seventeen to be Poor. Next he takes the Good pile and sorts these on the basis of a second reading into Outstanding, Very Good, and Good piles. In the Outstanding pile he might put only one essay, in the Very Good pile four, and the remaining twelve in the Good pile. Similarly he would sort the Poor pile into Appalling, Very Poor, and Poor with approximately the same numbers. Finally he would sort the Middling pile into three, Middling/ Good, Middling, and Middling/Bad in the proportion of about twenty, twenty-five, and twenty. This sorting gives a ninepoint scale which has been arrived at by a double marking involving an element of overlap. Obviously if the second reading requires a Middling/Bad essay to go into the Poor pile or a Poor essay to go into the Middling Pile such adjustments can easily be made. This technique has been shown to give good consistency as between different markers and the same marker over time.

If this technique is then combined with multiple marking, that is to say getting a second or third marker to re-read the essays and to make adjustments between piles, the results are likely to be even more consistent and reliable. There is a very cogently argued case for multiple marking made out in *Multiple Marking of English Compositions* by J. Britton *et al.* Techniques such as these acknowledge the fundamentally subjective nature of the assessments being made, but they exploit the psychological realities of judgement-making in a controlled way and this is surely sensible and useful. The time required for multiple marking is no greater than that required for using a conventional analytic mark allocation system and there seems little justification for clinging to the well worn and substantially discredited ways.

All of the above is almost by way of being preliminary. When the fundamentals of what assessing progress in learning a foreign language really involves are considered it becomes clearly apparent that it is the underlying theoretical view of what language is and how it works that is most important.

Discrete item tests

If language is seen as a kind of code, a means by which 'ideas' may be expressed as easily by one set of symbols as by another, then it is likely that the bilingual dictionary and the grammar will be seen as the code books by means of which the cypher may be broken. Knowing a language will be seen as the ability to operate the code so assessment will be in terms of knowledge of the rules – the grammar – and facility in transferring from one set of symbols to another – translation. It would seem that the great majority of foreign language examinations in Britain today still reflect this as their underlying theory. The typical rubric of an assessment of language seen in this way is 'Translate the following into English' or 'Give the second person plural of the preterite of the following verbs.'

If language is seen as an aggregate of 'skills' of various kinds, then assessment is likely to be in terms of a classification of 'skills'. So there might be tests of the ability to hear, to discriminate between sounds or perceive tone patterns or comprehend intellectually what is spoken; tests of the ability to speak, to produce the noises of the language correctly, to utter accurately, fluently and coherently, tests of the ability to understand the written form of the language, to read quickly, accurately and efficiently, to skim, to look up information; tests of the ability to use the graphic symbol system and its associated conventions, or to generate accurate, fluent and coherent language in the written medium; tests of the ability to interrelate media, to read aloud, to take dictation; and so on. Virtually all theoretical approaches to language take a skills dimension into account and in the examples which occur later in this chapter it will be observed that part of the specification of the type of test being illustrated relates to the skills involved.

If language is seen as a structured system by means of which the members of a speech community interact, transmitting and receiving messages, then assessment will be seen in terms of structure and system, of transmission and reception. Robert Lado's substantial work *Language Testing: The Construction and Use of Foreign Language Tests* is full of examples of the kind of test item this view engenders. Since language is seen as a number of systems, there will be items to test knowledge of both the production and reception of the sound segment system, of the stress system, the intonation system, and morphemic system, the grammatical system, the lexical system and so on. The tendency is to give prominence to discrete items of language and relatively little attention to the way language functions globally. There is a tendency, too, for assessments made with this theoretical background to have a behavioural dimension and to be designed to be marked objectively. Some examples of the kind of thing involved follow:

> *Recognition of sound segments. Oral presentation/ written response. Group.*

The examiner will read *one* of the sentences in each of the following groups of sentences. Write the letter of the sentence you heard in the space provided on the right hand side of the page.

(i) A. I saw a big sheep over there.
      B. I saw a big ship over there.
etc.

> *Recognition of correct grammatical structure. Written presentation/written response. Group.*

Each item below contains a group of sentences. Only one sentence in each group is correct. In the blank space at the right of each group of sentences write the letter indicating the correct sentence.

(i) A. What wants that man?
     B. What does want that man?
     C. What does that man want?
     D. What that man does want?

(ii) A. I have finished my work, and so did Paul.
     B. I have finished my work, and so has Paul.
     C. I have finished my work, and so Paul has.
     D. I have finished my work, and so Paul did.
etc.

> *Production of correct vocabulary. Oral presentation/ response. Individual.*

Examiner asks the question. The candidate must respond

with the correct lexical item. Only the specified item may be accepted as correct.

    (i) Q. What do you call a man who makes bread?
       A. A baker.
    (ii) Q. The opposite of concave is . . .
       A. Convex.
   etc.

Clearly discrete item tests of this kind have certain disadvantages. Testing ability to operate various parts of the system does not test the interrelated complex that is a system of systems − an important implication of the underlying theory − and the need for global tests which do interrelate the various systems apparent. Using discrete item tests is a bit like testing whether a potential car driver can move the gear lever into the correct positions, depress the accelerator smoothly, release the clutch gently and turn the steering wheel to and fro. He may be able to do all of these correctly and yet not be able to drive the car. It is the skill which combines all the sub-skills, control of the system which integrates the systems so that the speaker conveys what he wishes to by the means he wishes to that constitutes 'knowing a language' in this sense, just as it constitutes 'driving a car'. Attempts were therefore made to devise types of global tests which could be marked objectively. Two of these appear to have achieved some success, these are dictation and cloze tests.

Dictation

Dictation was, of course, used as a testing device long before Lado and the structuralist/behaviourist nexus became influential. Lado in fact criticised dictation on three grounds, first that since the order of words was given by the examiner, it did not test the ability to use this very important grammatical device in English; second, since the words themselves are given, it can in no sense be thought of as a test of lexis; and third, since many words and grammatical forms can be identified from the context, it does not test aural discrimination or perception. On the other hand it has been argued that dictation involves taking in the stream of noise emitted by the examiner, perceiving this as meaningful, and then analysing this into words which must then be written down.

On this view the words are not given — what are given are strings of noises. These only become words when they have been processed by the hearer using his knowledge of the language. This argument that perception of language, whether spoken or written, is psychologically an active process, not purely passive, is very persuasive. That dictation requires the co-ordination of the functioning of a substantial number of different linguistic systems spoken and written, seems very clear so that its global, active nature ought to be accepted. If this is so then the candidate doing a dictation might well be said to be actually 'driving the car'.

Cloze tests

A cloze test consists of a text from which every n^{th} word has been deleted. The task is to replace the deleted words. The term 'cloze' is derived from Gestalt psychology, and relates to the apparent ability of individuals to complete a pattern, indeed to perceive this pattern as in fact complete, once they have grasped the structure of the pattern. Here the patterns involved are clearly linguistic patterns. A cloze test looks something like the following:

In the sentences of this test every fifth word has been left out. Write in the word that fits best. Sometimes only one word will fit as in 'A week has seven . . . . . .' The only word which will fit in this blank is '*days*'. But sometimes you can choose between two or more words, as in: 'We write with a . . . . . .' In this blank you can write '*pen*' or '*pencil*' or even '*typewriter*' or '*crayon*'. Write only one word in each blank. The length of the blank will not help you to choose a word to put in it. All the blanks are the same length. The first paragraph has no words left out. Complete the sentences in the second and following paragraphs by *filling in* the blanks as shown above.

'Since man first appeared on earth he has had to solve certain problems of survival. He has had to find ways of satisfying his hunger, clothing himself for protection against the cold and providing himself with shelter. Fruit and leaves from trees were his first food, and his first clothes were probably made from large leaves and animal skins. Then he began to hunt wild animals and to trap fish.

In some such way . . . . . began to progress and . . . . . his physical problems. But . . . . . had other, more spititual . . . . . − for happiness, love, security, ... divine protection.' etc.

Like dictations, cloze tests test the ability to process strings of aural or visual phenomena in linguistic terms such that their potential signification is remembered and used to process further strings as they are perceived. Cloze tests are usually presented through the written medium and responded to in that medium too, but there seems no reason why oral cloze should not be possible, and indeed there have been attempts to devise such tests. (See the University of London Certificate of Proficiency in English for Foreign Students, Comprehension of Spoken English, 1976.) Cloze tests too are global in nature demanding perceptive and productive skills and an integrating knowledge of the various linguistic systems, grammatical and lexical since some of the words left out will be grammatical and others will be lexical. There is a good deal of discussion still going on about the technicalities of constructing cloze tests but useful pragmatic solutions to many of the problems have been found and it would seem that cloze offers a potentially very valuable way of measuring language proficiency.

There are, however, two substantial criticisms to be made of all tests which have a fundamentally structuralist/ behaviourist theoretical base, whether they are discrete item tests like those of Lado, or global tests like dictation and cloze. The first of these criticisms is that such tests rarely afford the person being tested any opportunity to produce language spontaneously. The second is that they are fundamentally trying to test that knowledge of the language system that underlies any actual instance of its use − linguistic competence in Chomsky's terms − they are not concerned with the ability to operate the system for particular purposes with particular people in particular situations. In other words they are testing the basic driving skill, as does the Ministry of Transport driving test, not whether the driver can actually use the car to get from one place to another quickly and safely and legally – as the Institute of Advanced Motorists test does.

Testing communication

If 'knowing a language' is seen as the ability to communicate in particular sorts of situation, then the assessment will be in terms of setting up simulations of those situations and evaluating how effective the communication is that takes place. Situations are likely to have to be specified in terms of the role and status of the participants. The degree of formality of the interaction, the attitudes and purposes of the participants, the setting or context and the medium of transmission used – spoken or written language. The productive-receptive dimension will also enter in since this is often relevant to the roles of participants. A lecturer does all the talking, his audience only listens; but a customer in a dress shop is likely to be involved in extensive two-way exchanges with the sales assistant. It is of course possible to devise discrete items, objectively scored tests of communicative ability, but it would seem in general that global, subjectively marked tests are more likely to make it possible to match the task on which the assessment is based fairly closely with the actual performance required. The 'situational composition' used as a testing device is probably the most familiar example of this, and has been part of the Cambridge Local Examinations Syndicate's paper in English Language for East Africa for many years. The sort of thing that is used is exemplified by the following:

Write a reply accepting the following formal invitation:

Mr and Mrs J. Brown
request the pleasure of the company of
Mr Alfred Andrews
at the wedding of their daughter
Sylvia
to
Mr Alan White
on Wednesday 6th April 1977 at 2.00 p.m.
in St Martin's Church, Puddlepool, Wessex
and afterwards at the Mount Hotel, Puddlebridge, Wessex.

18 The Crescent   R.S.V.P.
Puddlepool
Wessex.

There are however a great many other possibilities and one of the most interesting explorations of what these might be is Keith Morrow's *Techniques of Evaluation for a Notional Syllabus* (RSA 1977 — mimeo) from which the following examples are taken.

> *Identification of context of situation. Oral — tape recorded presentation written response. Group.*

Listen carefully. You are about to hear an utterance in English. It will be repeated twice. After you have heard the utterance answer the questions below by writing the letter of the correct reply in the appropriately numbered box on your answer sheet. The utterance will be repeated twice more after two minutes.

Person: 'Excuse me, do *you* know where the nearest post-office is, please?'
   (i) Where might somebody ask you that question?
      A. In your house
      B. In your office
      C. In the street.
      D. In a restaurant.
   (ii) What is the person asking you about?
      A. The price of stamps.
      B. The age of the post-office.

155

C. The position of the post-office.

D. The size of the post-office.

etc.

Question (i) here relates to the *setting* of the utterance

(ii) to the *topic*,

(iii) would relate to its *function*

(iv) to the *speaker's role.*

(v) to the *degree of formality* of the utterance,

(vi) to the *speaker's status*, and so on,

to cover as many different dimensions of the context of situation as may be thought appropriate.

Asking questions. Mixed oral/written presentation/ and response. Individual.

The examiner is provided with a table of information of the following kind:

KINGS OF ENGLAND

Name	Came to the throne	Died	Age	Reigned
William I	1066	1087	60	21
William II	1087	1100	43	13
Henry I	1100	1135	67	35
Stephen	1135	1154	50	19

Candidates are supplied with an identical table with blanks in certain spaces. The task is to complete the table by asking the examiner for specific information. To ensure that the examiner treated each question on its merits a number of different tables would be needed with different blanks at different places for different candidates. The candidates would be assessed on a number of related criteria. First, success. Does the candidate actually manage to fill in the blanks correctly? Second time. How long does it take the candidate to assess the situation and perform as required? Third, productive skill. If he fails to ask any questions, or if his question is unlikely to be understood by the average native speaker of English: no marks. If the question is comprehensible but unnatural: 1 mark. If the question is appropriate, accurate and well expressed:

4 marks. Candidates may be scaled between the extremes by using as principal criterion how far the candidate's faults interfere with his ability to cope with the situation.

Clearly test items of this kind can have an almost limitless range of variation, what has here been exemplified as oral presentation could be purely written, information which is here exemplified as being presented in tabular form could just as well be presented pictorially — sets of pictures of the 'Spot the difference' kind for example, and it is not unlikely that a good deal of exciting experimentation in this field will take place in the next few years.

In the last resort most formal assessment of English as a foreign language nowadays is a combination of elements from a wide range of all the different kinds of test discussed above, probably reflecting some kind of consensus view that language does involve code, system, skill and communication.

Four kinds of assessment

If the question asked above has been 'What kind of a thing is it that is being assessed?' the next question must be 'What is the purpose of making that assessment?'

There are at least four different sorts of purpose that assessment may serve. First, one may wish to assess whether a particular individual will ever be able to learn any foreign language at all. An assessment of this kind is an assessment of *aptitude*. The question being asked is 'Can he learn this at all?' Tests designed to measure aptitude must largely be only indirectly specific language orientated. There appear to be no tests to determine whether a foreigner has the aptitude to learn English as such. Aptitude test batteries include items like tests of the ability to break or use codes, to generate or create messages on the basis of a small set of rules and symbols, tests for memory of nonsense syllables, tests of additory discrimination and so on. A standardised test battery *The Modern Language Aptitude Test* has been devised by J. B. Carroll and S. M. Sapon. Such a test looks only forward in time from the point of the test and nothing lies behind it in terms of English language teaching.

Second, assessment may be made to determine how much English an individual actually knows with a view to how well he might be able to function in situations, which may be more or less closely specified, often quite outside the language learning classroom. The basic question being asked is 'Does he know enough English to . . .?' '. . . follow a course in atomic physics?' '. . . act as waiter in a tourist hotel?' and so on. Assessment of this kind is assessment of *proficiency*. Tests of proficiency look back over previous language learning, the precise details of which are probably unknown, with a view to possible success in some future activity, not necessarily language learning but requiring the effective use of language. Proficiency tests do, however, sometimes have a direct language teaching connection. They might, for example, be used to classify or place individuals in appropriate language classes, or to determine their readiness for particular levels or kinds of instruction. The question here is a rather specific one like 'Does he know enough to fit into the second advanced level class in this institution?' Thus selection examinations, and placement tests are basically proficiency tests. The title of the well-known Cambridge Proficiency Examination implies proficiency in English to do something else, like study in a British institution of further education.

Third, assessment may be made to determine the extent of student learning, or the extent to which instructional goals have been attained. In other words the question being asked is 'Has he learned what he has been taught?' Indirectly of course such assessment may help to evaluate the programme of instruction, to say nothing of the capabilities of the teacher. If he has learned what he has been taught the teaching may well be all right; if he hasn't, the teaching may well have to be looked at carefully and modified and improved. Assessments of this kind are assessments of *achievement*. Tests of achievement look only backwards over a known programme of teaching. Most ordinary class tests, the quick oral checks of fluency or aural discrimination that are part of almost every lesson are achievement tests, and so too should be end of term or end of year examinations.

Lastly, assessment may be undertaken to determine what errors are occurring, what malfunctioning of the systems there may be, with a view to future rectification of these. The question being asked is 'What has gone wrong that can be put right, and why did it go wrong?' Assessment of this kind is *diagnostic.* Diagnostic tests look back over previous instruction with a view to modifying future instruction. The details of past instruction may be known or not, so some kinds of diagnostic test will be like proficiency tests, some will be like achievement tests in this regard. However, it is important at all times to bear in mind the basic question which is being asked, and to realise that items which may be very good tests of actual achievement may be very poor diagnostically. A diagnostic test ought to reveal an individual's strengths and weaknesses and it is therefore likely that it will have to be fairly comprehensive, and devote special attention to known or predicted areas of particular difficulty for the learner. Diagnostic tests are most often used early in a course, when particular difficulties begin to arise and the teacher wants to pin down just what is going wrong so that he can do something about it. Such tests are almost always informal and devised for quite specific situations.

The four terms *aptitude, proficiency, achievement,* and *diagnostic* are very frequent in the literature on testing and it is well to get their meaning clear. It is also worth noting the characteristic usages which these terms have. A learner may *have* an *aptitude for* English language learning; if he does he may quickly *attain* sufficient *proficiency in* English *for* him to be able to study mathematics; this means he has *achieved* a satisfactory *standard*, but a *test* may *diagnose* certain *faults in* his English or in the teaching he has received.

Test qualities

There remains one other important question to ask about any assessment of knowledge of the English language — 'Does it work?' Here again there may be at least four different ways in which this question may be interpreted. The first of these is revealed by the question 'Does it measure consistently?' A metre stick measures the same distance each time because it is rigid and accurately standardised against a given norm. A piece of elastic with a metre marked on it is very unlikely

159

to measure the same every time. In this case the metre stick can be said to be a *reliable* measure. In the same way reliability in instruments for measuring language ability is obviously highly desirable, but very difficult to achieve. Among the reasons for this are the effects of variation in pupil motivation, and of the range of tasks set in making an assessment. A pupil who is just not interested in doing a test will be unlikely to score highly on it. Generally speaking the more instances of pupil language behaviour that can be incorporated into a test the better. It is for this reason that testing specialists have tended to prefer discrete item test batteries in which a large number of different instances of language activity are used, to essay type examinations where the tasks set are seen as more limited in kind and number. Variations in the conditions under which tests are taken can also affect reliability – small variations in timing where precise time limits are required for example, a stuffy room, the time of day when the test is taken, or other equally trivial-seeming factors may all distort test results. Perhaps most important of all in its consequences on test results is the reliability of the marker. This reliability may be high in objectively marked tests – like multiple-choice tests – but can be low in free response tests – like essays – if a structured approach or multiple marking are not used. Determining test reliability requires a certain amount of technical know-how and familiarity with the statistical techniques which permit the calculation of a reliability coefficient. Guidance to these will be found in the books referred to for further reading at the end of this chapter.

The second way in which the question 'Does it work?' can be made more precise is by rephrasing it as 'Does it distinguish between one pupil and another?' A metre stick may be a suitable instrument for measuring the dimensions of an ordinary room, but it would not be suitable for measuring a motorway or the gap of a spark plug for a car. In one case the scale of the object to be measured is too great, in the other it is too small. Not only should the instrument which is used be appropriate to the thing being measured but the scale on the instrument should be right too. A micrometer marked only in centimetres would not permit accurate measurement of watch parts, the scale needs to be fractions of millimetres.

Tests which have the right sort of scale may be said to *discriminate* well. Tests which are on the whole too easy or too difficult for the pupils who do them do not discriminate well, they do not spread the pupils out since virtually all pupils score high marks or all pupils score low marks. Ideally the test should give a distribution which comes close to that of the normal distribution curve.

One needs to be careful in reading the literature on testing when the term *discrimination index* is encountered. This has little to do with discrimination in the sense discussed above. It refers rather to the product of statistical procedures which measure the extent to which any single item in a test measures the same thing as the whole of the test. By calculating a discrimination index for each item in a test it is possible to select those items which are most efficient in distinguishing between the top one-third and the bottom one-third of any group for whom the test as a whole is about right. In other words it will help to establish the measuring scale within the limits of the instrument itself and ensure that that is about right, giving a proper distribution of easy and difficult questions within the test. But a *discrimination index* has no absolute value; to get the overall level of difficulty of the test right requires a pragmatic approach with repeated re-trials of the test items, accepting some and rejecting others until the correct combination has been achieved. Again details of these technical matters will be found in the books for further reading.

The third way in which the 'Does it work?' question may be more fully specified is by asking 'Does it measure what it is supposed to measure?' A metre stick is very practical for measuring cloth but it is irrelevant for measuring language ability. 'What it is supposed to measure' in the case of English language tests is presumably ability in English language, and the only way that the extent to which a test actually does this can be determined is by comparing the test results with some other outside measurement, some other way of estimating pupil ability, a way which ought to be at least as reliable and accurate as the test itself. Where the results of the outside measure match the results of the test reasonably closely the test can be said to have *empirical validity*. Suitable outside measures are difficult to come by.

So far the best criterion which seems to have been found is a teacher's rating. An experienced teacher who knows his class well can rank pupils in order of merit with considerable reliability and accuracy. Thus tests whose results correlate well with teacher ratings can be regarded as empirically valid, and the correspondence between the two measures can be expressed as a *coefficient of validity*. Testing specialists like such coefficients to have a value higher than 0·7 − perfect correlation would give a coefficient of 1·0.

It is clear of course that empirical validity is unlikely to be achieved unless a test is constructed in accordance with some respectable theory of language. It is also unlikely to be achieved unless the test adequately samples the knowledge and activities which are entailed by showing that one knows a language. However, a theoretical base and adequate sampling do not guarantee empirical validity − to gain that, the test must be set against some external criterion.

There is one final kind of validity which is sometimes discussed in the literature on assessment. This is 'face validity'. This is a matter of how the test appears to the pupils being tested, to teachers, administrators and so on. If the form or content of a test appears foolish or irrelevant or inconsequential, then users of the test will be suspicious of it; those in authority will be unlikely to adopt it, pupils may be poorly motivated by it. Thus test makers must ensure that a test not only tests what it is supposed to test, reliably and accurately but that it looks as though that is what it does.

A final characteristic of a good language test is *practicability*. By this is meant the extent to which the test is readily usable by teachers with limited time and resources at their disposal. Such factors as the cost of the test booklets, the amount of time and manpower needed to prepare, administer, invigilate, mark and interpret the test, the requirements for special equipment and so on must all be taken into account. For example a standardised test which employs re-usable test booklets with separate answer sheets is likely to be much cheaper to run than one which uses consumable test booklets. Tests which take relatively little time to work and process are likely to be preferred to those which take a lot of time, those which can be given to many pupils simultaneously are usually more practicable than those which require individual administration. Simple paper and pencil tests may well be preferred to those which require elaborate audio- or video-recording equipment. Up-to-date tests whose cultural content is unexceptional are evidently better than those which are out of date and contain culturally inappropriate or objectionable material, those with clear instruction manuals are better than those with obscure manuals, and so on. The test maker needs to bear all such factors in mind, but he should also bear in mind that the testing of some kinds of activity relevant to some dimensions of 'knowing a language' may require the use of elaborate equipment or individualised methods and a proper balance must be struck.

In the classroom the teacher finds himself faced with having to assess the progress of his pupils, to judge their suitability for one class or another and so on. He must decide out of the whole complex of considerations which has been outlined above what kind of assessment he wishes to make, of what aspects of his pupils learning, with what kind of reliability and what kind of validity. Once those decisions are made he can go ahead with devising his instrument for making the assessment. For help with that he will find J. B. Heaton's *Writing English Language Tests* a useful book along with the book by Lado mentioned earlier, and that by Rebecca Valette listed below.

The last matters to which it would seem appropriate to give some attention here concern standardised English language tests, and the public examinations systems.

A number of standardised tests exist. Among these the Davis test has been widely used. More recently Elizabeth Ingram has published *English Language Battery* but the American tests in this area seem to be more readily available. Among the best known of these are Robert Lado's *English Language Test for Foreign Students* which developed into the *Michigan Test of English Language Proficiency* and the TOEFL, Educational Testing Service, *Test of English as a Foreign Language.* Further information and discussion of such tests will be found in *The Seventh Mental Measurements Yearbook*, ed. O. Bures.

Public examinations

The public examination system tends to vary from country to country. One of the tasks which every teacher has when he takes up an appointment in a new country is to discover just what the requirements of the public examination system are. He needs to obtain copies of syllabuses, past papers, regulations, and the reports of the examiners, where these are published, and to familiarise himself with them. From this he should be able to discover what real linguistic skills are required of examination candidates and what kinds of examination techniques they will need to have mastered. It is then possible to concentrate substantially on teaching the language skills and, in about the last one-tenth of the course, to teach the necessary techniques for passing the examination. Most teachers devote far too much time to practice examinations — pupils often seem to like it, but it is rarely in their best interests since many good examining techniques do little to foster greater learning — dictation is a good case in point.

For information about the public examinations most widely taken in Britain, one can do little better than consult J. McClafferty's *A Guide to Examinations in English for Foreign Students*. In this there are useful hints on preparing for the examinations, details of the various examinations offered by the boards and summaries of regulations and entry requirements. It covers the examinations of the Cambridge Local Examination Syndicate, the Royal Society of Arts, the London Chamber of Commerce, and the ARELS Oral Examination, and has a supplementary list of other examinations in English for foreign students — altogether a very helpful document. Much of the preliminary investigatory work suggested in the previous paragraph has been done for the teacher by this book, there remains only the task of analysing past papers and consulting the annual reports of the examiners.

There are a number of types of examination or methods of assessment which have not been discussed at all in this chapter but which a teacher may come across from time to time. One of these is assessment by using a structured interview schedule. Here the test takes the form of an interview and the linguistic tasks demanded of the candidate are progressively elaborated according to a fixed programme. The point at which the candidate begins to fail in these tasks gives him a rating on the schedule. Such examinations are usually entirely oral – though clearly there is no absolute necessity that they should be so – and the rating is usually arrived at by subjective judgment against a fairly detailed specification of performance features, sometimes by a panel of judges. Another type of test is that involving simultaneous translation – usually reserved for assessing interpreters – but there are a number of such techniques and it is wise to keep an open mind towards them for they might well turn out to be useful some day.

The final word is – avoid too much assessment; resist pressures which might make examinations dominate teaching.

Suggestions for further reading

J. P. B. Allen and S. Pit Corder, *The Edinburgh Course in Applied Linguistics, Vol. 4, Testing and Experimental Methods*, Oxford University Press, 1977.

A. Davies, *Language Testing Symposium: A Psycholinguistic Approach*, Oxford University Press, 1968.

D. P. Harris, *Testing English as a Second Language*, New York: McGraw-Hill, 1969.

J. Oller, *Language Tests at School*, Longman, 1979.

R. M. Valette, *Modern Language Testing: A Handbook*, 2nd edn, New York: Harcourt Brace, Jovanovich, 1977.

Chapter 11

Young Children Learning English

The learning of English by younger children is by no means as common as at later stages and the nature of the younger learner probably affects content and methods more than with other age groups.

English in the primary school

The learning of English as a foreign language by the children of wealthy parents who engaged an English 'Miss' is a tradition as long-standing in Europe and elsewhere as the importation of a 'Mademoiselle' or a 'Fraulein' into upper-class households in Britain. And although this amateurish Anna-and-the-King-of-Siam type of language teaching to the young has a long history it was not until the 1950s that the early-start movement was established in state primary schools. In France, Sweden and Holland, independent experiments with classes of children starting English from ages between 7 and 9 years old demonstrated that enthusiastic teachers using oral methods could achieve excellent results, particularly in pronunciation, with little or no effort. Large schemes in the 1960s in Germany, France and Italy (paralleled by the experimental teaching of French in British primary schools) established in the growing climate of educational democratisation that success in foreign language learning need not be limited to the more intelligent child, though different rates of learning were a fact of academic life.

The teaching of Foreign Languages in the Elementary School – the FLES movement, to use the American label – attracted strong support from the Council of Europe and flourished in a number of countries during the 1960s. The economic crisis of the following years, however, had a major impact on the early teaching of English in state schools: not only was it felt to be something of an educational luxury, but it required specialised materials and teacher training. Although a number of FLES schemes continue to flourish in France, Germany, Italy and Yugoslavia, among others, major enterprises have been halted; the French Ministry of Education has banned further experiments, the ambitious plans to make Holland a bi-lingual nation by 1980 have been shelved.

But the twenty years of English teaching in foreign state primary schools must be seen against a much longer background of English language teaching to young children in second language situations. In East and West Africa, in Cyprus and Malaysia, in Fiji and Hong Kong, the long tradition of teaching English to young children continues. But primary school English in second language areas was for long a sectional filter for secondary, English-medium, education; and was frequently taught by semi-formal intelligence-bound methods. It was the twenty years of experimentation, research and enthusiasm of the FLES movement which gave clearer identity to the aims and methods appropriate to the primary classroom.

The optimum starting age

As millions of children have witnessed in the bi-lingual areas of the world, a second and even a third language can be acquired from the very earliest ages, without any seeming effort or retardation of the mother tongue. What is more, this is shown to occur to all normal children, irrespective of levels of intelligence. In a situation, therefore, when two or more languages are in natural use, they are best acquired together from the cradle. Children of mixed parentage often grow up happily using one language with the mother and another with the father and perhaps friends. A somewhat similar, 'natural' situation occurs where very young children are placed in a new language setting in which they, seemingly unconsciously, pick up a foreign language. Punjabi immigrant children who attend English nursery and primary schools, Spanish-speaking infants in English-speaking convent classes in Argentina and French 4-year-olds in Parisian *écoles maternelles* with native English teachers all show — after an initial period of settling down — how the very young child can learn totally fluent and natural English, without strain, embarrassment or even effort.

Teachers of English in the foreign primary school have argued that their children are uninhibited, positively enjoy most of the repetitive kinds of language activities and are ready for situational (as opposed to intellectual) learning. Interference from the mother tongue has been shown to be less before the age of 10 and neuro-physical clinical investigations suggest that the speech learning centre of the brain is at its maximum capacity between the first and ninth year of life. Socio-cultural arguments for an early start emphasise the breaking of the traditionally parochial character of the primary school, with the introduction of an international element that today is more essential than it has ever been.

Against all the evidence of ready foreign language learning in the young, must be set the balanced demands of the curriculum. Most school experiments have determined that starting a foreign language at the age 8–9 on the one hand does not fail to catch 'the teachable moment', and on the other gives time for the basic mother tongue skills to have been firmly established. Ideally a child should not be taught to read and write English before he is literate in his mother tongue, and the basic concepts of his first language are normally useful stepping stones to those of another.

The young learner

The nature of the very young learner does not appear to vary noticeably from nation to nation, and this suggests that the same general psychological and methodological principles hold good for teachers of the youngest children wherever they are.

For example the limited span of attention noted by

Ginsberg in her 5–6 year olds learning English in Leningrad is found in all young children. Consequently English 'lessons' must be short, though regular. Twenty to thirty minutes each day is ideal for children between 5 and 7, and a longer daily period, up to forty-five minutes for older primary school children. Equally, if not more important, it is necessary to switch frequently from one activity to another during the course of lessons: ten minutes is the longest time for which many primary children can sustain an interest in one activity, and for infant and kindergarten learners, the period is even shorter.

As Rivers points out, young children 'Love to imitate and mime; they are uninhibited in acting out roles, and they enjoy repetition because it gives them a sense of assurance and achievement.' This being so, an essentially oral approach is ideal, using patterned activities like games, songs and short dialogues which lend themselves to repetition. Young children are physically active. The injection into primary English teaching of physical movement for the sole purpose of letting off steam is an acknowledgment only of childish restlessness. But purposeful activity: action songs, dramatisation, the colouring and drawing of pictures, manipulating real objects and puppets, action games like 'Simon Says', quieter games like 'Picture Dominoes', the kind of role-playing found in children's play: these are the very stuff of the exploratory and expressive activity natural to the young child.

There are certain language functions which appeal to children of this age. And unless the language activities allow the learners to talk about what concerns them, English will soon be felt to be irrelevant and boring. Kindergarten children are 'set' to name things, a fundamental kind of control over and relationship with their environment. Therefore the earliest activities should be unashamedly lexical, with structural items playing a purely incidental and formulaic role. Hence 'Put your finger on your . . . . .' should follow from a song naming:

Two eyes and two ears and one mouth and one nose
Two arms and two legs, ten fingers and ten toes.

The ability to name things leads to claiming and collecting. So talking about 'My things' and 'I've got . . .' is naturally attractive, just as games involving collecting — finding hidden items, gathering things that go together, shopping, dressing dolls — have a strong appeal.

If naming objects and possessing them is satisfying to the infant ego, so is having private knowledge and wresting that knowledge from others. Hence the popularity of guessing games, which are rapidly modifiable for language teaching purposes — and played with no less pleasure for being in a foreign language. Indeed, the touchstone for successful activities in English is the harnessing of activities which are natural to the child's maturational level, those which he pursues normally in his own language. The result of this is that English is being used instrumentally for an enjoyable end and gives a constant surrender value and the developing oral skill. No learner should be pressed to learn aspects of the foreign language which are more advanced than his current level of command of his own language, although junior courses in English have been constructed on a structural basis originally designed for adults.

The love of repetition, common to all young children, is a feature of their natural games, stories and groups which is usefully applied to learning English. Therefore games like 'What time is it, Mr Wolf?' and songs of the 'Old MacDonald' variety are ideal. To teach traditional English nursery rhymes, however, is of questionable value. The acknowledged virtues of their attractive tunes and rhymes cannot justify their unusual vocabulary and syntax, let alone their frequent total lack of meaning. It is true that when operating in a foreign language most learners will tolerate a drop in sophistication and motivational levels. But whilst the adult learner is often prepared to listen to or record an anecdote in a foreign language which he would disdain in his mother tongue, he is vaguely aware of the psychological gap which exists. On the other hand, the 8 year old French boy singing 'Twinkle Twinkle Little Star' has few clues to tell him that the song is appropriate to English children half his age, and it is arguably doing as much a disservice to teach him it as it is to encourage items like *puffer-train* and *doggy*.

The readiness with which primary children form groups and participate in team activities is a quality which lends itself to the English lesson. Not only does group work give children more chance to talk to each other – no one can have a conversation with a taperecorder and semi-natural practice is difficult in a class-teaching situation – but it harnesses the purposeful and instrumental use of English. Colouring and drawing activities are best done in small groups where talk about the work in hand can take place naturally. Games with picture cards – picture dominoes, picture bingo, 'Happy Families' – call for small groups, which can also be the basis for dialogues, dramatisation and role-playing activities.

Language Content

But what topics should be the basis of the games and activities of the primary classroom? What centres of interest are commonest in children between 5 and 11? At the younger end of the primary spectrum, the most attractive items are those with potential rather than intrinsic interest. It is what the child can do with a thing, rather than what it is, which matters. Things to hold, drop, throw or carry, things to build with, to colour, to wear, to give and take, to hide and find are what matter when the child is growing experimentally in relationship to his environment. The activity is all important, though bright colours, manageable size and sympathetic textures are compelling. This being so, the earliest choice of objects to be named should be portable (balls, balloons and bags) wearable (coats, hats and shoes) and manipulative (bricks, dolls, and small items of furniture). Gradually the vocabulary of the immediate natural surroundings can be built up – the familiar lexis of home, toy cupboard, family, of streets and shops and play. The need to name things is best harnessed by learning lexical sets – parts of the body, clothes, furniture, food, toys and animals and so on – and the manipulative appeal may be supplied by simple drawing and colouring activities followed up by games which use these objects – real or represented – as tokens for touching, collecting, finding, counting or constructing, as appropriate.

The natural developmental patterns of the primary school child, then, suggesting an initial concern for naming things – nouns – and identifying where things are – prepositions – and doing things to things – verbs – opens up the world of action and role-playing. Giving, and taking and holding grows into helping in the house; collecting and carrying becomes shopping; playing with clothes develops into getting ready to go out and the putting and taking, the pushing and pulling, the hiding and finding crystallise into the simulated activities of parents, animals and work-people of the familiar world. The sex-role stereotyping of the maturing young child – little girls *are* by nature more interested in dolls and kitchens, little boys are more interested in boats and trains and lorries – is something to be exploited in the language activities, rather than shaped by the sociologically zealous teacher. Whatever is a natural topic in the mother tongue is a suitable topic for English.

The introduction of reading and writing in English should not take place until a fluent oral foundation has been established and, in foreign language situations, not until the children are familiar with the printed word in the mother tongue. Indeed, many teachers of primary English, using activity methods, prefer to withhold reading and writing for up to two years. Such concentration on spoken English pays dividends in fluency, pronunciation and the natural use of English, but demands considerable expertise from the teacher. It is true that once children can read and write English their language practice and experience is no longer totally reliant upon the teacher as a model and initiator. It is also true that in the more formal systems of primary education, and those second language situations where English is being developed as an academic instrument, the printed word is properly introduced at about the end of the first year of study. But in any case, reading, and later writing, are best woven gradually into the fabric of an oral/activity methodology.

There can be no doubt that primary school children can and do learn English with remarkable ease, enthusiasm and naturalness. Perhaps the saddest aspect of the FLES movement has been the problem of continuity; for unless the early learning of English is designed and functions as part of a process which continues unbroken in secondary schooling the sense of frustration in both children and teachers is considerable. It is basically for this reason that French in British primary schools has proved disappointing, and that the English teaching in French primary schools has been discouraged. On the other hand, where English is taught in a co-ordinated and unbroken sequence from primary through secondary education, and where the language teaching is vigorously non-selective, as in Sweden and Malta for instance, the results are a very high percentage of the population who are bilingual. It need hardly be added that in scores of private schools in many countries where children learn English from the age of 6 or 7, and continue in the same establishment for their whole school career, standards of spoken and written English tend to be most impressive. The reason lies not in the selective nature of these schools, in superior teaching methods or smaller classes, but in the un-broken sequence of teaching English which (it is taken for granted) every child can and does learn for both instrumental and integrative purposes.

The degrees of proficiency in the different languages of a multi-lingual speaker vary. That is to say, it is not uncommon for a foreign learner to have a lesser competence in speaking English than in reading and writing it. This often proves to be the case where English has been taught indirectly by trans-lation from the mother tongue, or where the teaching has been book-centred — foreigners who 'speak written English' are all too common. Perhaps one great advantage of an early start to learning English is that this danger is avoided: the young learner, unhampered by folk-myths about foreign lan-guages, is put into the position of thinking in English from the very start far more readily than the older beginner. What is more, the foreign language grows with him as an active part of his thinking and talking, and having first encountered English in its oral form he is never likely to regard the spoken word as inferior to print.

Suggestions for further reading

O. Dunn, *Beginning English with Young Children*, Macmillan, 1983.

O. Dunn, *Developing English with Young Children*, Macmillan, 1983.

R. Freundenstein (ed.), *Teaching Foreign Languages to the Very Young*, Pergamon, 1979.

H. H. Stern and A. Weinrib, 'Foreign Languages for Younger Children: Trends and Assessment', *Language Teaching and Linguistic Abstracts*, vol. 10, no. 1, Cambridge University Press, 1977.

Chapter 12

Learning English in the Secondary School

The purpose of this chapter is to relate the general principles discussed elsewhere in the book to the specific needs of the secondary school. In part, this means relating principles to the adolescent language learner's needs, and in part to the administrative constraints imposed by educational systems at secondary level.

Broadly, English is likely to be taught in three types of situation at secondary level. The teacher may be dealing with a class of students who are learning English solely because the school system demands it, with anything between one and five periods a week to contend with, and very little strong motivation. Alternatively, students may be quite strongly motivated in a foreign language situation, perhaps because they see themselves as specialists in English, or because they anticipate having to use it for university level work, or because there is an obvious role for English to play in the community outside school. Usually with classes of this kind the teacher has quite a number of periods, between three and eight, say, to use every week. Finally, there is the situation in which English is a medium for all or part of the instruction in the school. In circumstances like this the teacher is obviously able to develop more advanced work than in the other two situations. In classroom management and organisation the same principles apply to all three types of situation, but the appropriate goals for each course will vary according to its type.

Classroom management

The characteristic secondary school class is large (anything upwards of twenty-five students), and because of its size, it usually reflects a wide range of ability. Some would say that it is also characteristically unmotivated for hard work in learning a language, and it is certainly true that there are situations in the world in which the reasons for learning English are not self-evident, so that students may well feel less commitment to language work than to – say – geography or physics. The school cannot overcome single-handed problems which arise from administrative decisions, and if the wrong language is being taught to the wrong people in the wrong size of class for the wrong periods of time, it is not the teachers or the pupils who should be blamed for the failure of the system to produce fluent English speakers. But at the same time there are many ways in which the teacher can make the best of the situation that he is faced with, especially if he bears in mind that there is no teacher in the world who is satisfied with the conditions which he is asked to teach in.

The teacher's duty is to make sure that his teaching is *appropriate* to his class, that is *organised* systematically, and that it is *exciting.*

These three features interlock with each other, but it is worth noting that, while the first two are the easiest to attain, they are probably less often pursued than excitement. Yet a teacher who uses appropriate and well-organised materials usually has little difficulty in generating enthusiasm in his class. Let us examine each of these ideas in a little more detail.

Appropriacy

There are two stages in producing appropriate teaching, first in the preparation and selection of materials, (course books, exercises, visuals, etc.) and second in classroom organisation while the lesson is in progress. Materials used may, of course, be selected by a Ministry of Education or a head of department and be to some extent beyond the control of the classroom teacher, but someone somewhere needs to make the decisions. Whoever makes the initial selection of the material, it is the duty of the teacher to adapt it to the needs of his individual class as far as he can. First, the material must be considered for level: is it appropriate for the class linguistically (will the syntax, lexis, stylistic range be within the class's grasp without being so simple that they will be bored)? Is the material appropriate culturally, or does it demand that they know aspects of British or American life which it would be unrealistic to expect? Is it appropriate intellectually (and it is worth noting that much EFL teaching material presupposes an intellectual level of about 5 years old)? Is the material about the right length for the activities it will be used for? Is it something which the students will find interesting? And so on. If any part of the material is unsatisfactory in any of these respects, the teacher will need to make a decision, either to change the material and find something more suitable, or to organise his class activities so as to make the work appropriate by means of teaching techniques. For example, material which is far too simple in intellectual terms can be made exciting (and also demanding on pupils' thinking) when it is used as a game and gone through at great speed. And this brings us to the second stage of classroom organisation. All the time in the class the teacher will have to decide how to introduce his material (indeed *whether* to introduce his material), how much time to spend on each stage, when to vary the activity, how serious he should be at any one moment in the lesson, and so on. The more experienced the teacher becomes, the more likely he is to be able to anticipate the requirements of his class, particularly when he knows them well, but no teacher can anticipate everything. and all good teaching demands thinking on one's feet: the good teacher will always be sensitive to whether the class is alert or sleepy, whether discussion is appropriate or irrelevant, whether he is being ignored or listened to.

All of this applies to any teaching situation, but it is of particular importance to the secondary school, because when classes are large, and when motivation is not high (and a teacher who has a class which is interested most of the time can consider himself either very lucky or very successful), the teacher must always be flexible and sensitive. If he is not, the class will become extremely bored, or — worse still —

extremely undisciplined. A pleasant manner is simply not enough when teaching a large class.

Organisation

Decisions about organisation will partly have to be taken at the school level, but each teacher needs to operate systematically within the school system, and this means being organised personally. Sometimes teachers say that their own 'style' is to be disorganised as if this is rather charming and of very little importance to the student. While it is no doubt true that there have been brilliant teachers who have been very disorganised, there is a great deal of arrogance in thinking that one is brilliant oneself: nobody will suffer from being systematic.

What is meant by 'being systematic'? First, the teacher should become familiar with the work of the school as a whole and relate his own work to the total picture. This means that he should prepare a general scheme of work for himself for each class he teaches, within the overall scheme that the school uses. Within this general scheme, which may be organised on a termly or an annual basis, he should prepare teaching units which will vary in size from two or three periods to half a term or more. Within these units the individual lessons will be planned.

Of course not every teacher needs to spend all his time working out long-term schemes. These are activities which are best done in co-operation with colleagues. Nor do they necessarily have to be very detailed (though in some countries very precise details are demanded from teachers for the whole year's work). It is sensible, however, for every teacher to have notes which will tell him more or less what he is going to teach, with some reference to the basic materials he expects to use, and some reference to the order of teaching. This is the basis for his teaching; though certainly not an iron law, for a good teacher will always adapt when he discovers that his class generally knows more than he had anticipated, or when unexpected problems occur. Some people insist in putting in the timing for each item in the scheme of work but there are strong arguments against this, which are discussed in Chapter 14.

It is essential in the secondary school situation that the teacher should know for every moment of the lesson exactly what he is expecting each pupil to be doing, and of course what he should be doing himself. Whether the work is silent, like writing or reading, or controlled oral activity at class or group level, or free group activity, the teacher should know exactly what kind of behaviour he is expecting from the class, and how that relates to the teaching aims of the lesson. This means that, at the beginning of his career, the teacher will certainly need to spell out in great detail the aims of the lesson and the activities which will help to realise those aims. If the teacher starts by doing a training course which provides teaching practice, there is usually time to prepare lessons in detail and to consult with tutors and fellow-students, so that the process of preparation is developed carefully and systematically. But not all teachers are lucky enough to be able to do this. Nevertheless, in the early years of teaching such careful preparation is essential, and some teachers prefer to work as carefully as this throughout their working lives.

This means that a lesson plan is likely to contain several different types of information, which need to be clearly distinguished. First, it will contain the main points in the organisation of the lesson for the benefit of the teacher: then it will also contain detailed organisational information about class activities; finally it may contain a great deal of 'content' material which the teacher cannot expect to remember — like the detailed forms of oral exercises, or a passage to be read to the class, or a list of points which will be put on the blackboard for a writing exercise. A good lesson plan will not mix up these different types of information, but will lay them out so that the teacher can use them easily in class without the class being aware that notes are being consulted all the time.

An example of a workable lesson plan is given on page 179.

It will be seen from the lesson plan that the teacher has two main aspects to consider: the selection of materials, and the choice of classroom procedures. The problems of the selection of materials relate partly to the overall level of the class and the nature of the school's syllabus or scheme of

<u>CLASS 2A</u>   *Friday 12th May*   *9.30 – 10.15*

AIMS =

A <u>*LANGUAGE*</u> = {
  1 *Revise 'giving directions'*
  2 *Punctuation of direct speech via picture story*
}

B *INTERACTION*   3 *Pair practice = fluency*

TAKE IN   Direction cards

Plan of 'Balloon dialogue'   *Pictures in textbook*
pictures and story

	Teacher	<u>Pupils</u>
I	(a) ASK 3 pupils 'How can I get to the football pitch, please?'	Listen and answer if asked
approx. *10 mins*	+ chemistry lab. Secretary's office	
	(b) GIVE OUT DIRECTION CARDS EXPLAIN = work in pairs, like last week GO ROUND GROUPS	Work in pairs with cards
<u>II</u> *not more than 10 mins*	(a) TELL picture story and WRITE dialogue on board	Listen
	(b) Quick DRILL of story (as on attached sheet)	Choral and individual
5 mins	(c) ORGANISE pupils in threes - 2 to retell story and other to check: then move around	Work in threes
5 – 10 mins	(d) TELL to write story rapidly 5 mins (COLLECT DIRECTION CARDS WHILE THEY WRITE)	Write
	(e) TELL to check for punctuation of speech in pairs NB <u>Ask</u> me if there are problems	Check in pairs
10 mins +	(f) (if time) – go through in class	

work, and these are discussed elsewhere in this chapter, but they also relate partly to the classroom procedures which are used.

When teaching large classes, particularly, the teacher has to think very carefully about the most appropriate ways of enabling *every* pupil to participate as fully as possible in the lesson. In planning his teaching, he has to decide at each stage on the answers to two main questions. The first is – Do I want the whole class to be doing exactly the same piece of work at the same time? and the second is – Do I want them all to be working as one group, centred on me or the blackboard, or do I want them to be working in a number of independent groups? Note that these are not two versions of the same question: there will be many occasions when the class may usefully work in small groups, all simultaneously practising the same piece of language or preparing the same piece of written work. Let us first of all consider the advantages of breaking the class into small groups.

Many of the advantages of breaking the class down into smaller units are general educational ones, but some of them proceed from the nature of language itself and are especially important in language teaching. For example, if we want to develop natural conversational ability, we are far more likely to achieve this by means of face-to-face contact in small groups than through speeches made in public in front of the whole class – the more informal the situation, the more natural the interaction. We also need to recognise that the use of language – even a foreign language – is a very intimate activity for the user, and it is much easier to develop the necessary confidence in a comparatively private situation than in the public gaze of the full class: the art of addressing a large group, as any teacher knows, is very different from that of talking privately. But at the same time a number of other benefits result from working in small groups. The groups provide much more intensive opportunities for practice than any full class situation can, and they are potentially much more flexible. It is harder for a lazy pupil to opt out of group activity than out of full class activity, and pupils can learn a great deal from each other – far more than most people suppose.

In some ways, however, group work poses problems which

not all teachers are happy to face. It is often argued that classes become too noisy, that (in mono-lingual situations) they are liable to use the mother tongue, and that it is not possible for the teacher to check the accuracy of the work which is being carried out in groups. While it is perfectly true that bad use of groupwork can result in all these problems arising, it must be borne in mind what the advantages are, and particularly the advantage in intensity of work. What teacher can truthfully say that everyone is concentrating, even for three-quarters of the time when a large class is being taught as a full group? Yet it is easy to achieve concentration for most of the time with well organised group activities. The most important points to remember are that the class should be introduced to group work procedures gently, that the activities should be clearly related to the aim of the lesson, and that the reasons for working in groups should be made absolutely clear. Given these conditions, there are very few occasions when teaching will not be more effective in small groups than in whole-class work. Consider again the example on p. 13.

Thus the teacher may start by presenting a new item to the whole class, may follow with a very rapid choral practice to reinforce the pattern, and then immediately ask the class to practise repeating the pattern in pairs, each one checking carefully that the other is getting it right. (Note that one of the advantages of working like this is that pupils gain practice in correcting and helping each other.) This activity need not last longer than two or three minutes and should be stopped before this if the task has been completed or if the class is losing interest and not doing it properly. This routine may be followed by a little more full-class work, with more short sessions of pairs practice, and may lead into a communicative game to be played in groups of three or four, or alternatively may be followed by written work which can be prepared in groups and then written individually, or – if the teacher is confident that they will be able to do it successfully – written individually and then revised and corrected in pairs or groups. During all this process the teacher will go round the groups, encouraging, checking that everyone is doing the task properly, helping those in difficulty, and generally being available for consultation.

181

All in all, even with teaching sessions of an hour or more, the break from full-class to small-group to individual work means a reduction of monotony and an increase in pupil concentration.

It is also possible to use the small group system to enable pupils to work at different levels during the same lesson. In schools where there is a very wide range of ability within the same class this has sometimes been successful but it can lead, if badly planned, to undesirable results. It is not generally a good idea to break a class into more or less permanent groupings of good and less good unless there is an enormous divergence between groups (as perhaps when half the class has come from English-medium primary schools and the other half has not). Even in these extreme situations the educational disadvantage of establishing a permanent feeling of inferiority in the less good group may outweigh the short-term advantage of enabling the fast group to rush on without being slowed up by the other. Perhaps the ideal situation is when the teacher is able to persuade the class to work in mixed ability small groups so that the good students can – for part of the time at least – help those who are less competent. In fact, though, such an extreme situation is very rare and in few classes are the differences between the two halves so great that they are not better off working together than working apart. Particularly in exercises which are aiming at fluency rather than accuracy there are great advantages in mixing abilities, for it is not necessarily the pupil with the best formal knowledge of English who is the most skilful communicator.

None the less, there are occasions when pupils should be allowed to advance at their own pace, particularly with extensive reading, and there is certainly a place in the classroom for individualised programmes, based, for example, on reading laboratories or work-cards which enable particular difficulties to be dealt with by the pupils who are affected by them.

Beginners and false beginners

One of the greatest weaknesses of secondary school syllabuses is ambition: frequently they try to teach far more than is possible in the time available. In general, in language teaching, thorough teaching is more important than wide-ranging teaching. This is so much the case that in at least one country the secondary school language work improved greatly once it was admitted that the goal was merely to teach the primary school syllabus again, but effectively!

The secondary school language course, for one reason or another, will necessarily be going over a lot of old ground, all the time, because that is the only way of constantly reinforcing the language which has already been learnt, making it increasingly fluent. At the same time, it is a good idea systematically to go back over the basic stages of the language for all students, even if they should have covered them in primary school. If no great difficulty emerges, very little time needs to be spent; if some areas do give difficulty, the revision will be valuable.

If English is being started in the secondary school, exactly the same point applies, except that the revision starts a little higher up the school, but all language learners need constant practice and reinforcement of the early stages of their course.

More advanced work

As pupils progress through the school, their work in English will become more directed in two ways. First, if there is a terminal examination, to some extent the work will be geared to its demands. Second, as the pupils develop intellectually they will, quite rightly, be more critical about the goals of their English teaching, and it will become increasingly necessary to provide not merely a general English course, but one which is directed towards the needs in English that they are going to have. This may mean orientating the English teaching towards study skills and work at an advanced educational level, or it may mean concentrating on English for technical subjects, or – in second language situations – relating it to the work being carried on in other subjects in the school.

To some extent younger pupils will accept English because it is in the curriculum, but after adolescence they will need to be persuaded that it has specific value to them, and this means that the course must recognise the justice of their concern.

Organisation in the secondary school

Much of what is mentioned in this section is expanded on in Chapter 14. It is important to emphasise, however, that departmental organisation is probably more important in the secondary school than in any other type of institution. The reason for this is that secondary schools tend to be large and to keep pupils over a period of several years. The English department must be organised so that control is maintained over the many classes, and continuity is maintained from year to year.

The kind of scheme of work which was discussed earlier in the chapter is the responsibility of the department as a whole, and therefore ultimately the responsibility of the head of the department. While it is recognised that different institutions organise themselves in different ways, it must be insisted that it is highly irresponsible not to be able to offer a new teacher clear guidance on the level of work to be expected in classes to be taken over and on how that relates to the total work of the school. This means a great deal more than merely giving page numbers of a textbook.

The ideal scheme of work for a school will consist of two parts: a series of stages through which all pupils are expected to pass, going right from entry into the school up to the time that they leave, and a checklist of other items which cannot be ordered but which should be covered during the work of each year. The stages should cover all aspects of language work, but should also specify what sort of subject matter, and what sort of language interaction skills should be expected. At the same time, as appropriate, the checklist should provide a note of, for example, relevant pieces of cultural information which should be touched upon at some stage (a country with close links with the USA would expect to include relevant information about travel prospects, for example), or of basic syntactic errors which are not so important that they will be covered by the core course, but which should be revised during the year if the need arises. Thus, while the teacher should be able to know that a class which has reached stage 12 will have covered stages 1–11 in that order, he will have to see what has been crossed off the checklist to see which of the more incidental parts have been touched on.

The scheme of work, then, acts both as a guide and a record. If every class has a record kept of its activities, at the end of each term it will be possible at a glance to see how individuals and classes are progressing.

The preparation of the scheme of work for the department, and of materials to back it up, provides the basis for the professional development of the English teaching staff. No materials or scheme are likely to last for very long, because they express a relationship between pupils, teachers, and English learning needs. All of these are likely to change from year to year, and any scheme should be in a process of permanent, slow revision. Even when, as in most schools, the staff are pressed for time, the benefits of working together on a regular basis cannot be exaggerated.

The department in a secondary school has one other important role to play, however, and that is as a source for materials. There are some sorts of materials which can only exist efficiently on a departmental basis (for example wallcharts and aids of many kinds). It may also be true that no extensive reading can be effectively organised in the school without co-operation between all the English teachers. For example, if the school has funds to spend on class libraries for silent reading, these need to be organised in such a way that the maximum number of suitable books can reach the maximum number of pupils. This implies some kind of rota system between classes, and it is much more efficient for this to be organised than for it to be left to chance. And even in schools where there are no funds for this sort of book, pupils can be encouraged to lend books for such a purpose.

The final important activity at department level in the secondary school is the provision of information to staff and pupils. It is astonishing how often it is assumed that

185

teachers below examination classes do not need to know about the examination syllabus. Circulars from Ministries of Education, lists of books, anything which is of any relevance whatsoever to the English work of the school should be permanently accessible to all staff, and it should be assumed that they will want to see everything. No one can work efficiently if he feels that discussion relating to his work is going on in his absence. And to some extent the same principles apply to the pupils. Certainly those who are in examination classes should have access to – and ideally receive – copies of the official examination syllabus, and in general the higher up the school pupils rise, the more they should have the reasons for all activities of the department explained to them.

A final, important point is worth making. The organisation of a department is not solely the concern of the head of the department. Someone has to take responsibility and there must be a leader, but the running of the department and the administrative chores associated with it should as far as possible be a co-operative endeavour. Only then will the members of the department work as a team, and the activities function satisfactorily when the head of the department leaves or has to be absent for any time. Perhaps more than any other subject in the school curriculum, English teaching is a co-operative activity, and the considerations discussed in Chapter 14 are most vital at the secondary level.

Suggestion for further reading

The best general and detailed account of the secondary school (in a second language situation) is:

J. A. Bright and G. P. McGregor, *Teaching English as a Second Language*, Longman, 1970.

Chapter 13

Teaching English to Adults

Adults learning English bring to the task a mature personality, many years of educational training, a developed intelligence, a determination to get what they want, fairly clear aims, and above all strong motivation to make as rapid progress as possible. These are formidable qualifications which far outweigh any disadvantages, and make teaching adults a challenging and satisfying experience.

An adult is no longer constrained by the educational system or parental pressure to learn English, so the problems of dealing with conscripts do not exist. Since people choose to be present in an English class, the opposite is more the case — the tertiary teacher's task is to utilise and channel his student's motivation so that his specific needs and aims are optimally fulfilled. There is considerable diversity in the tertiary sector and the rest of this chapter looks at some of the important areas and their problems.

Higher education in the state system

Many English teachers find themselves in or attached to university or polytechnic English departments throughout the world in the capacity of assistants or lecturers. Generally speaking, the framework of the studies is fixed and the syllabus, usually preparing for a final examination, settled. The teacher's challenge is to bring to life the language, literature and civilisation it is his charge to teach.

The proficiency in English language on entrance to the English department varies from country to country throughout the world. In countries close to England with long traditions of English teaching and an efficient secondary feeder system, the standard of the new entrants is likely to be generally high. There will always be room for advanced English teaching, with specialisation in certain areas. Beyond improving the advanced student's use of the language, it should be possible at this level to increase his knowledge about English — that it is English as a content subject as well as a skill. Many departments offer a course in the history of English, which provides valuable insights into why English is the way it is today. A higher priority is a description of contemporary English presented as a formal system in as much detail as time will allow. Strongly to be recommended for this purpose is R. Quirk and S. Greenbaum's *University Grammar of English*. A good new grammar is S. Chalker's *Current English Grammar* from Macmillan. It is also worth reading through an introduction to the principles of language – R. Hudson's *Invitation to Linguistics* or J. Aitchison's *Linguistics* are fairly basic; somewhat more advanced are D. Bolinger and D. A. Sear's *Aspects of language* and V. Fromkin and R. Rodman's *An Introduction to Language*.

Many less developed countries pose different problems. Often the intake is of very mixed ability. A few people may have spent several years in Britain or America, others may have attended the English department because other departments of their first choice had no more places available, and their knowledge of English is very poor. Yet these people, and many in the middle, find themselves in the same class. There are two main ways to deal with these heterogeneous, very mixed ability groups — one administrative, the other pedagogic. Administratively it is best to devote all the class hours to intensive language work directed towards a Language Barrier exam which everyone must pass before going on to the degree course proper. Those who can pass it immediately should be allowed to proceed — but it is important to pass in all areas. Many people who have spent years in an English-speaking country may be orally fluent but quite incapable of expressing themselves in writing. The Language Barrier exam should be set as early as possible, but it is very common that one year's intensive English, and in some countries two years' study, is required before a student is in a position to do any justice to the subject matter of an advanced level degree course.

The pedagogic solutions for mixed ability classes are varied. It is useful to discover just how great the range is by using a diagnostic test. There will certainly be a large block in the middle of the ability range who can be separated off as a group for some parts of the lesson, or for some lessons, and will form a more homogenous teaching group. If this strategy is adopted, the poor ones and the better ones must receive their due time and attention. Individual work is essential for each person not in the main group, with the emphasis on bringing the weak ones up to standard to join the main group. A planned scheme of work using available textbooks and particularly class tape recorders and the language laboratory is vital in individualised learning of this type. A great deal of time, probably outside class hours, will need to be spent coaching the weak ones. There is one advantage, however, in that the weak ones may well not be proficient in English through lack of practice or opportunity, but they should, through the very fact of being selected for Higher Education, be intelligent and able. With care and attention they should always be capable of catching up with the others.

A danger of splitting a heterogeneous group in this way is that the very act of division may intensify rather than alleviate the difficulties. So it is probably better to have the whole class together for the majority of the time, and use techniques which involve each person at his own level. With, say, oral questioning, it is possible to ask the more difficult questions of the able students at a speed that will tax them and the easier questions of the less proficient and at a slower pace. Similarly, there might be a choice of titles for the composition, some more difficult than others, to cater for different levels of proficiency. One effective technique here is group work, where the good students are asked to be group leaders and given the task of helping along and getting the best out of the others. In general terms, the teacher's task is to provide each student with a learning experience at his own level and a challenge to improve, so that the initially heterogeneous class becomes over time a more homogeneous unit.

The problems are quite different where English is not the major subject of study. A student in the English department who usually has integrative motivation, identifies to at least some degree with the subject of his study and wishes to make his own the good things he find in the cultural, literary and aesthetic life of English-speaking countries. On the other hand, many scientists, for example, are interested in English simply as a tool, an instrument to make them better at their job by giving them access to the extensive scientific literature in English and by allowing them to speak to their English-speaking colleagues from around the world. With the growth of English as an international language, there has been a corresponding increase in the teaching of specialised English.

Teaching English to non-specialists in tertiary state education is just one branch of English for Special Purposes. English for Academic Purposes (EAP) is a growing branch of ESP peculiar to Higher Education. This can of course be radically different from country to country, especially when English is the medium of instruction for a scientific subject, as it is in large parts of Africa and the Indian sub-continent. The local languages do not have widespread acceptance amongst all the students concerned, they do not have the lexis to cope with the technical terminology, and there is very little in print of a specialised nature, hence English is the medium of instruction. The main problem here is to ensure that the level of English is sufficient to deal with the complex subject matter and with the demands of the learning system — listening to lectures, note-taking, reading textbooks, coping with tutorials and seminars, writing reports, essays and exam papers, and ultimately carrying out the research leading to a thesis. And of course all this must be done in English. The teacher's task here is to foster his student's study skills. There are several helpful courses available, such as J. B. Heaton's *Studying in English* (Longman, 1975).

In many other countries in the world, particularly where English is a foreign, rather than a second, language, it is very common for a teacher to be confronted with a group of medical students or engineers who have little existing knowledge of English and demand to be taught how to read their technical books and journals, and nothing else. They have no need to write in English nor even to speak it. Their need is for a course in reading technical English. It is not impossible to provide this by starting with very elementary examples of the written word and by taking the students through a carefully graded sequence of texts with copious commentary in their mother tongue.

A better approach is to argue, first, that this is in fact a misguided, short-term view of what is needed. There is always an opportunity to use the skills of writing, speaking and listening, whatever one's immediate circumstances. Many write reports or articles for publication in international reviews, others must talk to and understand expatriate colleagues and visiting lecturers. With the ease of travel today, many must surely travel outside their own country to international conferences and courses, where English will certainly be widely used. And it is a necessary precondition for many scholarships that the candidate has a good level of English.

The second argument is pedagogic. It may well be that the best way to learn to read efficiently in English is to pay particular attention to this skill only after the successful completion of a general course in all the skills. This is a very important premise, with implications for all ESP teaching, and there is considerable debate about it. One possible solution is illustrated by the following case.

A group of Spanish shopkeepers wanted to learn enough oral English to deal with British tourists. They were given a course in general English with certain special provisions. There was considerable oral emphasis, but written work and reading were insisted on too – partly for variety as it is quite possible to tire very quickly of a lot of oral work, and partly because the written word consolidates and reinforces what has been learnt orally. The basic grammatical structures that were taught remained essentially the same as in the regular courses, as did the emphasis on clear but natural pronunciation. However, the lexical items taught to fill the slots in the grammatical patterns were very carefully chosen to meet the needs of the shopkeepers – often statistically infrequent, but in this case useful, items were taught before the more generally common words.

The content of what was taught was also determined on a

functional basis – how to make requests, answer requests, persuade people to buy things and other similar notions of direct relevance to the shopkeeper. The teaching strategy was to make extensive use of situations familiar to the students and of role-playing and simulation exercises within those situations. This case illustrates how a course in general English can be adapted to the specific needs of a given group of learners. A tailor-made course is nearly always essential.

ESP is by no means restricted to the institutional framework of state-run Higher Education. There is enormous expansion currently in ESP in evening institutes of a semi-official nature, and primarily in private language schools in England and abroad. The field is wide and infinitely varied, and not given to easy generalisations. P. Robinson's *English for Specific Purposes* provides a bibliographical survey. More recently, C. Kennedy and R. Bolitho's *English for Specific Purposes* gives a good introduction to the theory and practice in this field.

The private sector

In many countries far more adults learn English in the private sector than in state-run institutions. As has just been mentioned, the private sector is prominent in providing ESP courses, and one of its characteristics is its flexibility in responding to a perceived demand. Clearly, however, private language schools and institutes cater principally for students wanting a more general grounding in English. Their clients often begin with no knowledge, or a very rusty and hazy knowledge of the English they did years before in secondary school. This often produces beginner classes of very mixed ability, and the remarks made earlier in this chapter on this problem largely apply here. Not only may ability in the class be very mixed – for the only entry requirement is the capacity to pay the fee – but aspirations may be very different. At one extreme there is the housewife who does not want to stagnate at home, at the other there is the businessman who wants to make very rapid progress. As a general rule it is best to segregate administratively these different types into homogeneous groups by enrolling the housewife into an afternoon or morning class which meets two or three times a week, and by putting the go-getting businessman with his peers in a daily intensive course.

It is quite conceivable, however, that both courses could use similar materials, though at a different pace, especially at the initial stages. But it is very important to make sure each group is using an appropriate course — relevant to the intellectual level and age of the group, suitable for the life-style of the country (sophisticated western life is not appropriate for less developed countries). As for the materials, the best policy to adopt in private schools is to take a modern course, of which there are many reputable ones on the market, and use it as a basis for the teaching, often right up to intermediate level and beyond. The Teacher's Books are full of sensible and practical advice, and the students are usually willing to buy the Student's Book, and other ancillary readers, workbooks, etc., that may be necessary. To these basic aids, the teacher himself must bring his professional expertise in using them and in supplementing them where necessary with material specially produced for local needs.

A key factor — perhaps even more so in private schools (where clients demand value for money and 'vote with their feet') than in state schools where it is obligatory to attend English classes — is the teacher's relationship with his class. In all teaching, the teacher's personality is the single most important influence in learning. Nowhere is this more important than in guiding his pupils with skill and professionalism through the first stages of learning in private schools and institutes. A teacher's good humour and sympathetic understanding of his problems have stopped many a student from withdrawing from a course when faced, as many are, with the pressures of a full-time job and English classes several nights a week.

Private sector students have chosen to be where they are because they feel this is the best way to achieve the goal they have in mind for themselves. They have usually specific aims in learning English and it is sound practice to make them see during the course just how they are attaining them. Progress should be made, and be seen to be made. One way to do this is to work towards an examination as the ultimate target.

This is a potentially dangerous procedure, since what is taught is dictated by what is tested. And what is tested is not necessarily what it is desirable to teach. However, there is often very strong pressure to pass examinations. This is a fact of life which cannot be avoided, and must be catered for. And it is reasonable that the student should be able to demonstrate by a pass certificate that he has reached a given level in English. Indeed, 'credentialling', as the process is sometimes called of issuing a student with a certificate stating publicly what his level of achievement is, is vital to the student. Very probably one aim he came with was to be able to show to his superiors or future employers that he could reach a given proficiency in English. Better jobs and increased salaries are strong motivating forces.

At intermediate level and above, particularly, the examination toward which one is working is of paramount importance, as it will tend to mould, and even dominate, the syllabus for months or years beforehand, and its international integrity and good name will be very important. There are very many examination options available, both local and international, at every level of learning, and an increasing number dealing with specialist English needs (secretarial English, translation, interpreting, etc.). A good guide to what there is can be found in J. McClafferty, *A Guide to Examinations in English for Foreign Students*, referred to on p. 164. One example of a complete range of examinations from the post-elementary to English degree level are those set by the Institute of Linguists. Far better known world wide are the three examinations set by the University of Cambridge Local Examinations Syndicate: the First Certificate in English, the Certificate of Proficiency in English, and the Diploma in English Studies. These are taken by many thousands of students each year and have currency all over the world.

A teacher faced with the task of teaching for the intermediate First Certificate is in a fortunate position. All the big international courses of the major publishers get the students to the level of the examination without preparing specifically for it. In addition there are more and more courses coming on the market which are purpose-written for the last year or so before the examination. Many of the more modern

194

ones serve their purpose admirably, and are a solid base for the teacher to build upon. His professional skill is called on to a greater degree at proficiency level, as there are few good books on sale and the demands of the syllabus and the students on him are greater.

A great advantage of the Cambridge Examinations is that they are international. The same test is taken at the same time in scores of countries throughout the world, and the standard of language of a Frenchman with a pass certificate is comparable with that of a Brazilian or a Thai with the same piece of paper. Within individual countries, this comparability of standards is important, especially where national examinations, often locally set on leaving secondary school or at university degree level examination, are subject to variation in standard both from place to place and from year to year. The problem of harmonisation of standards has been approached in a very interesting way by the Council of Europe. With the impetus of European integration and the freer movement of people between member states of the European Community it became progressively more obvious that some means to compare standards of attainment in English, French, German, etc., had to be devised. The Unit/Credit system is designed for this purpose. It aims to establish a Threshold Level (T-level) in these languages, which can best be defined in terms of the functions of language (not just the grammatical structure) the student has learnt.

Problems in teaching Advanced English

Most learners of advanced English are adults, and they require a different teaching strategy from that used with younger age groups. On the whole they will learn more quickly as they have been trained in learning for many years. Less demonstration is called for, and more explanation, since an adult mind demands reasons for things and a clear formulation of the principles involved. Hence the constant requests from an adult class for the 'rules' of English grammar. New knowledge and skills are integrated into his personality rapidly, although there is often the much greater rigidity which comes with age and mature thought patterns and habits to take into account. An adult learning a language from scratch will always have an accent, a child may not. The danger in a predominantly explanatory approach is that the adult might quickly pick up what he needs to know *about* English, but his actual skill in *using* the language falls far behind. This must not be allowed to happen, unless he intends to become a theoretical linguist or grammarian! Again, the teacher's problem is to present his material in varied and challenging ways. The following notes deal with a limited selection of the difficulties widely experienced by advanced learners. Most of them in fact are problems of spoken, conversational English, and much of what is said in Chapters 5 and 6 is relevant in dealing with them.

Register

Nearly all advanced learners have been schooled in standard and formal English: very few in the informal registers. This is all very well in the classroom, in business or any other fairly formal situation of everyday life. But it is less than useful in talking to a native speaker at anything beyond the most polite level, and in listening to native speakers talking to each other. If the student is not aware of this already, it is worth playing a tape (e.g. that accompanying Crystal and Davy's *Advanced Conversational English*) of Englishmen talking naturally together to demonstrate how useless the book English acquired over so many years of painful study really is in actual practice. A major task of the teacher is to develop an awareness of different styles of English. This awareness must then lead to sensitivity to appropriate use in different social situations.

The feeling for appropriacy can only be developed over a considerable period. There is no short cut. Students should be encouraged to question as words arise and to assign style labels to them. The teacher also must ask where a new expression might normally be found and how it is used. Apart from developing in his students a general sensitivity to the register of words, the teacher will have to spend a good deal of time plugging the gaps in his students' knowledge. This will often mean, for instance, teaching colloquial English and contrasting it with the standard or formal, which will be already known. One way to do this is to take a text with a high incidence of colloquial lexis and structures (a play, or transcript of a conversation) and read it through first for general meaning. Then, by judicious questioning, the meaning of the new vocabulary can be elicited from the class, and explained where necessary. It is always useful to compare what other modes of expression the author or speakers might have used in a contrasting situation (an office, a school, a formal reception, a lecture, a church) to put across the same meaning. It is valuable then to give other contexts where the new lexis is used, to build up in the learner's mind its meaning and associations. Practice is very important, so an exercise to rewrite the passage being studied in more formal style and writing natural dialogues using the new words are both useful devices. A more difficult exercise is to attempt to rewrite a formal passage in familiar and intimate style.

A sense of appropriacy is not of course restricted to informal/formal language. There are many other varieties of English which exhibit their own peculiar characteristics. Newspapers, particularly the more popular ones, use a distinctive variety of English of their own, 'journalese'. Sentences are short in length and not very complex in structure, the vocabulary is concrete and direct. Quite the opposite is the language of the Church and the Law, with its antiquated flavour expressed by unusual words (oblation, genuflection, tort, etc.) and complicated syntax. At the more advanced levels, the student needs at very least an awareness of these varieties and others. A basic book for the teacher is D. Crystal and D. Davy's *Investigating English Style.*

Vocabulary

At first sight, vocabulary does not seem to be a problem for many advanced foreign learners. In fact, their vocabulary range is often greater than that of many native speakers. The deficiencies lie, however, in two main areas. First, there is the gap mentioned above under Register. The problem is not simply one of teaching 'kid' instead of 'child', but of speaking natural rather than stilted English. Two ways amongst many in which this can be rapidly improved are by instilling a mastery of the use of the phrasal verb and by teaching a selective use of idiom. Very few students come to English with any familiarity acquired from their mother tongue with forms analogous to the phrasal verb. The need at an advanced level is to familiarise them with the problem, demonstrate current English usage, give copious practice and insist on the students' regular production of these forms. An allied problem is the use of idioms — not simply the use of the colourful phrase such as 'it's raining cats and dogs', but the teacher must develop a sensitivity to the less obtrusive yet very vital idiomatic restrictions on tense usage of many expressions, and to the difficulties of their semantic interpretation.

The second problem is the advanced student's lack of awareness of the connotations (that is, the associations, the allusive qualities) of the vocabulary they use. The strict meaning (the denotation) is usually known, but the 'feel' the word carries to a native speaker is usually not. Occasionally dictionaries help by attaching labels such as 'pejorative' to words like *frog* or *wog*; but there is not much more formal help. As in the case of register in the previous section, the teacher can only hope to begin to put things right over a long period of time. Similar teaching procedures can be adopted as to those outlined above, but in the last analysis the advanced student must develop his own associative semantic networks in English — nearly always different, if only subtly so, from those in his mother tongue — by prolonged repeated exposure to words in a variety of illustrative contexts. This is best done through extensive reading, and the building up of a set of index cards of words and phrases with illustrative examples of new connotations and associations. Only in this way will his intuitions approximate closely enough to those of native speakers, and only in this way will he appreciate the nuances of English and be able to respond equally sensitively.

Pronunciation

At the advanced level, a reasonable accuracy in the pronunciation of individual sounds has certainly been achieved. Rather than striving for an unattainable perfection in this area, it is infinitely more valuable to turn one's attention to stress, rhythm and intonation. This will probably have been neglected. If the teacher does no more than get his students to use the strong forms and weak forms in all the right places, he will have done them an inestimable service, for their spoken language will to the untutored native's ear give a much more accurate reflection of the learner's status as an advanced student of English. So often a person with years of learning and impeccable knowledge of grammar and vocabulary will appear like a raw novice when he produces too carefully articulated sentences.

Apart from the teaching techniques suggested in Chapter 5 to deal with this sort of problem, it is worthwhile suggesting to adults that they read a non-technical book such as J. D. O'Connor's *Better English Pronunciation.* The chapter 'Words in Company' in this book makes very valuable corrective reading. When made aware of a problem, an advanced student, with guidance, is often his own best teacher.

There is a great deal to be said at advanced levels for the teacher assuming more and more the mantle of tutor. At the early stages of learning, the teacher is responsible for choosing the material to be taught, presenting it and ensuring to the best of his ability that it is learnt. The advanced student brings with him an already considerable history of language learning, and probably a keen awareness of his own strengths and weaknesses. He is therefore more able to share in the choice of material to be covered and in the learning process. Once alerted, for example, to the importance of register and connotations of words, he will learn as much from the extensive reading of English newspapers and novels as he will from any formal lesson his teacher may give him on these topics. The teacher-tutor's business, therefore, is to point to the difficulties, give guidance as to how they might be tackled, and monitor progress, but it is less and less to teach a particular topic and assume it is then dealt with.

Adults live in a world where English is very important to them. Professionally, it may be quite essential. Socially it is likely to be very useful with the increasing mobility of societies. Even in the home, there may be a need for English — even if it is just dealing with the children's homework or watching an American film on TV without subtitles. The need is widespread and likely to persist throughout life. But most people are not in the position to contemplate English lessons throughout life. So one of the most essential services the teacher-tutor can perform for his students is to equip them to help themselves after they leave him, to equip them to shoulder the whole responsibility for their future progress. Going to see the latest Oscar-winning film in English at the cinema is then an end in itself, but also a continuation of a learning process of which they are in control. The trend towards permanent education, as it is called, must surely be right, as the world never stands still, nor should one's knowledge of it. The teacher of advanced students must prepare for the future as much as teach for the present.

Chapter 14

The English Department

There has been very little discussion in the past of the role of the English department in promoting good language learning conditions, yet those who visit schools frequently can immediately tell when there is a well-organised department because of the feeling of commitment and excitement which is generated by the members of the department, and this usually communicates itself to the students as well. The role of the department is to enable all English teachers to operate as effectively as possible by providing all necessary support and encouragement, and the role of the head of department is simply to cause this to happen. In the rest of this chapter, a large number of suggestions are made of ways in which a department can be organised most effectively. Each situation has its own problems, and no list will exhaust the possibilities, but it is fair to say that any institution which does not provide the following support for all its English staff is making life unnecessarily hard for them:

(a) a nominated person who will be responsible for running the department;
(b) a range of as many as possible appropriate textbooks for consultation by staff, and machinery for easy access;
(c) access regularly to duplicating facilities, and support for co-operative development of materials for all aspects of language work;
(d) a range of basic books suitable for reference by students (like the *Advanced Learner's Dictionary*, which may be too expensive for individual students to buy);

(e) materials suitable and in sufficient quantity for extensive reading work by students;
(f) a reference library for teachers;
(g) basic audio-visual equipment (according to the facilities
available), with a minimum in most institutions of one
large taperecorder and a number of portable cassette
recorders, plus spare tapes and cassettes;
(h) a place to use as a base for the department's possessions,
at least a few shelves and a cupboard, and ideally somewhere where members of the department can meet as well;
(i) access to a range of simple visual materials, like wall
charts, flashcards, portable blackboards and pieces of
softboard, *realia*, etc.

Obviously not all institutions are rich enough to be able to
afford all these facilities, but they are a minimum to aim at,
and most of these items are not expensive to gather and
maintain over a period of several years.

General organisation

In the first instance, it will be the responsibility of the head
of department to set up a satisfactory organisation, but it
is most important that he should feel — as soon as possible —
that he is entirely dispensable. The system that is set up
should be sufficiently open for the department to be able to
be carried on totally efficiently by the other members, even
if the head is suddenly whisked off at ten minutes' notice to
another post or another country! However, particularly in
institutions where there is no strong tradition of working as
a team, the initial stages of building up a departmental feeling
may require a lot of tact and a lot of careful planning and
discussion.
    The two basic aims of departmental organisation are

(i) to ensure a consistent and sensible policy in English
teaching throughout the institution, and
(ii) to keep the administration of the department running
smoothly.

To achieve these aims a good head of department will ensure

that all useful information is made rapidly and easily available to all staff teaching English and will also delegate responsibility wherever this will not impair efficiency (that is, most of the time), and will always be accessible to criticism, either of himself or of the system. Finally, he will never be contented, the department will be in a perpetual process of self-assessment and self-renewal, without losing the basic framework on which its continuity and efficiency rests.

'A consistent and sensible policy'

Teaching is the art of the possible. However up-to-date or valuable the ideas of anyone in the department may be, they will be valueless if they alienate either staff or students. If the department is seen as an organisation which achieves the most efficient possible deployment of facilities, people and ideas, then all members of the department must be in a position to understand what the basis of discussion and innovation is. This suggests that part of the work of a department consists of clarifying its concept of why and how it is teaching English. Such a discussion should not take place in a vacuum, however, and nor should it be separated from the fundamental work — that of teaching. There are certain key documents which every institution should provide for itself, which can be used as a basis for more general discussion. Every teacher, for example, should possess a syllabus or a scheme of work for the whole institution which will show how his own work fits in with that of classes below, above and parallel to those which he teaches, and if possible how the work in English relates to work in other subjects, particularly other languages which are taught. Such a scheme of work should specify briefly in the introduction the role of English in the country, and the basic needs which it may have to serve. These may be related to education, business, tourism, for example, and they may be expressed through emphases predominantly on speaking, or on listening, or on reading and writing, or on any combination of these. It should be pointed out which of these needs are for use within the school, which for concurrent use outside the school, and which are simply predictions of probable needs of students after leaving school. All this can be done simply, briefly and straightforwardly, leaving the rest of the scheme for a summary of the stages of work within the school.

The organisation of this scheme may take a number of forms. Sometimes there will be units allocated by time, so that each week's work is fully described. Sometimes the scheme will be no more than a checklist of items to be taught, in more or less any order. Sometimes it will be a kind of ladder giving a sequence of stages to be mastered, without any specific time recommendation. Similarly, there are a number of ways in which the scheme may describe the topics to be taught — for example in relation to structures, situations, items of vocabulary or notions. It is impossible for a scheme to specify everything which will be taught, so a selection needs to be made. But a syllabus needs to be cumulative, so that the order needs to be established on the basis of some sort of appropriate criterion. A department may decide that the order should be on the basis of what sort of language interactions are likely to be needed most quickly by the students, or what structures are most accessible, or what structures in a remedial situation have been observed to cause difficulty most frequently. Decisions of this kind will determine the ordering of the elements of the scheme, as well as what elements to include. At the same time the school which uses a syllabus which is basically structural may well also require a checklist of extra structures to be drilled if necessary, but which are not important enough to be in the core scheme, or it may wish to have a checklist of situations or notions which should be covered at some stage in the programme, but which will not fit neatly into an ordered, basic pattern. So in practice, the scheme will probably consist of a core of work which is ordered, together with a checklist of other items, which may or may not be optional.

It will be noticed that very little has been said about timing. This is because the dangers of a carefully timed scheme of work probably outweigh the advantages in any but the short-course situation. In general, as thorough a coverage of any one stage of the scheme as is compatible with student boredom is desirable (assuming that the group continues to find difficulty with the work). The ideal scheme of work would provide an ordering sequence, but would leave it to the individual teacher to determine when the students should advance to the next stage. It is not possible (especially in the remedial situation of all post-beginners' work) to predict exactly how long is appropriate for any one section of the syllabus. What is absolutely essential is that a clear record should be obtainable of what each student has covered, with a fair degree of certainty that to have covered the work means that it has been well assimilated, either for active or receptive use, according to the requirements of the particular stage. In language work, it is far more important to be thorough than fast.

We have, then, a scheme of work, with an introduction, a series of stages and a checklist. There are two other possible additions. One is a series of sections of advice on teaching procedures in the classroom, and the other – which is much more important – is some kind of indication of appropriate materials to use at each stage. This may mean linking the stages to particular textbooks (indeed many schemes of work are based in practice on textbooks), or to exercises in a variety of textbooks, or to exercises being produced by the school or neighbouring schools. Either way, the emphasis should be on the quality of the materials and methodology used. Good materials, whether published or unpublished, should be freely available, and teachers need not hesitate to steal good ideas from textbooks, other teachers or from any source whatever – but acknowledge the theft!

On the basis of a document such as this, produced by all the English teachers in an institution co-operating with each other, the kind of general framework for thinking about English teaching, referred to above, will be rapidly established. The document will certainly require revision – slightly, every year – and a major overhaul should be necessary every three to five years, but once the basis is set up the process of revision will be easy. Without such a document, it will not be possible for teachers to see how their own work fits in with that of others, nor will it be possible for outsiders to be shown easily what the school does. Above all, on the basis of such a scheme, the department will be able to keep a public record of the varying progress of different classes and will be able to clarify its own ideas in discussion on what everyone is doing. Being forced to compile such a

205

scheme of work concentrates the mind wonderfully on all sorts of problems which would otherwise have remained deep in the subconscious mind.

The scheme of work suggested above may be a useful basis for the kind of professional discussion which will be going on all the time in a good English department, but it will not in itself be enough to ensure full commitment by all staff. They will only have time to be committed if the administrative machinery runs as smoothly and effortlessly as possible, and many of the items discussed later in the section on administration have a direct bearing on professional efficiency. Before that, however, there are a number of minor, but still important, points which need to be made.

Just as the head of department will expect to be able to spread some of the more routine chores, so he should be prepared to spread the discussion and policy-making, both major and minor, in the department. Whether it is discussing what books to teach from, attitudes to discipline in the classroom, or who should teach what class, members of the department have a right to expect to be consulted. But all these decisions will only make sense if they are taken within a framework of educational priority and service to the needs of the students. Discussion of these aspects of the work will occur inevitably in the course of examining syllabuses and schemes of work, and on this foundation can develop discussion of administrative matters. Thus staff have a right to be kept informed of all matters relating to the teaching of English, whether it is an important circular from the Ministry of Education, or a trivial request for students to enter an essay competition in English. There should be some sort of file on permanent open access, into which all relevant items of recent correspondence can be put. At the same time, there is a great deal of information which should be permanently in the possession of all English teachers in addition to the school scheme of work. Copies of external examination syllabuses and some past papers should be in the possession of all teachers, lists of all textbooks, recordings, aids, etc. available, and any information which a teacher might ever need to ask for. If each new teacher, on arrival at the school, is handed a file containing all the information that he needs to know, a great deal of time will be saved, and the teacher will at once realise that he is coming into a professional organisation with high standards.

Even in a big department staff should have the opportunity to contribute all the time towards the development of efficient teaching. Small things can help in this. For example, it is a good idea to have a permanent book available in which staff comments on the textbooks they use can be entered, and all staff should be encouraged to examine and evaluate the usefulness of new books as they appear. The department should subscribe to some of the basic periodicals concerned with EFL teaching (a list appears on page 220), and some discussion of ideas in these may be a feature of department meetings. Indeed, staff, individually or collectively, should be encouraged to contribute to these periodicals if and when they have anything original to say.

The department should meet regularly — probably two or three times a term. Ideally, these meetings should be informal but serious (it is probably unnecessary to keep minutes, but some record should be circulated of what people have agreed to do, and some check made in subsequent meetings that what was agreed has actually been done). Above all, the meetings should not become dominated by the day-to-day administration. If necessary, hold separate professional meetings, but make sure that professional matters are discussed. In a good department the activities of all members will be discussed with each other, in and out of meetings. The head of department should be aware through the meetings of everything that is going on in the department. Existing methods should be discussed in meetings and suggestions for improvement of all kinds should be discussed, and perhaps experiments carried out on improving the work in a variety of directions. Different members of staff will have different interests (though there should be no one who is unwilling to take an interest in every aspect of the work), and while one may wish to experiment with a method using drama in the classroom (to report back on the work after a term or two), another may be developing materials for controlled writing or listening comprehension. All these activities will be improved by discussion, observation by fellow-teachers, and consultation, and the department should make all this as easy as possible. It may be, also, that some department meetings could involve discussion of more theoretical issues, with or without outside speakers, and certainly members of the department (including the head) should assume that they will be expected to report back on courses, conferences and meetings that they have attended. Each group of teachers will develop their meetings in a different way, and the nature of the activity is probably less important than the fact of activity. The new teacher should feel that he is joining a community of professionals, and not a group of people who happen to be working in the same building.

Administration

Administration is very important, and inefficient organisation may kill a department, but it is less important than the professional aspects, and no department can claim credit for merely being well organised: that should be taken for granted. In the following paragraphs a number of suggestions are made about organisation, but obviously not all departments will be responsible for the same things, and each one must adapt the general principles to its own needs. Listed below are some of the main areas for which English departments may be responsible:

1 Reception, stamping and storage of new books and equipment.
2 Maintaining inventories of all equipment.
3 Preparation of orders for new equipment.
4 Running external and internal examinations.
5 Filing all information of importance to staff and students, so that it is readily accessible.
6 Maintaining records of students' progress.

Each institution will vary in its approach to each of these problems, but the English department, in self-defence, should know what happens in each of these areas, and should be prepared to take it over if it is being inefficiently done elsewhere. It seems worthwhile, however, to make a few comments on the last of these areas.

It is a good idea to keep a check on classes collectively as well as on individuals. An easy way of doing this is to have an exercise book as a record book to accompany each class through the institution. In this can be entered for each pupil his examination marks, details like reading speed if they are tested, and report comments. General comments on the class can also be included, together with the stages in the scheme of work reached at the end of each term, books which have been used, comments on particularly successful books and exercises, and so on. In this way there is a convenient way of handing on information about a group which changes hands, especially if this happens unexpectedly. It is necessary for the head of department to insist that details are filled in conscientiously every term, but any serious teacher will see the advantage of the system and be prepared to co-operate. The book can be completed with an entry of external examination results, where appropriate, and stored for reference as a complete record of the work of a class. In this way continuity is maintained.

Other areas where the English department may be able to offer administrative help are in organising libraries of class readers, appropriately graded for level (by content as well as language), and in liaison with other institutions. In general, any matter where several heads are better than one will work well at department level, whether it is a highly skilled issue of how to solve a teaching problem, or a large administrative chore like cataloguing library books related to English language.

The head of department

Much of what has been described in this chapter is only possible if the head of department is able to be an efficient and inspiring leader who is willing to act not as a dictator but as leader of a team. Ideally, he will be able to hold the trust of his department by his willingness to do the hard and boring work as well as the prestigious decision-making. Too often one hears of heads of department who will never teach the difficult classes (or who even allocate them to student teachers on teaching practice!) and who seem to regard their position as an excuse for taking all the interesting decisions but not doing too much of the routine work. When this happens, it is unlikely that a department will ever attain the level of interest that has been described in this chapter. But it is only fair to say that every teacher of English has a right to expect the sort of support which has been outlined here, and to fail to provide it is to make everyone's task far more difficult than necessary. A good department can produce outstanding results from a mediocre teacher, but a bad department, insensitively run, can drive good teachers out of the profession.

Appendix 1

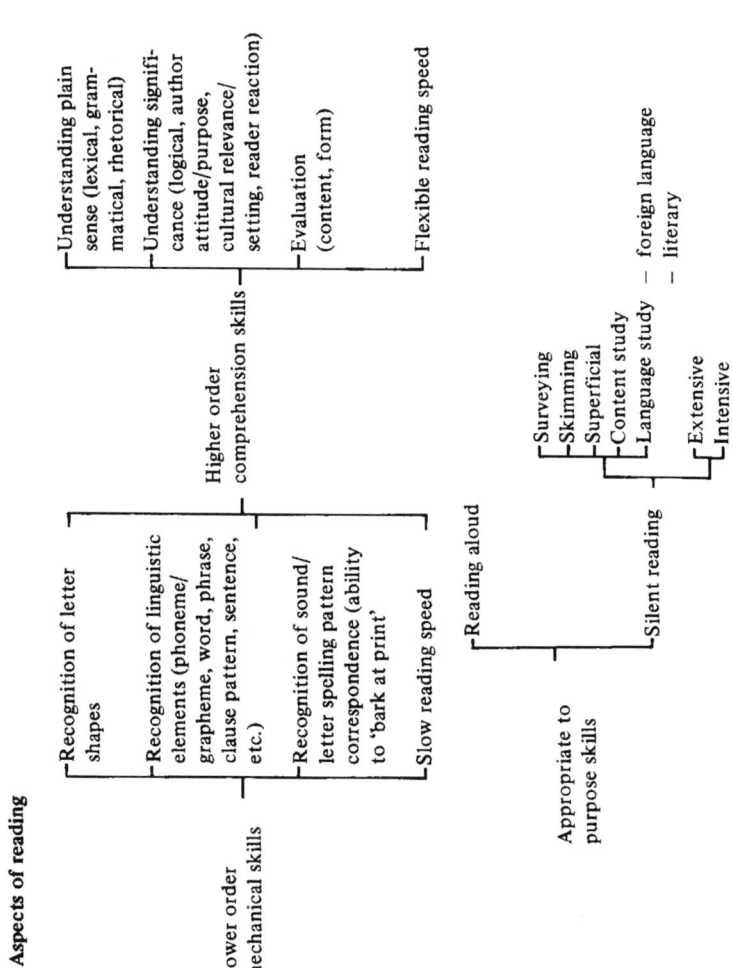

Aspects of reading

Lower order mechanical skills
- Recognition of letter shapes
- Recognition of linguistic elements (phoneme/grapheme, word, phrase, clause pattern, sentence, etc.)
- Recognition of sound/letter spelling pattern correspondence (ability to 'bark at print'
- Slow reading speed

Higher order comprehension skills
- Understanding plain sense (lexical, grammatical, rhetorical)
- Understanding significance (logical, author attitude/purpose, cultural relevance/setting, reader reaction)
- Evaluation (content, form)
- Flexible reading speed

Appropriate to purpose skills
- Reading aloud
- Silent reading
  - Surveying
  - Skimming
  - Superficial
  - Content study
  - Language study — foreign language — literary
  - Extensive
  - Intensive

Appendix 2

Text
The cruel big man beat the little donkey with a heavy stick because the animal refused to carry him over the river.

		Answer type			
Comprehension skill	Yes/No	Expected minimum answer: phrase/content word	Expected minimum answer: clause/sentence	True/False	Non-linguistic
Understanding plain sense					
Lower order: mechanical recognition of linguistic elements/patterns	Did the man beat the donkey? The man beat the donkey. The man beat the donkey. The man didn't beat the donkey, did he?	Who beat the donkey? Did a man or a boy beat the donkey?	Why did the man beat the donkey? Did the man beat the donkey or feed it hay?	A small man beat the donkey.	1. The donkey was large. 2. The donkey was big. 3. The donkey was little. 4. The donkey was heavy.
Higher order: recognition of lexical meanings/patterns	The *animal* refers to the donkey? Does *the animal* refer to the donkey?	Which word or phrase in the first part of the sentence does *the animal* refer to? Does *the animal* refer to the man or to the donkey?	What does *the animal* mean this sentence? Does *animal* here mean the man or does it mean the donkey?	The *animal* refers to the man.	1. The *animal* refers to the man. 2. The *animal* refers to the donkey. 3. The *animal* refers to a feline creature. 4. The *animal* refers to the heavy stick.
Recognition of grammatical meanings/patterns	Does *him* refer to the donkey? *Him* refers to the donkey, doesn't it?	What does *him* refer to in this sentence? Does *him* refer to the man or to the donkey?	How do we know that the donkey refused to carry the man over the river?	*Him* refers to the man in this story.	1. *Him* refers to the man. 2. *Him* refers to the donkey. 3. *Him* refers to the stick. 4. *Him* refers to the rivet.
Recognition of rhetorical structure	Is this text a bit of narrative? Does the second clause show the purpose for which the man beat the donkey?	Which is the most important phrase in the first clause? Is this text a bit of narrative or part of an argument?	How do you know which is the most important phrase in the first clause? What difference would it have made to the sentence if the author had put the *because* clause first?	This text is a piece of narrative.	1. This text is a piece of narrative. 2. This text is a piece of poetry. 3. This text is part of an argument. 4. This text is part of a joke.
Understanding significance					
Higher order: recognition of logical structure/inference	Did the man hurt the donkey? Had the man crossed the river when he beat the donkey?	What did the donkey feel when the man beat him? Was the donkey angry or hurt when the man beat him?	What makes us think that the man hurt the donkey a lot?	When the man beat the donkey it felt great pain.	When the man beat the donkey, the donkey felt: (1) great pain. (2) quite cheerful (3) very content (4) rather happy
Recognition of author attitude/purpose	Does the author regard the man favourably? Is the author's purpose in writing this story to amuse us?	How does the author describe the man? Does the author regard the man favourably or unfavourably?	Why do you think the author did not intend us to be amused by this story?	The author regards the man in this story favourably.	The author regards the man as: (1) good (2) kind (3) unkind (4) wicked
Recognition of cultural relevance/setting	Do you think the text was written about life in London today? Is it likely that this text was written by a middle class English woman?	Which word in the text especially might have been chosen by someone sympathetic to the aims of the RSPCA?	Why do you think this text was not written about life in London today?	This story is about life in a big American city.	This story is about life: (1) in the country. (2) in a small town. (3) in a big city. (4) on a big ship.

Recognition of reader reaction	Do you think that the man was cruel?	Do you feel kinder towards the man or towards the donkey in this story?	How do you feel about the man in the story?	I feel sympathetic towards the man who beat the donkey.	I feel: (1) angry with the man. (2) sympathetic towards the man. (3) indifferent about the whole thing. (4) irritated with the author.
Evaluation *Higher order*: evaluation in terms of content/ knowledge of the world	Is it true that big men sometimes beat little donkeys? Have you ever seen a man beat a donkey?	How many times do you think the man hit the donkey?	What would you do if you saw a man beating a donkey?	It is true that men sometimes beat donkeys.	(1) I have never seen a man beat a donkey. (2) I have once seen a man beat a donkey. (3) I have often seen a man beat a donkey. (4) Donkeys have to be beaten to make them go.
Evaluation in terms of impact of the message/form	Is the writer's message in this text clear and unambiguous?	Is it sensible or foolish to write about a donkey being beaten?	Why does it matter that acts of cruelty should be written about in books?	This writer uses too many adjectives in his writing.	(1) This account favours the donkey. (2) This account contains too little detail. (3) The account of the event is unbiased. (4) The account of the event favours the man.
General questions		*Wh-* questions; alternative questions	Why? How? questions; alternative questions	Rubric: State whether each of these statements is true or false.	Rubric: Choose the one statement in each set of four which is correct with regard to the text.

Question Type

Glossary of Selected Terms

In addition to mainstream topics in ELT, we have indicated wide suggestions for reading. The following is a glossary of terms which may be encountered in further reading or in discussion.

accent (1) A variety of English pronunciation, usually based on geography, e.g. Australia, Liverpool, Scotland, Yorkshire and/or social class. See *RP*. Cf. *dialect*. (2) The pattern of prominence of stress, pitch, quality and length in words and connected speech.

acceptability Usually contrasted with grammaticality, e.g. 'The man thrown the ball kicked it' is grammatical and acceptable whereas the sentence 'The man kicked the ball kicked it' is grammatical (has the same form) but is not acceptable.

accuracy see *fluency*.

acquisition A term used for language learning which is unconscious, i.e. without deliberate attention to rules. Some writers contrast acquisition with learning, i.e. conscious, deliberate learning. See *monitor*.

active vocabulary Words, phrases, etc., which a learner can use in speech and writing. Cf. *passive vocabulary*.

AILA Association International de Linguistique Appliquée.

allophone see *phoneme*.

analytic syllabus A syllabus which provides the student with authentic texts from which he makes his own analysis. Structural considerations are secondary to the use to which he puts the language. See *synthetic syllabus*.

anomalous finite A verb which forms the interrogative and negative without the auxiliary *do*, e.g. can, might, have, be. Cf. *modal verb*.

anomie A feeling of disorientation often experienced by immigrants through being unable to identify either with the users of the home language or with the host community.

214

applied linguistics Studies of the relationship between theoretical disciplines of language and related disciplines, on the one hand, and their practical problems, on the other. The main application is considered to be language teaching, but the term is also applied to machine translation, lexicology, etc.

appropriacy The fitting of an utterance into the development of a discourse as a whole, so as to achieve a communicative purpose. Usually contrasted with formal 'correctness', where the aim is to produce correct sentences.

approximative systems A learner's transitional knowledge at any point moving towards his competence in the target language; cf. *interlanguage*.

ARELS Association of Recognised English Language Schools; i.e. recognised by the Department of Education and Science.
Address: 125 High Holborn, London WC1.

aspect With tense and mood, one of the grammatical categories of the verb. Refers to the way in which the action of the verb is experienced or regarded, mainly used to distinguish forms like 'I break' from forms like 'I am breaking' and 'I have broken'.

audio-lingual A development of the mimicry-memorisation method. See *mim-mem*. An approach to teaching where oral imitation, memorisation and drilling precede spontaneous speech, extensively using recorded dialogues and drills. Derived from structuralism and now much less common than in the 1950s and '60s.

audio-visual As for audio-lingual but with the added extensive use of visual materials. Audio-visual aids include tape recorder, OHP, films and slides. Classic examples of audio-visual programmes have been developed by CREDIF (q.v.).

authentic materials Spoken or written materials not specially written for classroom use but taken from the media or real life.

autonomous learning Learning in which the learner becomes independent of the teacher, working with his own momentum.

AVA Audio-visual aids.

BAAL British Association for Applied Linguistics.
Address: c/o CILT, 20 Carlton House Terrace, London SW1.

behaviourism A psychological theory emphasising the importance, in studying human behaviour in general and language in particular, of verifiable facts from measurable data. Much in vogue in the 1940s, '50s and '60s. Cf. *mentalism*; *S-R*.

bilingual education/schooling This is where two languages are used in the school and some, at least, of the content teaching, e.g. Mathematics, Geography, is in the less familiar one.

bilingualism Having command of two languages. Until recently the implication was that both languages were spoken with equal proficiency.

black English A variety of English associated with black communities in the USA with its own characteristic phonology, grammar and lexis.

body language The largely unconscious communication between people by non-verbal means, such as posture and gesture. See *para-language*; *kinesics*; *proxemics*.

CAL Centre for Applied Linguistics.
Address: 1717 Massachusetts Avenue NW, Washington DC 20036, USA.

cardinal vowels A system of eight vowel sounds which does not describe any particular language; cardinal in that it specifies fixed points which serve as a standard of comparison within a language and between different languages.

case grammar A generative theory of grammar on a semantic rather than syntactic base, proposed by Fillmore in the late 1960s. The name comes from the use of 'deep' semantic cases such as agentive, instrumental, locative, etc. See *deep structure*.

chaining In drilling, the linking of one response to the next round the class. 'Back-chaining' refers to the pronunciation drill which works back through the sentence, e.g.:

Teacher: Tomorrow	Class: Tomorrow
Teacher: Go there tomorrow	Class: Go there tomorrow
Teacher: He'd go there tomorrow	Class: He'd go there tomorrow

CILT Centre for Information on Language Teaching and Research.
Address: 20 Carlton House Terrace, London SW1.

cloze test/procedure Consists of a written passage in which, after the first, introductory paragraph, every fifth (or sixth . . . or twelfth) word is left out for the student to supply. Used to measure the readability of texts, reading and listening comprehension, and general proficiency in English.

code (1) The inventory of signs and rules in a system. Refers to systems like traffic-lights and visual communications or to the formal aspects of human language. (2) In sociolinguistics. See *elaborated code* and *restricted code*.

code switching The usually unconscious movement from one language to another in the course of one utterance or even sentence. Also the changing of style or dialect within an utterance in one language.

cognitive code learning Emphasises the conscious learning of new items by deliberate attention to 'rules' rather than by the stimulus-response training of behaviourism.

coherence The relationship between illocutionary acts in discourse. There may be no obvious link between utterances as in:
A: There's the doorbell.
B: I'm making dinner.
Their coherence depends on their communicative value in context as request and excuse:

A: There's the doorbell. (Can you answer it please?)
B: I'm making dinner. (So I can't answer it.)

cohesion The overt signalling by means of formal links of syntax and semantics between sentences and their parts indicating the relationship between them. E.g. reference as in 'The man walked down the street. He was dressed in black.'

collocation The tendency for words to occur predictably with others; e.g. solve/problem. Fixed collations are very predictable; e.g. hearth and home; hop, skip and jump. See *idiom*.

common core Administratively the central part of a course, programme or syllabus which must be followed by everyone. The elements of the language essential to any language teaching programme.

communicative language teaching A teaching approach relating the teaching techniques (e.g. pair and group work), language content and materials (e.g. authentic material) to the communication needs of the students outside the classroom.

community language learning see *counselling learning*. Derived from counselling learning, it places the principles of learning above those of teaching in emphasising the security of the learner in the 'investment' phase and the discussion of the experience in the 'reflections' phase. The 'teacher' creates an atmosphere of permissiveness, warmth and acceptance and has the role of counsellor and informant.

competence An idealised speaker-listener's perfect knowledge of his own language in a completely homogeneous speech community. Contrasted with 'performance': all aspects of language use which are not accounted for by the concept 'competence'. These include mispronunciations, slips, and variation according to situation of language use. The distinction was first technically made by Chomsky.

componental analysis The analysis of word meaning into distinctive semantic features. E.g. boy = + human, + male, – adult.

content word A word with a full lexical meaning of its own, i.e. nouns, main verbs, adjectives and most adverbs. Cf. *function words.*

contextualisation Placing by the teacher or materials writer of an item to be learnt in a realistic and meaningful situation in order to facilitate its learning.

contrastive analysis Comparison of two languages at phonological, grammatical, lexical and cultural levels. Until recently, a syllabus was often based on contrasts between mother tongue and target language. Considered today to be useful to explain learners' errors rather than a predictive procedure for syllabus design. See *interference.*

controlled composition Oral or written composition in which the students follow exact instructions and should produce error-free writing, e.g. filling in blanks, combining sentences, etc. See *guided composition*; *free composition.*

core linguistics Phonology, syntax, lexis and semantics which are seen as the central concerns of linguistics, contrasted with linguistic studies which are related to other disciplines, e.g. psychology, sociology.

counselling learning A style of learning (associated with the work of Curran deriving from psychotherapy) in which for language learning a tutor helps groups of students to develop conversation by formulating what they want to say, but without overt language instruction. There is a heavy emphasis on establishing strong rapport between students and 'helpers' (not teachers). See *community language learning* for specific developments in language teaching.

CRAPEL Centre de Recherche et d'Applications Pédagogues aux Langues. Address: Université de Nancy II, 23 Boulevard Albert Ier, 5400 Nancy.

CREDIF Centre de Recherche et d'Etudes pour la Diffusion du Français. Address: 11 Avenue Pozzo di Borgo, 92211 Saint-Cloud, France.

creole A language, originally a pidgin, which has become the mother tongue of a community and expanded to fill all language needs. E.g. Sierra Leone Krio. See *pidgin.*

cue cards Cards with writing or pictures, used to elicit student response, either oral or written. See *flash card.*

culture Values and behaviour patterns common to people belonging to the same national, social or language community.

curriculum (1) A specification of all the subjects taught in an educational institution, or, (2) (1) above, plus any values, attitudes, etc., transmitted implicitly or explicitly by the institution.

deep structure A term in TG referring to the underlying syntactic and semantic structures which are revealed by analysis of sentences. See *surface structure.*

deixis/deictic A feature of words like *it, this, former,* which acquire meaning by pointing to something in the context of the discourse.

deprivation hypothesis The sociolinguistic view that some children are linguistically handicapped because they belong to social groups which have a poor linguistic repertoire.

dialect A variety of language used by members of a particular geographical region or social class. Sometimes, as with Chinese, mutually unintelligible languages are regarded as dialects because they share a common writing system. Cf. two varieties of the same language (or sometimes of two different languages) for 'high' (literary, liturgical, governmental) and 'low' (commonplace and familiar) purposes.

diglossia The use within one country of two languages or of 'high' and 'low' (classical and colloquial) varieties of one language for different social purposes, the whole population being bi-lingual. E.g. Spanish and Guarini in Paraguay, or High German and Swiss-German in Switzerland.

direct method Language teaching mainly through conversation, sometimes carefully arranged, but without explicit statement of grammatical rules or the use of the mother tongue.

discourse Any stretch of language in which communication is achieved in a coherent flow of spoken or written sentences, involving either one speaker or writer (e.g. lecture, book) or interaction between two or more participants. Hence *discourse analysis*: the study of how spoken or written sentences relate to each other so that they are coherent and effective. See *text*.

distractor Any of the unacceptable alternatives in a multiple-choice test.

drill The intensive choral or individual repetition of items to be learned.

EAP English for Academic Purposes.

elaborated code see *restricted code*.

ELTJ English Language Teaching Journal, published quarterly by Oxford University Press.

error analysis The systematic investigation of language learners' errors. See *contrastive analysis* and *interlanguage*.

ESL/E2L English as a second language.

ESP English for Specific/Special Purposes. E.g. medicine, commerce, nursing.

EST English for Science and Technology.

ETIC English Teaching Information Centre, British Council.
Address: 10 Spring Gardens, London SW1.

extensive reading General reading in which the aim is to read widely rather than to pay great attention to detail. See *intensive reading*.

extrinsic motivation Externally imposed motivation, not based on personal wishes or needs. E.g. examinations, etc. See *intrinsic motivation*.

false beginners/faux débutants Students starting elementary language courses but having had previous experience or study of the language.

FELCO Federation of English Language Course Organisers. An organisation concerned with Summer School courses in the UK.
Address: 43 Russell Square, London WC1.

first language Usually the mother tongue.

flash card A card with writing or a picture held up briefly by the teacher to illustrate a teaching point or elicit a response from a class.

FLES Foreign Languages in the Elementary School.

fluency Ability to speak or write as naturally and easily – but not necessarily as accurately – as the native speaker can.

form The shape patterns and structure of the substance of language, i.e. the sounds and letter shapes.

formal The adjective derived from either *form* or *formality*.

formality (1) The style of spoken or written language used to show respect, politeness or for public ritualistic speech. (2) Scale or level of formality: the scale from formal to informal as defined in (1) above.

free composition That kind of composition in which students write without controls and with minimum guidance. See *controlled composition*; *guided composition*.

free response A spontaneous, individual response, contrasting with mechanical responses as in drill.

free variation Language items are in free variation when they can be used interchangeably without loss, or significant change of meaning.

function The communicative purpose fulfilled by an utterance. A functional grammar would describe the communicative functions of the language. A functional syllabus is organised around functions rather than graded structures. In functional/notional syllabuses functions categorise language interaction whereas notions classify meaning. See *notion*; *structure*.

function words Words without lexical content with a grammatical role in the sentence. E.g. pronouns, prepositions, articles, etc. Also called structure words or empty words or operators. Cf. *content word*.

General Service List *A General Service List of English Words* by M. West, Longman, 1953. The most influential standard list of 2,000 frequently used English head-words.

generative grammar see *transformational/generative grammar*.

generative semantics The development of standard TG on a semantic rather than syntactic basis. Cf. *generative grammar*; *case grammar*.

Gestalt Literally (from the German) form, pattern, configuration. Gestalt psychology claims that learning is the mind's attempt to organise perceptions into satisfying complex patterns.

grading In syllabus construction, the classifying of language items according to their differences. Also loosely used for a similar classification in learning tasks. See *selection*; *sequencing*.

grammar (1) A specific theoretical approach to studying language. E.g. TG, case grammar, systemic grammar. (2) Most commonly Morphology (the structure of words) and ways in which words are arranged in sentences. See *selection*; *sequencing*.

grammar-translation A language-teaching method emphasising the memorisation of rules and the practice of translation.

grapheme A written symbol or symbols for a sound of a language. I.e. letters of an alphabet, or a character in picture writing.

guided composition Composition in which students are given detailed guidance and advice but can use their own words. See *controlled composition*; *free composition*.

IATEFL International Association of Teachers of English as a Foreign Language affiliated to the Fédération Internationale des Professeurs de Langues Vivantes.
Address: 87 Benwell's Avenue, Tankerton, Whitstable, Kent, England CT5 2HR.

idiom A fixed phrase whose meaning is not deducible from its constituent parts and which has some grammatical limitation. E.g. 'to smell a rat', 'to spill the beans'.

illocution/illocutionary force What language does rather than what it says. For example, 'Would you close the door please?' is an order though it has the form of a question. The term is derived from J. L. Austin, *How to Do Things with Words*, Oxford University Press, 1962.

individualisation An approach to teaching in which the specific needs of each learner are catered for so that he proceeds at his own rate, in his own way, with his own materials - used in contrast with 'lock-step' teaching. See *lock-step*.

information gap The situation in which different parts of a piece of information are known to different people who, therefore, need to communicate with each other to gain complete information and therefore fill the gap.

instrumental motivation Motivation to learn a foreign language such that the learner can carry out some clearly defined task through the medium of the target language. For example, the French waiter who wishes to learn enough English to be able to serve English-speaking tourists will have instrumental motivation. See *integrative motivation.*

integrative motivation When a learner wishes to identify with the target language community his motivation is integrative. When learners are instructed to learn language as an instrument for practical purposes, then motivation is said to be instrumental.

intensive reading Close reading of relatively short texts to derive maximum value from them.

interaction analysis Ways of describing the patterns of teacher–pupil behaviour in classrooms. A well-known scheme of this kind is that of R. F. Flanders, *Analysing Teaching Behaviours*, Addison-Wesley, 1970.

interference The effects that the knowledge of one language has on the attempt to produce or understand another. For example, French speakers frequently have problems producing the English /θ/ as in *th*eatre, because that sound does not occur in French and the *th* spelling is pronounced /t/; so the French pattern interferes with the English. Cf. *contrastive analysis.*

interlanguage Any one of the changing systems which a language learner develops as he moves from ignorance to competence in another language. Often such systems manifest features of both the learner's first language(s) and the target language - also referred to as *approximative systems* (q.v.).

intonation The patterns by which the pitch of the voice rises and falls in speech.

intrinsic motivation Motivation to learn derived from the inherent interest of the subject, or of the materials and procedures used in teaching. Cf. *extrinsic motivation.*

IPA International Phonetic Alphabet (or Association). Full details are set out in *The Principles of the International Phonetic Association*, 1949. Obtainable from International Phonetic Association, Department of Phonetics, University College, London WC1.

IRAL International Review of Applied Linguistics in Language Teaching. Published quarterly by Julius Groos Verlag, Heidelberg.

kinesics The study of body movements and postures as related to social behaviour usually associated with cultural factors.

L^1 Normally the mother tongue.

L^2 Usually any language learned rather than the mother tongue.

LAD Language Acquisition Device. An innate psychological capacity for language acquisition. A term associated with the work of Noam Chomsky. See *transformational/generative grammar.*

language laboratory A classroom in which pupils in separate booths are equipped with headphones for listening to a language teaching programme either broadcast from a central console or pre-recorded on tapes in the booths. Language labs may be simply audio-active (AA), where pupils listen and respond to the programme, or audio-active comparative (AAC), where in addition pupils may record their own performance with a view to comparing it with the model provided on the master tape of the programme.

langue/parole A distinction first made by Ferdinand de Saussure. 'Langue' is the conventionally accepted recognised system of linguistic elements by means of which the members of a speech community interact. 'Parole' is any given instance of actual individual linguistic behaviour. 'Langue' as system, can only be inferred from 'Parole', instances of actual practical use. See *competence.*

lexical item An item of the vocabulary of a language which has a single element of meaning. 'Lexical item' does not equal 'word'. Some lexical items consist of two or more words, e.g. to 'put up with'; some words may realise several different lexical items, e.g. 'bank' of a river and 'bank' for money.

lexical set A group of words related to one another by some semantic principle, a word family. For example, the names of colours - red, orange, yellow . . . - constitute a lexical set.

lexis/lexicon The vocabulary or stock of lexical items of a language. See *lexical item/lexical set.*

lock-step A pattern of teaching in which all pupils move forward at approximately the same rate, carrying out the same tasks and procedures at the same time - like soldiers marching together. See *individualisation.*

look and say An approach to teaching initial reading by concentrating on the general shape of the word and not on reconstructing it from the sound–letter correspondence.

macro-sociolinguistics The study of the use of language at the level of the speech community, the nation, etc., concerned with language planning, language policy, for example. Cf. *micro-sociolinguistics.*

marked form Marked forms are those linguistic items which manifest a contrast distinguishing them from an 'unmarked', 'neutral' or normal form. For example, *mare* and *stallion* are both marked forms – marked with regard to sex – as opposed to *horse*, which is unmarked. Similarly, *old* is the unmarked form in the age system in English – the question 'How old is he?' is neutral as opposed to 'How young is he?' which presupposes youth and so is marked.

MCQ Multiple Choice Question (q.v.).

mentalism A view of learning and thinking which sees the mind as a non-physical reality underlying observable human behaviour. Usually contrasted with behaviourism, which holds that such unobservable phenomena are by definition unscientific. Cf. *behaviourism.*

MET Modern English Teacher. A magazine of practical suggestions for teaching English as a foreign language, published four times a year by Modern English Publications Ltd, 33 Shaftesbury Avenue, London W1.

micro-sociolinguistics The study of the use of language at the level of interaction between individuals, typically concerned with such matters as the level of formality used, and the linguistic matters of relative status, personal attitude, etc.

micro-teaching A procedure used in teacher training wherein a small part of a lesson is taught to a small number of 'pupils' for a short length of time. 'Pupils' are often peers of the students who may or may not be assigned roles. Micro-teaching is often video-recorded allowing the teachers to watch themselves, and in the classic form of micro-teaching there is a revise and reteach phase as well.

mim-mem Mimicry and memorisation. Usually refers to a largely American method of teaching whose main procedures were extensive mimicry and mechanical repetition which was supposed to foster effective memorisation through imprinting the appropriate response. See *audio-lingual*; *S-R.*

minimal pair A pair of linguistic items differing by only one feature, most often phonological. For example, a pair like *pit* and *pet* are a minimal pair since the only difference between them is the vowel.

modal verb One of the auxiliary verbs. *Will/would, shall/should, may/ might, can/could, must, ought, need, dare*, and *used*. They are a subset of the anomalous finites.

model (1) The pattern of pronunciation or other form of (linguistic) behaviour offered as the example which a learner should follow in order to arrive at an acceptable performance. Thus RP (q.v.) is frequently suggested as a suitable model of pronunciation. (2) An abstract description of the nature of, for example, language, matter, society. A classic linguistic model is that of Chomsky. See *transformational/generative grammar.*

monitor A term coined by S. Krashen to describe a learner's self-conscious checking of his spoken or written language.

mood The realisation of a speaker's attitude to the content of what he is saying by means of verb forms: in English by use of modal verbs (q.v.).

morpheme The smallest unit of language which is grammatically significant. Morphemes may be 'bound' or 'free'. Bound morphemes are only found attached to some other morpheme. Thus *boys* consists of two morphemes, /boy/, which can occur alone and so is 'free', and /-z/ plural, which is bound.

MT (1) Mother tongue – the language learned at one's mother's knee; hence the language in which one feels most at home, though not necessarily one's mother's language. See *first language*; L¹. (2) Micro-teaching (q.v.).

multiple choice questions Test items framed in such a way that the learner has to choose from a number of options in order to respond satisfactorily. Sometimes there is an actual question to which four different answers are suggested; sometimes there is a stem to which four different completions are attached. The answers or completions which are not correct are referred to as distractors.

national language The language of a nation, especially one which is indigenous, and towards which members of the nation feel great loyalty. It may be contrasted with 'official language', which is a language authorised for use in parliament, government, education, etc., but towards which there may be little loyalty.

natural language Any of the several thousand known languages of the world, contrasted with 'artificial language', i.e. a language specially constructed or invented, for example, for use in symbolic logic, philosophy or international communication, e.g. Esperanto.

negotiation The process by which in interpersonal communication the participants make adjustments along such dimensions as presuppositions about shared knowledge, the purpose of the communication and the relative status or authority of the participants. Thus if A says 'John is going to London' and B responds 'John who?' and A replies 'John Henry', then they have negotiated agreement on the reference of 'John'.

notion A category of classification of meaning. E.g. time, quantity, space. Usually contrasted with *function* (q.v.). See also the work of Wilkins and the Council of Europe, especially van Ek.

objective question A question for which there is only one clear-cut answer, or an extremely limited range of specifiable alternatives. Often used for multiple choice questions, but there are other types. An objective *test* is one consisting entirely of objective questions. The question is 'objective' only in the marking. The choice of *what* is to be answered is normally made subjectively by the setter of the question or test.

official language The language which is adopted by a country or institution through administrative or judicial decision: usually the language of parliamentary debate, lawcourts, education, broadcasting, etc. See *national language*.

OHP overhead projector.

operator see *function words*.

oral/aural Term used for methods of teaching which concentrated on developing the skills of speaking and listening in the first instance (c. 1950–70). Cf. *audio-lingual* and *direct method*.

oral composition A story, or other extended piece of speech, composed in class, usually by co-operative class effort.

pair work A procedure for intensive class work in which students co-operate simultaneously in pairs (also called dyads) for discussion or practice.

paradigm, paradigmatic (1) In traditional grammar, the list of forms a word can take, e.g. boy, boys, boy's, in written English. (2) In post-Saussurean linguistics the possible choices in a particular slot; e.g. each slot in 'She can swim' can be filled respectively by I, you, he, it, we, etc., may, will, might, etc., hop, jump, run, write, etc. Cf. *syntagmatic*.

para-language Systematic communication associated with language, but not realised in grammar or lexical choice. May include 'ums' and 'ers', significant pauses, 'uhuh' and – some would say – intonation. Some people extend this definition further to include other signalling systems. See *semiotics*; *body language*.

parole see *langue*.

passive vocabulary The vocabulary which a student is able to understand as distinct from what he or she is able to use. 'Receptive' is often preferred, as the operation of understanding is not a passive activity.

pattern Any regular organisation which can be perceived: used in grammar. E.g. sentence patterns; phonology and semantics. Cf. *structure*.

pattern practice A teaching procedure associated with audio-lingualism which enables students to practise sentence patterns in order to acquire the grammatical 'shape' without any reference to meaning or use.

pedagogical grammar A grammar of a language modified so that it is suitable for effective teaching; this may be based on an adaptation of a descriptive grammar, or on an analysis of the natural order in which a learner or learners acquire items in a foreign language.

pedagogics A term more frequently used outside Britain than inside, for the systematic analysis and study of teaching procedures.

peer group The group of people which occupies the same position in

225

the hierarchy as the person being talked about; in an educational context, usually students of the same age and level.

performance see *competence*.

performative According to the philosopher Austin, words like *promise* in which the saying of the word is the doing of the act. 'I promise I will' is to make the promise, but 'I eat the bread' is not to eat it.

perlocution A perlocutionary act is one which has an effect on the person communicated with, thus if I *scare, convince, persuade* or *inspire* someone, I have not merely done something to them but I have changed them in some way. Cf. *illocution*.

phoneme The smallest unit of sound which can be used in meaningful contrast with other sounds in a particular language. Thus the sounds contrasted by *a* and *u* in *bad* and *bud* or by *b* and *m* in *bad* and *mad* are phonemes of English.

phonetics The study of sounds used in speaking. Usually divided into articulatory phonetics (the study of the organs of speech in use) and acoustic phonetics (the study of the physical properties of the sounds used). Cf. *phonology*.

phonetic transcription The written record of the sounds used in speech requiring a special alphabet. A phonemic transcription limits itself to the sound distinctions necessary to distinguish words meaningfully. Phonetic transcriptions attempt more precisely to indicate the exact quality of the sounds produced. See *IPA*.

phonics An approach to teaching reading which concentrates on building up the sound of the word from the sounds associated with the individual letters. Cf. *look and say*.

phonology The study of the way in which the sounds in a language are organised to express meaning. See *phoneme*; cf. *phonetics*.

phrase structure In TG the rules which form the base component of the grammar, and show the basic structure of the sentence, using categories to be found in many other grammatical descriptions. Example of PS rule:

NP	$\longrightarrow$	Det	+ N
i.e. Noun Phrase consists of determiner			+ noun
e.g.		the	girl

pidgin A limited language which is developed for (usually commercial) contact between two groups of speakers of different languages. Cf. *creole*.

pitch The high or low sound quality of the voice, measurable in frequencies. This will vary over an extended stretch of speech, and movement in pitch may convey grammatical meaning, e.g. He spoke? v. He spoke. In tone languages, the same sounds may be spoken at different pitches to produce words of totally different meanings.

practice stage In most language teaching, follows the presentation stage (q.v.) and consists of opportunities for students themselves to master the new item(s).

presentation stage The point (usually at the beginning of the lesson) when new material is introduced by the teacher. Followed by practice stage.

production stage The part of the lesson where students use language meaningfully, following presentation and practice stages (q.v.). Sometimes used for any occasions when students either speak or write, however uncommunicatively.

proxemics The study of how human beings position themselves in relation to each other. Much communication is subtly adjusted by distance, where and how people touch, what posture they adopt, etc. Varies from culture to culture. Cf. *body language*; *kinesics*.

psycholinguistics The study of all psychological issues relating to language, particularly first and second language learning, the relationship between language and concept formation, and language disorders.

reading laboratory A box of graded exercises, scientifically tested, to develop reading skills, and printed on separate cards so that they can be used for individual work.

realia Common, everyday objects, e.g. bus tickets, menu cards, fruit, brought into the classroom to assist language work.

redundancy A feature of all languages whereby some information is provided more than once. Thus in the sentence 'She met her son yesterday' both *she* and *her* mark her sex, and both the past form of the verb, *met*, and *yesterday* mark the event as being in the past.

register A widely used but imprecise term for variation in language associated with the use to which it is being put. Sometimes called 'functional dialect', it reflects features like formality (q.v.), e.g. addressing superiors, addressing friends; topic, e.g. legal v. religious language; and mode, e.g. letter-writing v. telegram-composing.

reinforcement In EFL, provision of extra language use and learning opportunities to enable items which have been presented and practised to be fully internalised.

remedial work In language teaching, generally all work which is aimed at putting right existing mistakes – hence most work after the earliest stages is arguably remedial. Often, used outside language teaching only for work for particularly backward learners.

restricted code In Bernstein's early work, a mode of language use heavily dependent on situation, marked by, e.g., much use of pronouns, and used in situations where explicit linguistic indication of precise meaning is unnecessary. Allegedly, all groups use it some of the time, but working-class groups more, so that they have more difficulty adjusting to the school environment, which demands extensive use of elaborated code. This is language suitable for precise and wide-ranging expression of meanings and functions allegedly used by educated speakers. Still frequently cited, this distinction is lacking in empirical evidence, and would be accepted in simple form by no linguist.

rhetoric Traditionally the study of how to speak or write persuasively. Relates to discourse studies (q.v.) in its concern with the functional organisation of texts.

rhythm The pattern of sound length and stress in speech.

role play An activity, either for teaching or therapeutic purposes, in which someone acts out a role in a more or less improvised fashion; sometimes distinguished from simulation (q.v.) in that people may be asked to act as a person with a different sex, age, or function from their own.

RP Received pronunciation, 'generally used by those who have been educated at "preparatory" boarding schools and the "Public Schools"' (Daniel Jones, 1918).

RSA Royal Society of Arts, 18 John Adam Street, London. The main examining body for certifying teachers of EFL/ESL outside the formal, full-time certification by the British Department of Education and Science; also sets English Language examinations.

scale and category An earlier name for what is now usually called systemic grammar. There were four fundamental categories (unit, structure, class, system) and three scales (rank, exponence and delicacy).

scheme of work A plan for a sequence of lessons, within a syllabus. It may be based on time units, e.g. a term, a year, or on some kind of organisation through topics.

segment An isolable sound unit in the stream of speech. Segmentation, i.e. the dividing up of material into minimal units, may also be used in analysis of grammar or semantics. See *componental analysis*; *suprasegmental.*

selection see also *sequencing*; *grading*. The decision about which items should be taught in the syllabus for a particular course.

SELMOUS Universities preparing Special English Language Material for Overseas University Students. C/o CILT (q.v.).

semantic field The general area of meaning covered by particular lexical items in relation to other items. (1) The item *plant* belongs to two fields: (a) that including tree, bush and grass, and (b) that including machinery, factory and industry. (2) *Uncle* in English contrasts with *aunt* in covering male siblings of both mother and father. Cf. *lexical set.*

semantics The study of meaning and how it is expressed through language and in particular languages.

semiotics The science of signs. Saussure saw linguistics as a part of semiotics, in that language is only the most intricate of a number of systems, e.g. gesture, proxemics (q.v.), but also architecture, clothing, etc., which structure communication between human beings. Sometimes loosely used to include only gesture, or only language-related systems. Cf. *para-language.*

sequencing In syllabus design, the establishing of an order for the teaching of items which have been selected. Criteria may include frequency of usage, complexity, generalisability. Cf. *selection*; *grading.*

sign language (1) A system of gestures as an alternative to spoken language, invented to assist deaf people. This may simply translate the alphabet into movements of the hands and arms, or may use signs to represent particular ideas directly, without spelling out words. (2) (Loosely) the use of gesture to communicate by human beings, e.g. nodding, beckoning, etc.

silent way A language teaching procedure associated with Gattegno. Groups of learners are introduced to a new language through a highly structured programme of intricate techniques. The teacher is encouraged to restrict his speech to the minimum so that students are forced to become fully engaged in creating and establishing successful language behaviour themselves.

simulation A teaching technique in which students act out language-using situations with or without preparation. Sometimes distinguished from role play (q.v.) in that in simulation students are expected to behave appropriately in the setting, but the emphasis is not on the adoption of a different personality.

situational approach Based on selected situations as settings for language to be taught. Situational syllabuses might organise learning through a sequence of situations. Situational compositions require learners to produce writing appropriate to the demands of specific situations.

skill A psychological term loosely used in EFL to cover any learned ability. The 'four skills' are listening, speaking, reading and writing. Behaviourist psychology regarded language learning as the acquisition of skills by habit formation.

SL Second language.

sociolinguistics The study of language in its social setting; typical concerns are class dialects, appropriacy of style and register (q.v.), and social function.

speech act What a language user does with a particular utterance; three common speech acts are assertion, question and command. See *illocution*; *perlocution.*

spiral syllabus A syllabus in which, instead of the traditional linear sequence, the planned course returns regularly to selected areas which are developed and extended.

SQ3R A study technique for reading comprehension, consisting of the sequence: survey, question, read, recite, and revise.

S-R Stimulus response: a basic concept of behaviourist learning theory.

Any utterance can be regarded as an automatic response to a stimulus which may be verbal, physical, etc.

stress In phonetics, the degree of emphasis or loudness, measurable in terms of intensity, muscular activity or air-pressure. Word-stress is concerned with patterns of stressed and unstressed syllables, cf. |photo, pho|tography, photo|graphic; sentence stress is concerned with the pattern of stresses within the utterances which tend to be placed in the words carrying the burden of the actual meaning.

stress-timed In English the rhythmic beats occur at fairly regular intervals of time, making it a stress-timed language. Cf. syllable-timed language, like French, where each syllable needs to have equal stress.

structure (1) Structure is the way in which parts are formed into a whole. (2) Conventionally, a structure is a grammatical pattern. Structural linguistics is concerned with observable formal relationships and tends to discount subjective and semantic evidence. A structural syllabus or approach takes linguistic structure as its basis for selection, grading, sequencing and basic methodology. See also *deep structure* and *surface structure.*

study skills Language-related skills which aid study, e.g. use of reference books, note-taking, skimming, interpretation of data.

style In applied linguistics, the variation of language most often related to speakers and settings.

stylistics Broadly the linguistic analysis of texts in terms of social function; more narrowly, the application of linguistic insights and techniques to literary texts – stylistic analysis.

substitution table A device to demonstrate and practise a number of structurally related utterances displayed in a table, e.g.:

He is too	young drunk weak	to	enjoy this help you fight

suggestopedia An approach to learning and teaching developed by Lozanov in Bulgaria. It emphasises confidence and authority on the teacher's part (marked in language teaching by tightly organised materials and methodology) and relaxed learning (aided by comfortable seating, background music and role play).

suprasegmental The term for those features of utterances like stress and intonation which supplement the quality of individual sounds, and often extend beyond the limits of particular phonemes: length, pitch and degree of stress. They are also known as prosodic features. Features of pronunciation are not matters of individual sound segments (q.v.), but of the whole shape of the whole sound of the sentence or utterance. E.g. stress, intonation.

surface structure In modern grammar, the linear pattern in which an utterance appears, as opposed to deep structure (q.v.), which is the underlying structural representation which determines meaning. The ambiguity of the surface structure of 'Visiting aunts can be boring' is accounted for by two possible underlying deep structures: (a) Aunts pay visits. Aunts can be boring. (b) I visit aunts. My visits can be boring.

syllable-timed see *stress-timed.*

syntagmatic Along the horizontal dimension in grammar, as opposed to the vertical. See *paradigm.* In the sentences 'She goes' and 'He went' the relationships between subject and verb are syntagmatic, and the relationships between She/he and goes/went are paradigmatic.

syntax see *grammar.*

synthetic syllabus Wilkins' term for any syllabus which is the cumulative teaching of a sequenced inventory of items. E.g. a grammar-based syllabus.

systemic grammar A model grammatical description concerned with networks of systems which underlie an utterance; associated with the work of Halliday.

TEFL The Teaching of English as a Foreign Language.

TESOL The Teaching of English to Speakers of Other Languages. Also the American Association of that name. Address: School of Languages and Linguistics, Georgetown University, Washington DC, USA.

text A stretch of spoken or written language.

TG see *transformational/generative grammar.*

threshold level The Council of Europe term for the specification of a level of minimal competence in a foreign language. See van Ek, 1975.

tone group see *intonation.*

transfer The influence of the knowledge of one language on the learning of another. Where the two are similar, positive transfer may take place. Negative transfer, or interference (q.v.), may be found where the two are different.

transformation In transformational/generative grammar, the rule-governed process of producing a surface structure (q.v.) from another, underlying structure. A passive transformation of 'The dog ate the bone' is 'The bone was eaten by the dog'. See *deep structure; surface structure.*

transformational/generative grammar A model of grammar, largely developed by Chomsky, which seeks to account for all possible sentences in a language by a system of transformational rules operating on a small number of basic structures.

unit/credit system A Council of Europe scheme to standardise among member states the objectives and validation of foreign language learning by adults.

utterance A stretch of spoken or written language, in speech usually marked off by silence before and after. An utterance may vary in length from a single word to a succession of sentences.

Glossary

vernacular The language spoken by the population at large; the indigenous language.

VTR Video-tape recording.

weak form The qualitative variation of certain syllables or words in unstressed positions. Some common words like *at*, *of*, *an*, *was* most frequently occur in their weak forms /ət, əv, ən, wəz/, rather than in their strong forms / æt, ov, æn, woz/.

Bibliography

Aitchison, J. (1972) *General Linguistics*, English Universities Press.

Aitchison, J. (1978) *Linguistics*, Hodder & Stoughton, 2nd edn.

Alexander, L. G. (1971) *Guided Composition in English Teaching*, Longman.

Allen, J. P. B. and Corder, S. Pit (eds) (1974) *The Edinburgh Course in Applied Linguistics, Vol. 3, Techniques in Applied Linguistics*, Oxford University Press.

Allen, J. P. B. and Corder, S. Pit (1977) *The Edinburgh Course in Applied Linguistics, Vol. 4, Testing and Experimental Methods*, Oxford University Press.

Anderson, W. L. and Stageberg, N. C. (1966) *Introductory Readings on Language*, New York: Holt, Rinehart & Winston.

Argyle, M. (1972) *The Psychology of Interpersonal Behaviour*, Penguin, 2nd edn.

Austin, J. L. (1962) *How to Do Things with Words*, Oxford University Press.

Bach, T. and Harris, F. L. (eds) (1968) *Universals in Linguistic Theory*, New York: Holt, Rinehart & Winston.

BBC/British Council (1976) *Teaching Observed*, 13 films with handbook.

Binham, P. (1968) *How To Say It*, Longman.

Bloomfield, L. (1935) *Language*, Allen & Unwin, revised British edn.

Bolinger, D. (ed.) (1972) *Intonation*, Harmondsworth: Penguin.

Bolinger, D. (1975) *Aspects of Language*, Harcourt Brace Jovanovich 2nd edn.

Bolinger, D. and Sear, D. A. (1981) *Aspects of Language*, Harcourt Bruce, 3rd edn.

Bright, J. A. and McGregor, G. P. (1970) *Teaching English as a Second Language*, Longman.

Bright, J. A. and Piggott, R. (1976) *Handwriting, A Workbook*, Cambridge University Press.

233

Brittan, K. (1974) *Advanced Listening Comprehension Practice in English*, Hamish Hamilton.

Britton, J., Martin, N. and Rosen, H. (1966) *Multiple Marking of English Compositions*, Schools Examination Bulletin no. 12, HMSO.

Bromhead, P. (1974) *Life in Modern Britain*, Longman, 4th edn.

Broughton, G. (1977) *Know the British*, Hutchinson.

Brown, G. (1977) *Listening to Spoken English*, Longman.

Brumfit, C. J. (1977a) 'Correction of Written Work', *Modern English Teacher*, September.

Brumfit, C. J. (1977b) 'The Teaching of Advanced Reading Skills in Foreign Languages with Particular Reference to English as a Foreign Language', survey article in *Language Teaching and Linguistics: Abstracts*, vol. 10, Cambridge University Press.

Bures, O. (ed.) (1972) *The Seventh Mental Measurements Yearbook*. New Jersey: Gryphon Press.

Burstall, C. (1970) *French in the Primary School*, Slough: National Foundation for Educational Research.

Byrne, D. (1976) *Teaching Oral English*, Longman.

Byrne, D. and Wright, A. (1975) *What Do You Think?*, Longman.

Carroll, J. B. (ed.) (1956) *Language, Thought and Reality: Selected Writings of Benjamin Lee Whorf*, Cambridge, Mass.: MIT Press.

Carroll, J. B. and Sapon, S. M. (1966) *The Modern Language Aptitude Test*, New York: The Psychological Corporation.

Chalker, S. (1984) *Current English Grammar*, Macmillan.

Chaplen, F. (1975) *Communication Practice in Spoken English*, Oxford University Press.

Cherry, E. C. (1957) *On Human Communication*, John Wiley.

Chomsky, N. (1965) *Aspects of the Theory of Syntax*. Cambridge, Mass.: MIT Press.

Christophersen, P. (1973) *Second Language Learning*, Harmondsworth: Penguin.

Close, R. A. (1974) *A University Grammar of English Workbook*, Longman.

Combe Martin, M. H. (1970) *Listening and Comprehending*, Macmillan.

Cook, V. J. (1974) *English Topics*, Oxford University Press.

Cook, V. J. (1968) *Active Intonation*, Longman.

Corder, S. P. (1978) 'Learner language and teacher talk', *AVLJ* 16, 1, pp.5-13.

Corder, S. P. (1973) *Introducing Applied Linguistics*, Harmondsworth: Penguin.

Corder, S. P. (1966) *The Visual Element in Language Teaching*, Longman.

Crystal, D. (1971) *Linguistics*, Harmondsworth: Penguin.

Crystal, D. and Davy, D. (1969) *Investigating English Style*, Longman.

Crystal, D. and Davy, D. (1976) *Advanced Conversational English*, Longman.

Curran, C. (1972) *Counseling-Learning: A Whole-Person Model for Education*, New York: Grune & Stratton.

Curran, C. (1976) *Counseling-Learning in Second Languages*, Illinois: Apple River Press.

Davies, A. (1968) *Language Testing Symposium: A Psycholinguistic Approach*, Oxford University Press.

De Cecco, J. P. (1969). *The Psychology of Language, Thought and Instruction*, New York: Holt, Rinehart & Winston.

Defoe, D. (1709) *Robinson Crusoe*.

de Freitas, J. F. (1970) *To Start You Talking*, Macmillan.

Dickens, C. (1838) *Oliver Twist*.

Dodd, W. A. (1970) *The Teacher at Work*, Oxford University Press.

Dykstra, G. *et al.* (1968) *Ananse Tales*, Columbia: Teachers' College.

Educational Testing Service *Test of English as a Foreign Language*, Princeton, New Jersey.

English Teaching Information Centre (1974) *Information Guide No. 3. Recorded Material for Teaching English*, British Council.

English Teaching Information Centre (1976) *Information Guide No. 2. English for Specific Purposes*, British Council.

Eynon, J. (1970) *Multiple Choice Questions in English*, Hamish Hamilton, 2nd edn.

Fillmore, C. (1968) 'The Case for Case', in Bach and Harris (eds).

Fromkin, V. and Rodman, R. (1983) *An Introduction to Language*, Holt, Saunders, 3rd edn.

Fry, E. (1963) *Teaching Faster Reading*, Cambridge University Press.

Gattegno, C. (1963) *Teaching Foreign Language in Schools*, New York: Educational Solutions.

Gattegno, C. (1976) *The Common Sense of Teaching Foreign Languages*, New York: Educational Solutions.

George, H. V. (1972) *Common Errors in Language Learning*, Newbury House.

Gimson, A. C. (1970) *An Introduction to the Pronunciation of English*, Arnold, 2nd edn.

Gurrey, P. (1955) *Teaching English as a Foreign Language*, Longman.

Halliday, M. A. K. *et al.* (1964) *The Linguistic Sciences and Language Teaching*, Longman.

Harris, D. P. (1969) *Testing English as a Second Language*, New York: McGraw-Hill.

Hartley, L. P. (1953) *The Go-Between*, Hamish Hamilton.

Hartog, P. *et al.* (1941) *The Marking of English Essays*, Macmillan.

Bibliography

Haycraft, B. (1970) *The Teaching of Pronunciation – A Classroom Guide*, Longman.

Haycraft, J. (1978) *An Introduction to English Language Teaching*, Longman.

Heaton, J. B. (1975) *Studying in English*, Longman.

Heaton, J. B. (1975) *Writing English Language Tests*, Longman.

Heliel, M. and McArthur, T. (1974) *Learning Rhythm and Stress*, Collins.

Hill, L. A. and Fielden, R. D. S. (1974) *English Language Teaching Games for Adult Students*, Evans.

Hogins, J. B. and Yarber, R. E. (1969) *Language, an Introductory Reader*, New York: Harper & Row.

Holden, S. (ed.) (1978) *English for Specific Purposes*, special issue no. 1 of *Modern English Teacher*.

Hornby, A. S. (ed.) (1974) *Oxford Advanced Learner's Dictionary of Current English*, Oxford University Press, 3rd edn.

Hudson, K. (1984) *An Invitation to Linguistics*, Martin Robertson.

Ingram, E. (1975) *English Language Battery*, Oxford University Press.

Institute of Education, Dar es Salaam (1969) *Handbook for English Teachers*.

Isaacs, R. (ed.) (1968) *Learning Through Language*, Tanzania Publishing House. (Macmillan).

Jones, D. (1918) *An Outline of English Phonetics*, Cambridge: Heffer.

Jupp, T. C. and Milne, J. (1968) *Guided Course in English Composition*, Heinemann.

Jupp, T. C. and Milne, J. (1972) *Guided Paragraph Writing*, Heinemann.

Kennedy, C. and Bolitho, R. (1984) *English for Specific Purposes*, Macmillan.

Lado, R. (1951–60) *English Language Test for Foreign Students*, Ann Arbor: Wahr.

Lado, R. (1961a) *Michigan Test of English Language Proficiency*, Ann Arbor: University of Michigan ELI.

Lado, R. (1961b) *Language Testing: The Construction and Use of Foreign Language Tests*, Longman.

Lawrence, Mary S. (1972) *Writing as a Thinking Process*, Ann Arbor: University of Michigan Press.

Lee, W. R. (1965) *Language Teaching Games and Contests*, Oxford University Press.

Leech, G. and Svartvik, J. (1975) *A Communicative Grammar of English*, Longman.

Leslie, A. (1971) *Written English Today*, Macmillan.

Levine, Josie (1972) *Developing Writing Skills*, Association for the Education of Pupils from Overseas.

Linden, E. (1974) *Apes, Men and Language*, Harmondsworth: Penguin.

Lozanov, G. (1978) *Suggestology and Outlines of Suggestopedy*, New York: Gordon & Breach.

Mackey, W. F. (1965) *Language Teaching Analysis*, Longman.
Mackin, R. and Dickinson, L. (1969) *Varieties of Spoken English*, Oxford University Press.
Mackin, R. and Whiteson, V. (1977) *More Varieties of Spoken English*, Oxford University Press.
Macmillan, M. (1965) *Efficiency in Reading*, British Council, ETIC Occasional Paper no. 6.
McClafferty, J. (1975) *A Guide to Examinations in English for Foreign Students*, Hamish Hamilton, 2nd edn.
McCree, Hazel (1969) *From Controlled to Creative Writing*, Lagos: African Universities Press.
Millington Ward, J. (1966) *Practice in the Use of English*, Longman.
Minnis, N. (1973) *Linguistics at Large*, Granada.
Moody, H. L. B. (1971) *The Teaching of Literature*, Longman.
Moody, K W. (1966) *Written English Under Control*, Oxford University Press.
Moon, C. and Raban, B. (1975) *A Question of Reading*, Ward Lock.
Morrow, K. (1978) *Advanced Conversational English Workbook*, Longman.
Morrow, K. (1978) *Techniques of Evaluation for a Notional Syllabus*, Royal Society of Arts.
Munby, J. *et al.* (1966) *Comprehension for School Certificate*, Longman.
Munby, J. (1968) *Read and Think*, Longman.
Musman, R. (1977) *Britain Today*, Longman, 2nd edn.

Nash, W. (1971) *Our Experience of Language*, Batsford.

O'Connor, J. D. (1967) *Better English Pronunciation*, Cambridge University Press.
O'Connor, J. D. and Arnold, G. F. (1967) *Intonation of Colloquial English*, Longman.
O'Neill, R. and Scott, R. (1974) *Viewpoints*, Longman.
Osborne, John (1957) *Look Back in Anger*, Faber & Faber.

Peterson, L. *et al.* (1974) *Work and Leisure*, Heinemann.
Peterson, L. *et al.* (1975) *Our Environment*, Heinemann.
Peterson, L. *et al.* (1978) *Other Worlds*, Heinemann.
Politzer, R. L. and Weiss, L. (1970) *The Successful Foreign Language Teacher*, Philadelphia: Center for Curriculum Development and Harrap.

Potter, S. (1960) *Language in the Modern World*, Harmondsworth: Penguin.

Quirk, R. and Greenbaum, S. (1973) *University Grammar of English*, Longman.

Redlich, M. (1977) *Everyday England*, Duckworth, 4th edn.
Richards, J. C. (ed.) (1974) *Error Analysis*, Longman.
Rivers, W. (1968) *Teaching Foreign Language Skills*, University of Chicago Press.
Robinson, P. (1980) *English for Specific Purposes*, Pergamon.

Sampson, A. (1971) *New Anatomy of Britain*, Hodder & Stoughton.
Sapir, E. (1921) *Language*, New York: Harcourt, Brace & World.
Saussure, F. de (1915) *Cours de linguistique générale*, English trans. 1966, New York: McGraw-Hill; paperback edn, Collins/Fontana.
Science Research Associates (1958, revised 1960) *SRA Reading Laboratories*, Illinois: SRA.
Selinker, L. (1972) *Interlanguage*, IRAL 10, 3, pp. 219-31.
Sillitoe, A. (1958) *Saturday Night and Sunday Morning*, W. H. Allen.
Smith, F. (1970) *Understanding Reading*, New York: Holt, Rinehart & Winston.
Smith, N. and Wilson, D. (1978) *Modern Linguistics*, Harmondsworth: Penguin.
Spencer, D. H. (1967) *Guided Composition Exercises*, Longman.
Stern, H. H. (1967) *Foreign Languages in Primary Education*, Oxford University Press.
Stern, H. H. and Weinrib, A. (1977) 'Foreign Languages for Younger Children: Trends and Assessment', *Language Teaching and Linguistic Abstracts*, vol. 10, no. 1, Cambridge University Press.
Stevick, E. W. (1976) *Memory, Meaning and Method*, Newbury House.
Strevens, P. (1977) *New Orientations in the Teaching of English*, Oxford University Press.

Templer, J. C. and Nettle, K. (1974) *Listening Comprehension Tests*, Heinemann, 2nd edn.
Templer, J. C. and Nettle, K. (1975) *Oral English Proficiency Tests*, Heinemann.
Trim, J. (1975) *English Pronunciation Illustrated*, Cambridge University Press, 2nd edn.
Trudgill, P. (1974) *Sociolinguistics*, Harmondsworth: Penguin.

Valette, R. M. (1977) *Modern Language Testing: A Handbook*, New York: Harcourt Brace Jovanovich, 2nd edn.
van Ek, J. (1975) *The Threshold Level*, Council of Europe; repr. 1980, Pergamon Press.

Wallwork, J. F. (1969) *Language and Linguistics*, Heinemann.

West, M. (1953) *A General Service Word List*, Longman.

Widdowson, H. G. (1971) 'Teaching of Rhetoric to Students of Science and Technology' in *Science and Technology in a Second Language*, CILT Reports and Papers no. 7.

Widdowson, H. G. (1976) *Stylistics and the Teaching of Literature*, Longman.

Widdowson, H. G. (1978) *Teaching Language as Communication*, Oxford University Press.

Wilkins, D. A. (1972) *Linguistics in Language Teaching*, Arnold.

Wilkins, D. A. (1976) *Notional Syllabuses*, Oxford University Press.

Useful Periodicals

ARELS Journal, 43 Russell Square, London WC1B 5DH.

BBC Modern English (Modern English Publications, International House, 40 Shaftesbury Avenue, London W1V 8HJ).

Culture and Language Learning Newsletter (East-West Center, Honolulu, Hawaii).

Educational Review (Birmingham University, School of Education). Occasional issues on language and education.

English in Education (NATE Office, Fernleigh, 10B Thornhill Road, Edgerton, Huddersfield HD3 3AU). Primarily mother tongue teaching.

*ELT Documents (ETIC, 10 Spring Gardens, London SW1A 2BN).

*English Language Teaching Journal (Oxford University Press).

*English Teaching Forum (US embassies).

*Language Learning (University of Michigan, Ann Arbor, Michigan, USA).

*Modern English Teacher (Modern English Publications, International House, 40 Shaftesbury Avenue, London W1V 8HJ).

TESL Reporter (Box 157, Brigham Young University, Hawaii Campus, Laie, Hawaii 96762).

*TESOL Quarterly (Georgetown University, Washington, DC, USA).

*especially recommended

Index

Index

threshold level, 195
transfer error, *see* interference from mother tongue
translatability, 28–30
translation, 78, 137, 149, 165, 173
transmission of information, 27

understanding, *see* comprehension
Unit/credit system, 195

varieties of English, 4–6, 10, 30, 31, 56, 57, 138, 196, 197
  choice of model in SL and FL situations, 6, 7, 56, 57, 138
video, 98, 163
visual aids, 23, 42, 71, 83, 107–9, 175, 202
  example of use, 13
vocabulary, 72, 101, 110, 119, 150, 170, 197, 199, 204; *see also* lexis
voice, voicing, 51, 58
vowel length, 51, 52, 58

wall charts, 42, 107, 185, 202
weak forms and strong forms, 54, 199
Wordmaster, 99
writing, 113, 149, 152, 154, 172, 173, 178, 188, 191, 293
  aims of, 116, 131
  assessment of, 157
  controlled, 119, 120, 128, 131, 207
  correction of, 139–41
  and 'creating', 130, 131
  free, 119–21, 127, 128, 131, 147, 160
  guided, 119, 120, 128
  methodology for, 121–30, 180, 181
  programme, 117–20, 126, 131; and its goals, 119, 120
  skills needed, 116, 117, 152
written language, *see* writing